TEXAS AND TEXANS IN THE GREAT WAR

TEXAS AND TEXANS IN THE GREAT WAR

Ralph A. Wooster

Cover photo by Belton, Texas, resident Lieutenant Robert Bruce Frazier, 90th Division. From the collection of Donald S. Frazier, Abilene, Texas.

Buffalo Gap, Texas

Library of Congress Cataloging-in-Publication Data

Wooster, Ralph A.
    Texas and Texans in the Great War / by Ralph A. Wooster.
    p. cm.
Includes bibliographical references and index.
ISBN 978-1-933337-37-1
1. World War, 1914-1918–Texas. 2. Texas–History–20th century. I. Title.

D570.85.T4W66 2009
940.4'09764–dc22

                                                        2009024030

Copyright © 2009, State House Press
All Rights Reserved

State House Press
P. O. Box 818
Buffalo Gap, TX 79508
(325) 572-3974
www.mcwhiney.org/press

Printed in the United States of America

ISBN 978-1-933337-37-1

Book designed by Rosenbohm Graphic Design

Contents

Preface vii
Chapter One: War Comes to Europe and the United States 9
Chapter Two: Mobilizing for War 35
Chapter Three: Texans in Wartime National and State Affairs 61
Chapter Four: Life on the Texas Home Front 83
Chapter Five: Over There: Texans in France 117
Chapter Six: Victory and Peace 147
Endnotes 169
Appendix I: Chronology 204
Appendix II: After the War 210
Bibliography 222
Index 249

Preface

The First World War, or the Great War, as it was known at the time, was a gigantic struggle that involved most of the European powers and ultimately the United States. Those four years of conflict saw more than 32 million casualties and 4 million deaths from battle and disease. At the end of the war, parts of France, Belgium, Austria-Hungary, Serbia, and Poland lay devastated; the German, Austrian, and Russian monarchies were no more.

Although the United States entered the war late, its contribution in terms of manpower, war materials, and money was substantial. In what President Woodrow Wilson called the "war to make the world safe for democracy," the United States mobilized more than 4 million men and suffered 364,000 casualties, including more than 120,000 who were killed or died from disease.

Nearly 200,000 Texans served in the American armed forces during the First World War. Texans who were killed or died from disease (many in the great influenza epidemic) in the war numbered 5,171. Thousands of other Texans contributed to the Allied victory by producing materials needed to win the war. They and other Texans supported the war effort through their purchase of war bonds and stamps, food conservation programs, and Red Cross, YMCA, and Salvation Army activities.

Numerous articles and specialized studies have described specific aspects of the Lone Star State's role in the Great War. Surprisingly, however, no overall study of the part that Texas and Texans played in the war has been previously published. In this book, I attempt to describe how the nation became involved in the war, how Texans reacted to our involvement, how they participated on the home front and the war front, and how the conflict changed the state.

Many people, most of whose works are cited in the endnotes and bibliography, have contributed to this work. I particularly want to thank my longtime friend and colleague in the Lamar University history department, Dr. Adrian Anderson. The biographer of Wilson's Postmaster General Albert Sidney Burleson and a fountain of knowledge concerning Texas and national affairs during the Progressive era, Andy first suggested that I undertake this study and has saved me from numerous pitfalls along the way.

Another friend, artist George Farrar, once again prepared the maps for this study. Theresa Hefner-Babb, documents librarian at Lamar, and other staff members helped me obtain inter-library loans and other materials. Tom Reid, former army master sergeant and author of several military studies, answered numerous questions concerning Army operations and records. Patty Renfro, secretary in the Lamar University history department; her husband, Mike Renfro, a public school history teacher; and Terry Rioux, instructor of history at Lamar, assisted in a number of ways. John Anderson, preservation officer at the Texas State Archives, provided the photos of Texas personalities that accompany the text. My appreciation is extended to these and others for their assistance.

As in all of my historical investigations, my family has contributed understanding and support. As always, my wife, Edna, has given me love and encouragement. My son, Robert, a military historian and student of the frontier Army, and his wife, Catherine, provided additional support for the project. Without their encouragement, I could not have completed this work.

Ralph A. Wooster
Beaumont, Texas, January 2009

CHAPTER ONE

WAR COMES TO EUROPE AND THE UNITED STATES

The events in Europe in the summer of 1914 that led to the outbreak of a major war seemed of little concern to most Texans. Local issues such as the weather, the cotton crop, and politics were of greater interest. Although the spring had been wetter and cooler than usual, June and July were hot and dry. As a consequence, Texans looked for shade trees and cool drinks to help defeat the oppressive heat. A bumper cotton crop was nearing harvest, and the economy was generally good. For the first time in two decades a Democrat, Woodrow Wilson, was in the White House; a Texan, Colonel Edward M. House of Austin, was the president's closest political adviser and confidant. Two Texans, Postmaster General Albert Sidney Burleson and Secretary of Agriculture David Houston, were in the Cabinet. A third Texan, Thomas Watt Gregory of Austin, would soon join the Cabinet as attorney general.

The state was also well represented on Capitol Hill. The state's senior senator, former Gov. Charles A. Culberson, was chairman of the Judiciary Committee in the upper chamber of Congress. Veteran lawmaker Robert L. Henry of Waco presided over the powerful House Rules Committee. Other House committees were led by John H. Stephens of Vernon, William R. Smith of Colorado, James L. Slayden of San Antonio, Alexander Gregg of Palestine, and Martin Dies of Beaumont.[1]

Texans were more interested in the contest for governor in the Democratic primary than events in Europe that summer. As part of the Democratic Solid South, the state had not elected a Republican governor since Reconstruction and would not do so for some years to come. Although the Greenback and People's parties occasionally provided a challenge in the late nineteenth century, the Democrats were always victorious in the governor's race.

With the adoption of the Terrell election law in 1905 requiring political parties that received more than 100,000 votes in the general election to select their nominees through direct elections, the Democratic primary held in the summer took on major importance. The nominees selected in these contests were assured victory in the autumn general election.[2]

Oscar B. Colquitt, first elected governor in 1910 and re-elected in 1912, was completing his second term as Texas' chief executive. Observing the two-term tradition, he was not a candidate in the 1914 primary. Many assumed that Thomas H. Ball of Houston, the candidate supported by the prohibitionist wing of the party and favored by President Wilson and Secretary of State William Jennings Bryan, would be chosen as the Democratic nominee. However, he was defeated in the July primary by a political newcomer, Temple banker James E. "Pa" Ferguson, who in the campaign emphasized the plight of the tenant farmer.[3]

Three days after Jim Ferguson's nomination, war broke out in Europe. One month earlier, on June 28, 1914, Archduke Francis Ferdinand, heir to the Austrian throne, was assassinated in the Bosnian city of Sarajevo. Ferdinand's death set off a series of events in which the principal European powers took steps leading to war. On July 28, Austria-Hungary declared war on Serbia. Two days later, imperial Russia, the protector of Serbia, mobilized its troops for war. On August 1, Germany, principal ally of Austria-Hungary, declared war on Russia. This led France, bound to Russia by an alliance, to mobilize. On August 3, Germany declared war on France. The next day, German troops entered Belgium as part of a plan to crush France before Russia could become a decisive factor in the war. This violation of Belgian neutrality caused Great Britain to declare war on Germany.[4]

The first reports of Francis Ferdinand's assassination received little attention in Texas. The event seemed to be just another tragic episode in the muddled affairs of the Balkan states. But as Austria sent an ultimatum to Serbia and as other European powers made threats and counter-threats, Texans expressed greater interest. The *Dallas Morning News* of July 24 reported that the Austrian ultimatum was "a matter of serious concern." The editor of the *San Antonio Express* on July 28 expressed the belief that the German attitude in the affair was "of paramount importance." The next day, the *Morning News* carried a banner headline across eight columns: "Austria-Hungary Formally Declares War On Serbia; Feeling Runs High." That same day, the *Austin Daily Statesman* reported, "If present conditions prove accurate Europe is on the brink of the greatest war of all history."[5]

Oscar B. Colquitt

The majority of Texans wanted no part in the developing war. Although most Texas newspapers criticized the German invasion of Belgium and reported allegations of German atrocities, they expressed the view that the United States should not become involved. They applauded President Wilson's statement that Americans remain "neutral in thought as well as in name."[6]

In the summer of 1914, Texas ranked fifth among the states in number of people, exceeded only by New York, Pennsylvania, Illinois, and

Ohio. Population increased from 3,048,710 in 1900 to 3,896,542 in 1910 and was more than 4 million by 1914. Although the majority of Texans still lived in rural areas, the number and percentage of urban dwellers were increasing, from 17.1 percent in 1900 to 24.1 percent in 1910. San Antonio, with 96,614 residents, was the largest city in the state, followed closely by Dallas with 92,104 people. Houston (which had been slightly larger than Dallas in 1900) and Fort Worth were the only other Texas cities with populations of more than 50,000 in 1910. El Paso, Galveston, Waco, Austin, and Beaumont were the only other Texas cities with more than 20,000 residents in 1910.[7]

In the early twentieth century, four of every five Texans were white. The black population, although growing in number (488,171 in 1890, 620,702 in 1900, and 690,049 in 1910), was declining in percentage of the total population (21.8 percent in 1890, 20.4 percent in 1900, and 17.7 percent in 1910). More than 90 percent of all Texans were born in the United States; three-fourths were native Texans. The majority of non-natives came from the states of the old Confederacy, especially Tennessee, Alabama, Mississippi, and Arkansas.[8]

Nearly 240,000 Texans in 1910 were natives of foreign countries; another 350,000 were children of foreign-born parents. Half of those born outside the United States—124,238, or 51.8 percent—were natives of Mexico; another 118,682 Texas residents were children of parents born in Mexico. One-fourth of Texans born outside the United States were Germans (44,917) and Austrians (20,566). Italians (7,190) were the fourth-largest foreign ethnic group in early twentieth-century Texas.[9]

In the decade preceding the war's outbreak, 60 percent of Texas adults were farmers or ranchers. The federal census of 1910 reported 417,700 Texas farm operators, an increase of slightly more than 65,000 from 1900. More than half of these, 219,575, or 52.6 percent, were tenant farmers. The census enumerated 195,863 Texans, or 46.9 percent, as owners of their farms; 2,332, or 0.5 percent, were listed as farm managers. Another 400,000 Texans worked as farm laborers.[10]

TEXAS CITIES WITH POPULATIONS OF 20,000 OR MORE IN 1920

City	1900	1910	1920
San Antonio	53,321	96,614	161,379
Dallas	42,638	92,104	158,976
Houston	44,633	78,800	138,276
Fort Worth	26,688	73,312	106,482
El Paso	15,906	39,279	77,560
Galveston	37,789	36,981	44,255
Beaumont	9,427	20,640	40,422
Wichita Falls	2,480	8,200	40,079
Waco	20,686	26,425	38,500
Austin	22,258	29,860	34,876
Laredo	13,439	14,855	22,710
Port Arthur	900	7,663	22,251

Source: *Fourteenth Census of United States, 1920. Vol. 1, Population, pp. 303-305*
[Eight other Texas cities had populations of 12,000 or more in 1920. In descending order, these were Denison (17,065), Ranger (16,205), Paris (15,040), Sherman (15,031), Marshall (14,291), Cleburne (12,820), Greenville (12,384) and Tyler (12,085).]

The total acreage on Texas farms actually declined during the first decade of the twentieth century, from slightly over 125 million acres in 1900 to just over 112 million in 1910—a 10.6 percent loss. The number of improved acres grew, however, from slightly over 19 million in 1900 to over 27 million in 1910—an increase of nearly 40 percent. The value of Texas farm property rose 130.5 percent in century's first decade, from $962 million in 1900 to slightly less than $2.22 billion in 1910.[11]

Cotton was the king of Texas agriculture. Nearly 10 million of the state's 13 million acres of cropland was devoted to cotton in 1909—a 42.7 percent increase from 1899. Although there was a slight decline in actual production, from 2,506,212 bales in 1899 to 2,455,174 bales in 1909, Texas remained the largest cotton-producing state, a position it held from 1879. As historian Lewis Gould points out, "these years were prosperous for cotton farmers, with prices fluctuating at around fourteen cents a pound in 1909 and 1910, well above the disastrous lows of the 1890s."[12]

On the eve of the First World War, cotton production was still concentrated in East and Central Texas. The cattle industry, on the other hand, was centered primarily in South and West Texas. Although the total number of cattle declined slightly in the first decade of the century (from 7,279,935 in 1900 to 7,139,400 in 1910), Texas still ranked first among the states in number of cattle.[13]

The discovery of the great Spindletop oil field near Beaumont in 1901 and subsequent strikes at Batson, Sour Lake, Humble, and Goose Creek ushered in a new era in the state's economic development. However, the main focus of exploration moved to Oklahoma in 1905. By 1910, Texas ranked seventh among the states in oil production. New discoveries at Electra, Mexia, and Wichita Falls just before the 1914 outbreak of war in Europe pushed the state's production up to 20 million barrels annually by 1914.[14]

Texas still lagged behind the other states in manufacturing, ranking twenty-fourth in 1899 and seventeenth in 1909 in value of goods produced. Slightly more than 80,000 Texans were employed in the state's 4,588 manufacturing establishments. Although there were more printing and publishing shops than any other businesses, meatpacking and slaughtering produced the highest value of goods—slightly over $42 million in 1909. Flour milling (with products valued at $32.4 million) and lumber (with products valued at $32.2 million) were the other leading industries.[15]

On the eve of the war, Texans enjoyed much better means of transportation than their parents and grandparents had. More than 14,000 miles of railroad track connected Texas towns and cities. Too, freight charges and passenger rates declined dramatically in the early twentieth century, benefitting Texans traveling or shipping goods across the state.[16]

Although most Texans still traveled short distances by horseback, buggy, or wagon, automobiles were becoming more common. By 1913, there were 32,000 automobiles in the state, and the number was growing each year. Approximately 130,000 miles of public roads, 3,591 of which were paved, made travel easier.[17]

Streetcars provided transportation for Texans within the major towns. Until the 1890s, these were pulled by horses or mules, but electric cars replaced them in the first decade of the century. Electric interurban railways also served the larger cities. By 1914, there were nearly 500 miles of track, mainly in the state's northern region—Fort Worth, Dallas, Denison, Cleburne, Corsicana, and Waco. An electric railway linked Galveston and Houston in 1911. That same year, electric interurban service began between Beaumont and Port Arthur.[18]

In an era before network radio and television, Texans depended heavily upon local newspapers for state, national, and world news. In 1910, the state had eighty-nine dailies, twenty-eight semi-weeklies, and 768 weeklies published in 550 different towns and cities. Several, including the *Galveston News*, *Victoria Advocate*, *San Antonio Express*, and *Bastrop Advertiser*, dated from pre-Civil War years. Others, such as the *Dallas Morning News*, *Houston Chronicle*, *Austin Daily Statesman*, *Fort Worth Star-Telegram*, *El Paso Herald*, and *Houston Daily Post*, were of more recent origin but had large audiences.[19]

Texas newspapers reflected the diversity of the state's residents. Twenty-three weekly newspapers owned or edited by African-

Americans, including the *Houston Texas Freeman*, *Dallas Express*, and *San Antonio Advocate*, were published in Texas. Twenty-nine German-language newspapers, eighty-six Spanish newspapers, and several Czech newspapers served Texas readers in their native languages.[20]

African-Americans and Mexican-Americans were the largest minorities in the state. Both suffered from various forms of discrimination. A series of laws passed in the late nineteenth and early twentieth centuries separated blacks from white Texans in public and private facilities including education, housing, amusements, and public transportation. The adoption of a requirement that only white Texans could vote in the Democratic primary, along with the requirement of payment of a poll tax for voting, effectively disfranchised black citizens from political participation. Efforts to challenge the system were met by physical intimidation and mob violence. Although the total number of lynchings declined in the twentieth century, eighty black Texans were lynched in 1900–09.[21]

Although they did not suffer from state laws that segregated blacks from whites, Mexican-American Texans faced many types of discrimination. Anglo Texans generally looked down upon Mexicans, whom they considered an inferior race. Housing in many residential sections of Texas towns and cities was denied Mexicans. Schools for Mexican children were usually inferior in South and West Texas. Signs declaring, "No Mexicans Allowed" were posted in some public buildings and business establishments. Ballots were printed only in English. A new state law prohibited the use of interpreters in voting. Mexicans were often excluded from voting in the Democratic primary. Where they were allowed to participate, their vote was often controlled by local political machines such as those of James B. Wells in Cameron County and Archie Parr in Duval County. Efforts to challenge Anglo control resulted in jail time or physical violence. Twenty-nine Mexican-Americans were lynched in 1910–19.[22]

The role of women in Texas society, whatever their color or race, was restricted. Although some held jobs outside the home as teachers, secretaries, and sales clerks, women were expected to marry, raise a family, and work in the home and on the farm. A state law passed in 1913 slightly expanded the rights of women to control their own bank accounts and income from rents, stock, and bonds, but husbands still retained control over community property. Although they worked through various organizations such as the Texas Federation of Women's Clubs, the Texas Congress of Mothers, and the Young Women's Christian Association to solve social problems, Texas women still did not have the right to vote. The Texas Suffrage Association, founded in 1903 and reactivated in 1913 under the leadership of Mary Eleanor Brackenridge and later Minnie Fisher Cunningham, worked for equal suffrage but faced major opposition in its efforts to secure voting rights for women.[23]

Many Texas women were involved in the struggle to eliminate alcohol abuse. The Woman's Christian Temperance Union, organized in Texas in 1882, worked with other organizations to prohibit the sale of alcoholic beverages. In 1887, a state prohibition amendment was rejected by a two-to-one ratio, but in 1911 a similar amendment was only narrowly defeated, 237,393 to 232,096.[24]

The drive for prohibition was supported by the state's largest evangelical churches. Southern Baptists, with 355,251 members, and Southern Methodists, with 315,812 members, were in the vanguard of the movement to make Texas dry. Leaders such as Baptist Joel H. Gambrell, who served as superintendent of the Texas Anti-Saloon League; his brother James B. Gambrell, editor of the *Baptist Standard*; and George C. Rankin, former pastor of the First Methodist Church of Dallas and later editor of the *Texas Christian Advocate*, were instrumental in focusing attention upon the evils of alcohol and in securing the adoption of "dry" ordinances in more than 100 Texas counties.[25]

Many of the state's 462,874 Roman Catholics (a large number of whom were Germans or Mexican-Americans) and the 191,243 members of the black National Baptist Convention, as well as members of non-evangelical Protestant churches, opposed efforts to adopt local dry ordinances and a statewide prohibition amendment.[26]

Prohibitionist hopes for success in Texas dimmed in 1910–12 with the election and re-election of Oscar B. Colquitt as governor. Colquitt—an East Texas lawyer, former railroad commissioner, and state senator—was an outspoken opponent of prohibition. As governor, he helped defeat the prohibition amendment in 1911. Texas drys were encouraged by the candidacy of Thomas H. Ball for governor in 1914. A well-known Houston attorney and former congressman, Ball unified Texas prohibitionists behind his candidacy. Although he was endorsed by President Wilson and Secretary of State William Jennings Bryan, Ball was defeated by Temple banker James E. Ferguson. Ferguson, who campaigned largely against the evils of farm tenancy, declared prohibition a false issue and promised to veto any prohibition legislation.[27]

Ferguson won the Democratic nomination three days before the outbreak of war in Europe, virtually assuring his election in November. Colquitt, who remained as governor until January 1915, meanwhile faced growing concern about a major drop in cotton prices. In an effort to cripple Germany in the war, the British imposed a naval blockade on all goods, including cotton, being imported by Germany. The British blockade and the spreading war in Europe temporarily destroyed the overseas market. Cotton sold for twelve cents a pound in early July but dropped to six cents during September and October. To make matters worse, Texas farmers, who produced one-fourth of the nation's cotton, had a bumper crop on its way to market.[28]

Colquitt called a special session of the Texas Legislature in late August to consider aid for Texas cotton farmers. At his request, lawmakers passed measures creating warehouses where farmers could store their cotton until prices rose. To provide needed credit for cotton producers until the economy improved. Colquitt attempted to get the Legislature to create a state bank to assist the farmers. When this and a proposal for mandatory acreage reduction failed, the governor denounced both the Legislature and the federal government for their inaction. He described the Wilson administration as "the greatest failure in the history of the Presidency" and predicted Democratic defeat in the 1916 election.[29]

James E. Ferguson

Southern congressmen attempted to get the federal government to assist cotton growers. Led by Rep. Robert L. Henry of Waco, they introduced a bill requiring the deposit of millions of federal dollars in cotton state banks. This money would enable farmers to borrow at a maximum rate of 4 percent. A cool reception of the idea by the Wilson administration, however, killed the measure.[30]

Southern (and Texas) dissatisfaction with the administration's lack of action during the cotton crisis mounted. Navy Secretary Josephus Daniels of North Carolina and Wilson adviser Edward M. House of Texas warned the president that failure to provide some form of assistance to cotton producers would have serious political consequences in the South.[31]

The Wilson administration gradually moved to placate Southern constituents. After prodding by Secretary of State Robert Lansing, the British government, not wishing to undermine the U.S. president, agreed to purchase cotton shipments that normally would have gone to

Germany and Austria-Hungary. This guarantee, along with increased needs for cotton in Europe and America, solved the problem. Cotton prices slowly went back up. By the summer of 1915, Texas cotton producers were getting nine cents a pound. By the end of the war, cotton was selling for more than thirty cents a pound.[32]

With the rise of cotton prices, the Texas economy improved. At the same time, however, there were increased concerns about the growing unrest and violence in the Rio Grande Valley. The 1910 revolution in Mexico brought political refugees and an increased number of immigrants into the area. Mexican revolutionaries and bandits plotted their activities, purchased weapons, recruited volunteers, and made raids all along the border. Colquitt concentrated Texas Rangers along the Rio Grande in hopes of stabilizing conditions in the region and asked President Wilson for additional troops to patrol the border.[33]

In January 1915, federal and state authorities uncovered a revolutionary manifesto supposedly written in the South Texas town of San Diego. This document, labeled the "Plan de San Diego," was actually written in a jail in Monterrey, Mexico. The plan called for an armed uprising by a "Liberating Army of Races and Peoples"—made up of Mexicans, African-Americans, and Japanese—to free Texas, New Mexico, Arizona, California, and Colorado from the United States. Once liberated, the states would be organized into an independent nation that might later join Mexico. The uprising, scheduled for 2 a.m. February 21, 1915, would be a violent race war. No prisoners were to be taken, and all male Anglos aged sixteen years or older were to be executed.[34]

Newspaper publication of the Plan of San Diego caused alarm in South Texas. Gov. Jim Ferguson, who succeeded Colquitt in January, called upon the federal government for more troops and increased the number of Texas Rangers along the border. Tensions eased slightly when the February insurrection date came with nothing more than another manifesto calling for the proletariat to revolt. In late summer, however, Mexican revolutionaries carried out a series of raids in South Texas in which prominent Anglo and Tejano landholders were attacked, barns, storehouses, and railroad bridges burned, and telegraph lines cut.[35]

The number of cross-border raids diminished in late October 1915 when the Wilson administration recognized the Mexican government of Venustiano Carranza, convincing many Texans that Carranza had encouraged the raids in order to pressure the United States for recognition. The violence in South Texas continued for some time, however, as Texas Rangers, local officials, and vigilante groups executed anyone suspected of siding or sympathizing with the raiders. In the atmosphere of hate and recrimination, several hundred Mexican-Americans were killed.[36]

In much of Texas and in the nation as a whole, the 1915 raids in South Texas were overshadowed by events on the high seas. In February, the German government announced that the waters around Great Britain were a war zone. All merchant ships entering the zone would be subject to sinking by submarines. The new German policy brought a sharp protest from President Wilson. When the British passenger liner *Lusitania* was sunk off the Irish coast on May 7, 1915, more than 1,200 lives were lost; 128 were Americans. Protests from the American government and the public demanded that Germany renounce its U-boat policy.[37]

Most Texans supported Wilson, who said the German government must disavow the sinking of the *Lusitania*, pay restitution, and prevent future sinkings. The *Fort Worth Star-Telegram* described the sinking as "just as brutal and just as cowardly as if the passengers have been taken one by one from the *Lusitania* and swung from the yard arm by some marauding pirate ship." State Sen. J. C. McNealus of Dallas offered a motion in the Texas Senate expressing "horror at and condemnation of this savage act of war against helpless, inoffensive non-combatants."

While expressing confidence in Wilson and his administration, McNealus believed it was the duty of the United States to sever diplomatic relations with Germany. The McNealus call for the breaking of diplomatic relations was not adopted, but both chambers of the Legislature did pass resolutions condemning the sinking of the *Lusitania* and pledging support for the Wilson administration in its handling of the matter.[38]

The May 9 editions of the *Dallas Morning News*, the *Galveston Daily News*, and the *El Paso Herald* all criticized the German actions. The editor of the *San Antonio Express* dismissed the German government's warning to the passengers of the *Lusitania*. The *Austin Statesman*, on the other hand, believed that the warning was sufficient to excuse Germany from Wilson's policy of strict accountability. The *Houston Chronicle* cautioned American citizens to be calm and deliberative in the crisis.[39]

The crisis eased somewhat in September 1915 when the German government pledged to limit submarine use. The threat to American neutrality, however, convinced Wilson that the United States must strengthen its military forces in the event the nation should become involved in the European conflict. In October, he submitted recommendations to Congress calling for substantial increases in the size of the Army and Navy.[40]

The president's proposals did not find favor with all members of Congress. Several Texas congressmen opposed the president's plans. Oscar Callaway from Comanche County led the opposition in the House to naval expansion. The West Texan, a former prosecuting attorney, believed that building new battleships was a waste of money. Noting that the battleship was made obsolete by the submarine, Callaway opposed the president's plan to build new capital ships. Callaway argued the nation was in no danger of foreign invasion. The West Texan declared that any military foe attempting invasion could be repulsed by citizen soldiers, pointing out that Sam Houston and his army of civilians had defeated a much larger professional army at San Jacinto. Callaway also criticized fellow congressmen who might profit from increased military spending. His remarks were so pointed that parts of his speech were expunged from the *Congressional Record*.[41]

Other Texans spoke out against military expansion. Rep. John H. Stephens, a veteran lawmaker from Vernon, noted that Democrats traditionally worked for peace and opposed war. He urged a vote against proposals he believed were leading to war. Rufus Hardy from Corsicana, another longtime congressman, agreed with Stephens and expressed his opposition to any measures that might lead to war. The colorful populist James H. "Cyclone" Davis, who had been elected to Congress in 1914, denounced millionaire bankers and steelmakers who were leading the nation to war. These conspirators, Davis believed, were manipulating Wilson into accepting the "rabid Republican program of militarism" that would lead to a military dictatorship.[42]

Rep. James L. Slayden from San Antonio, a former president of the American Peace Society and a longtime opponent of American imperialism, agreed with his Texas colleagues that munitions makers were pushing the United States to war. Had Americans forgotten the advice of George Washington that we should not become involved in foreign entanglements?[43]

Criticism of Wilson's preparedness proposals eased in the late spring of 1916, when the president abandoned his support for the so-called Continental Army plan recommended by the War Department. Under this plan, a 400,000-man force would replace the National Guard as the nation's primary military reserve. The Continental Army plan encountered strong opposition, not only from National Guard and state officials but also from congressmen such as Martin Dies of Beaumont. Dies, described by historian Dewey Grantham as "one of the most reactionary members of the Texas delegation," was a bitter foe of militarism and centralization of power. He denounced the Continental Army plan as a conspiracy foisted on the nation by the War Department.⁴⁴

Wilson's willingness to give up the Continental Army idea and support a House plan drafted by Rep. James Hay, chairman of the Military Affairs Committee, turned the tide. The Hay plan, which increased the size of the regular Army but made the National Guard the nation's primary military reserve, passed the House by a 402–2 vote on March 23, 1916. All Texans voted for the bill except Rufus Hardy of Corsicana and Alexander Gregg of Palestine, who were among the twenty-seven House members who abstained.⁴⁵

The U.S. Senate adopted an Army expansion measure similar to the Continental Army plan, but conferees worked out differences between the House and Senate bills. The Senate agreed to a bill incorporating concessions from both chambers on May 17, the House on May 20. As passed, the National Defense Act of 1916 thoroughly integrated an enlarged National Guard into the federal defense structure and authorized increasing the size of the regular Army from 5,029 officers and 100,000 men to 11,327 officers and 208,336 men.⁴⁶

Administration proposals for increasing the size of the Navy encountered less opposition in Congress. Both houses of Congress agreed that the Navy must be increased, but they differed on the extent and type of increase. The House version placed emphasis upon new battle cruisers instead of dreadnought battleships. The Senate plan, adopted after and influenced by the battle of Jutland (May 31–June 1), called for a larger Navy and more battleships. After some wrangling, the House capitulated and accepted the Senate "big Navy" expansion. Seventeen Texans in the House voted for the naval expansion bill. Only four Texans—Eugene Black, Martin Dies, Rufus Hardy, and James Slayden—voted against the bill.⁴⁷

In the midst of the debates over Wilson's preparedness program, the issue of German submarine policy arose again. Although Berlin pledged in September 1915 to limit submarine warfare, it reversed itself as a result of British steps to arm merchant ships. On February 10, 1916, the German government announced that its submarines would attack armed merchant ships without warning. This alarmed congressmen who feared that loss of American lives on such ships would bring the nation into war. Jeff McLemore of Houston, a former cowboy and newspaperman elected to Congress in 1914, offered a resolution in the House requiring that Americans traveling on armed belligerent ships be advised of the danger. A similar resolution was presented in the Senate by Thomas P. Gore of Oklahoma.[48]

The Wilson administration, fearing that any congressional action might upset delicate negotiations being conducted with the British and Germans over the issue of armed merchant ships, opposed the McLemore-Gore resolutions. Administration supporters, including Sens. Charles Culberson and Morris Sheppard of Texas, were able to table the Gore resolution by a 68–14 vote on March 3, 1916. Four days later, the House voted 276–142 to table the McLemore resolution. Twelve House members from Texas voted in favor of the tabling resolution. Among those opposing were McLemore, Eugene Black of Clarksville, James P. Buchanan of Gonzales, Oscar Callaway of Comanche, Joe Eagle of Houston, and James L. Slayden of San Antonio.[49]

Two days after the House tabled the McLemore resolution, attention shifted from the submarine to the Mexican border. On March 9, 1916, the Mexican revolutionary leader Francisco "Pancho" Villa, angry at the United States for recognizing the rival Carranza government, raided Columbus, New Mexico, burning the town and killing nineteen Americans. Demands by state officials, congressmen, and newspapers for reprisal and punishment of Villa were so strong that the federal government had to respond. President Wilson ordered American military authorities in Texas to assemble an expeditionary force to move into Mexico, capture Villa, and prevent further raids.

On March 11, Brigadier General John J. Pershing, stationed at El Paso's Fort Bliss, was given orders to lead such an expedition. At the same time, Wilson called the National Guards of several states, including Texas and Oklahoma, into federal service along the Rio Grande.[50]

For the next ten months, the Pershing expedition campaigned in northern Mexico. Despite several clashes with Villista and Carrancista forces, almost leading to a full-scale war between the United States and Mexico, Pershing's troops were unable to capture the elusive Villa. In January 1917, Wilson ordered the American troops to begin withdrawing from Mexico.[51]

Pershing's foray into Mexico was followed by a renewal of Mexican raids into Texas during the late spring of 1916. On May 5, Mexican raiders struck at Glenn Spring and Boquillas in the Big Bend area, killing four Americans and taking two hostages. In June, Mexican raiders crossed into Texas near Laredo and Brownsville. In response, Wilson ordered more National Guardsmen stationed along the lower Rio Grande. The raids ceased in late summer, but tensions remained high in South Texas throughout the year.[52]

The 1916 border raids occurred as Texans were campaigning for state and national offices in the Democratic primary. The renomination and re-election of Gov. Jim Ferguson seemed assured, so major attention focused upon the race for U.S. senator. Former Gov. Charles A. Culberson was completing his third term in the Senate. Suffering from poor health for many years, Culberson had spent the last six months convalescing in Maine and was considered highly vulnerable. At first, it appeared he would not make the race. However, he was urged by friends of Wilson—who feared the possible candidacy of Joseph E. Bailey, a conservative ex-senator—to run again. Reluctantly, Culberson, referred to by some as "the sick man of the Senate," announced himself a candidate for re-election.[53]

Bailey's expected entry in the 1916 Senate contest never materialized. As a result, Texas conservatives rallied around the candidacy of former Gov. Oscar B. Colquitt. A critic of prohibition as well as Wilson's policies, Colquitt conducted a vigorous campaign and led the six-man race in the first primary. Culberson trailed a poor second.[54]

In the August runoff, Wilson supporters, including Postmaster General Albert Sidney Burleson and Attorney General Thomas Watt Gregory, worked for Culberson's renomination. A few days before the voting, Gov. Ferguson—who had easily defeated prohibitionist Charles H. Morris of Winnsboro, a political unknown, in the July primary—endorsed Culberson. Most big-city Texas newspapers—even the *San Antonio Express*, which had criticized Wilson as being too pro-British—supported Culberson in the runoff. German-American organizations in the state endorsed Colquitt.

Colquitt ran well in the German counties of Central Texas but fared poorly elsewhere. Culberson won the renomination by more than 60,000 votes, and with it re-election was assured in November.[55]

Wilson forces in Texas won several other victories in the state that summer and fall. The president easily carried Texas in his successful bid for re-election, defeating Republican Charles Evans Hughes, 186,514 to 64,999. Several Texas congressmen who had criticized the administration were defeated in the Democratic primary. Rep. Oscar Callaway of Comanche, an arch-opponent of increased military spending, lost his bid for a fourth term, defeated by U.S. Attorney James C. Wilson of Fort Worth—largely on the issue of preparedness. Two other critics, James H. "Cyclone" Davis of Sulphur Springs and John H. Stephens of Vernon, were defeated in their re-election bids. Three other Texas congressional critics of the president—Jeff McLemore, Martin Dies, and James L. Slayden—were re-elected.[56]

With the elections out of the way, the Wilson administration turned its attention to the war in Europe, now in its third year. Most

Americans, and Texans, wished to remain out of the conflict, but many feared that the war's prolongation might cause the country to become involved. In late December 1916, Wilson sent a note to the European belligerents, calling upon them to define their objectives in the conflict. In a speech to the U.S. Senate on January 22, 1917, the president urged the European nations to end the fighting with a "peace without victory." Such a peace, Wilson argued, should be based upon the principles of the equality of all nations and the right of all people to govern themselves.[57]

Wilson's clarion call for peace and good will was favorably received by the American public. Hopes were high among war opponents that the president's speech would lead to serious peace discussions. Disappointment ensued, therefore, when the message evoked no positive response from the belligerent nations. This disappointment was followed by shock when the German government informed the United States that unrestricted submarine warfare would be resumed on February 1, 1917.[58]

The German decision to resume unrestricted submarine warfare was based upon the belief by their military and naval strategists that victory could be achieved by preventing American shipments to England. Even though such a policy risked the possibility of U.S. entry into the war, the German high command believed that England would capitulate before American manpower and resources could be effectively mobilized to influence the war's outcome.[59]

American reaction to the German notification was strong. Except for expressions of caution in German-American journals, most newspapers condemned the new German policy. The *Houston Chronicle* denounced the announcement as "a gigantic mockery of our efforts for peace." The *Galveston Weekly News* believed the German note to the United States to be "a declaration of universal warfare wherein Germany acknowledged the whole world as her foe." The *Fort Worth Star-*

Telegram asserted that "neutrality with honor" seemed no longer possible. The *Austin Statesman* lamented, "Germany stuns us with the challenge just when we were trying to be most friendly." The *Dallas Morning News* labeled the new policy "terrorism to be enforced by the murder of whosoever may remain unterrified." Even the *San Antonio Express*, which had been more sympathetic to the German position than most major Texas newspapers, asserted that the nation "would never submit to any German naval outrage against the United States."[60]

Wilson was saddened by the German announcement. On the morning of February 1, he expressed his disappointment to his good friend and confidant, Colonel House of Texas. "The President was sad and depressed," noted House, "and I did not succeed at any time during the day in lifting him into a better frame of mind." Wilson, he noted, "was deeply disappointed in the sudden and unwarranted action of the German government."[61]

Consultation with House, Secretary of State Robert Lansing, and other members of the Cabinet convinced Wilson that the United States must take a firm stand against the new German policy. On February 3, the president announced the United States was breaking diplomatic relations with Germany.[62]

Wilson's action was praised by most members of Congress and endorsed by the majority of newspapers, although a few like the *Houston Post* regretted the break and the inevitable consequences that would follow.[63]

Others questioned the break with Germany. Wilson biographer Arthur Link notes that the break in relations "spurred leaders in the peace movement to almost frenzied activity." Although most criticism in Texas was confined to German-American groups, massive demonstrations to protest the rupture were held in Northern cities. At one such meeting in Chicago, more than 10,000 people gathered in the Coliseum to hear lame-duck Texas congressman Oscar Callaway denounce the munitions makers, capitalists, military leaders, and big-city newspapers that the Texan believed were forcing the United States into the European war.[64]

Although the president continued to hope that the United States might yet avoid war, events in late February and March brought the nation closer to military involvement. In February, German U-boats sank two American merchant ships, but in both instances warnings were given and safety provided for the crews. However, the threat to sink all vessels entering the war zone caused several American firms to cancel sailing of passenger and cargo vessels. Under pressure from Cabinet members such as Secretary of Agriculture David F. Houston, the president asked Congress on February 26 for authority to arm American merchant ships. He also requested authority to "employ any other instrumentalities or methods" necessary to protect American ships and people.[65]

Reaction to Wilson's new requests was generally favorable. Texas congressmen and Texas newspapers voiced little opposition to arming ships. Although the House refused to give the president the broad powers to "employ any other instrumentalities or methods," it passed an armed-ship bill on March 1 by a vote of 403–13. In the Senate, however, a small group of anti-interventionists led by Robert La Follette of Wisconsin and George Norris of Nebraska staged a filibuster that prevented passage of the armed-ship bill before the 66th Congress adjourned on March 4.[66]

On March 1, while Congress debated the armed-ship bill, Wilson released to the press copies of a telegram sent by German Foreign Minister Alfred Zimmermann to the German minister to Mexico that proposed an alliance between the two nations (and Japan) if and when the United States and Germany went to war. The note indicated that at the end of the war, Mexico would be given back territory in Texas, New Mexico, and Arizona previously taken by the United States. The

Zimmermann message had been intercepted and deciphered by the British and given to the American government on February 15.[67]

Publication of the Zimmermann telegram caused strong reaction throughout the country. Texas newspapers concluded that a de facto war with Germany existed because of the message. In the public mind, the Zimmermann note was linked with the Carranza regime in Mexico.[68]

Public discussions of the armed-ship bill and the Zimmermann message were still going on when Wilson took the oath of office for a second term. Denouncing the "small group of willful men" who defeated the armed-ship bill supported by the majority in Congress and the American people, Wilson asked Attorney General Thomas Gregory if there were legal restrictions preventing the president from arming merchant ships without congressional approval. When Gregory responded that there were none, Wilson instructed the Navy to place guns and gun crews on American liners and merchant ships.[69]

There was little criticism of Wilson's unilateral decision to arm the ships. Indeed, some congressional opponents admitted that the president had the power to do so. More public attention at the time focused on events in imperial Russia, where the revolutionaries had forced Czar Nicholas II to announce his abdication. The end of autocratic rule and the creation of a provisional democratic government pleased most Americans.

Three days after the czar's abdication, newspapers reported the sinking of three American ships with the loss of American lives. Sentiment for a U.S. declaration of war was growing. Even with increased demands by interventionists such as former President Theodore Roosevelt for a declaration of war, however, Wilson hesitated.[70]

Two days after the news of the ship sinkings, the president met with the Cabinet to discuss the situation. Members of the Cabinet, including the three Texans, spoke in favor of a declaration of war. Secretary of

Agriculture David F. Houston, former president of the University of Texas and Texas A&M, was one of the first to speak. "Germany is now making war on us," he noted. "She has been making war on us for some time, sinking our ships, even our ships homeward bound, and killing our citizens. We see what she is trying to do against us in Mexico. We ought to recognize that a state of war exists."[71]

Attorney General Gregory joined Houston and other Cabinet members in urging that Congress be called at once and necessary steps taken to pursue aggressive action against Germany. Gregory expressed concern about German intrigues in North America and asked for additional laws to enable his department to meet the menace.[72]

Postmaster General Albert Sidney Burleson was among the last Cabinet officers to speak. A longtime congressman from Austin before he joined the Cabinet, Burleson had been more sympathetic to the German position than other Cabinet members, possibly because of the large number of German-Americans in his congressional district. In early Cabinet discussions on the issue of German violations of American neutrality, his had been a voice of moderation. As late as March 16, he criticized British interference with overseas delivery of American mail. But now he, too, recommended a declaration of war. "There are many personal reasons why I regret this step, but there is no other way," he declared. "It must be carried through to the bitter end."[73]

The day after the Cabinet meeting, Wilson requested that Congress meet in special session to receive a communication concerning "grave matters of national policy." Although he refused to say what he would recommend, there was little doubt that the president would ask for a declaration of war. During the eleven days that followed, he gathered materials and thoughts for his message to Congress, meeting twice with his closest adviser, Colonel House, to discuss the issues.[74]

On the morning of April 2, Wilson addressed Congress. He described the recent German submarine campaign as "warfare against mankind" and Berlin's current course as "in fact nothing less than war against the government and people of the United States." Our choice was clear—"we will not choose the path of submission," he declared. "Congress must accept the status of belligerent which has thus been thrust upon us."[75]

The president's address was well received. Newspapers throughout the country, including those in Texas, praised the message. Peace organizations and some German-American groups still hoped that war could be averted, but most Americans supported the president's position that action must be taken. The Senate Foreign Relations Committee moved quickly to approve a war resolution. On April 4, the full Senate approved the resolution, 82–6. The House of Representatives passed the resolution on April 6 by a 373–50 vote.[76]

Only one Texan, Jeff McLemore of Houston, voted against the declaration of war. Other Texas critics of Wilson's neutrality policies, including James L. Slayden of San Antonio and Martin Dies of Beaumont, voted in favor of the resolution. Among the Texas congressmen who voted for the declaration of war were three who would later attain national prominence: Tom Connally of Marlin (first term in Congress), John Nance Garner of Uvalde (eighth term), and Sam Rayburn of Bonham (third term).[77]

The United States was now at war with Germany. Eight months later, the United States declared war on Germany's principal ally, Austria-Hungary. There was no opposition in the Senate to this declaration. In the House, only Meyer London, a New York Socialist, voted in opposition. Wilson approved the resolution on the same day and on December 11, 1917, proclaimed that a state of war existed with Austria-Hungary.[78]

CHAPTER TWO

MOBILIZING FOR WAR

The day after the United States declared war on Germany, Secretary of War Newton D. Baker presented a bill to Congress proposing the creation of a million-man national military force through selective conscription. Under the Baker plan, the administration asked for authority to draft immediately 500,000 men between the ages of nineteen and twenty-five, with the addition of another 500,000 later. These would be in addition to the 222,663 authorized for the regular Army and 440,000 authorized for the National Guard by the National Defense Act of 1916.[1]

The decision to adopt conscription, or the draft, was made after weeks of discussion within the Wilson administration. The president and Baker had originally believed that a wartime Army could be raised through volunteers, but a combination of factors led the administration to support a selective draft as the best means of utilizing the nation's resources.[2]

The selective service proposals encountered opposition from many congressmen and citizens. The nation's first draft during the American Civil War had resulted in riots and bloodshed. Some predicted a reoccurrence if conscription was attempted again. Others argued that a draft insulted the patriotism of American citizens who would willingly volunteer if the nation went to war. The issue was further complicated by the request of former President Theodore Roosevelt that he be permitted to lead two divisions of volunteers in the fighting in France. Although some of Roosevelt's admirers favored such an idea, professional Army officers believed that the request had little merit, as Roosevelt had no experience or training in commanding large bodies of men in a modern war. Certainly Wilson was not pleased with the idea of turning over command to the former president, who had been his most vocal critic in the days preceding the declaration of war.[3]

While pacifists and socialists opposed any increase in the size of the military establishment, most Texans saw the need for a large Army if the war was to be won. Gov. Jim Ferguson initially criticized the selective draft proposal but later sent a telegram to the president announcing his support. Former Govs. Joe Sayers and Oscar Colquitt issued statements endorsing selective service. The Texas Senate adopted a resolution urging the Texas delegates in Congress to vote for the Army bill. A Texas House resolution that "unemployed and unproductive persons" be the first called into service was referred to a committee, where it died.[4]

Congress debated the selective service bill for six weeks before final passage was secured. Although Texas and other Southern congressional Democrats were at first cool to the idea of conscription, most came to support some version of a draft. Much of the delay over passage was caused by arguments about the age limits of those conscripted and the question of volunteer divisions commanded by Roosevelt. As finally passed, the measure set the age limitations for conscription at twenty-one to thirty years. The raising of a volunteer force under Roosevelt's command was left to the discretion of the national administration. To no one's surprise, Wilson chose not to give Roosevelt the command he sought.[5]

The Army act passed by Congress provided that on June 5, 1917, all male American citizens aged twenty-one through thirty would appear at local centers throughout the country to register for military service.

Although there was some concern that widespread resistance to registration might occur, the process went off smoothly in Texas and elsewhere. On the assigned date, nearly 10 million young men registered, 418,160 of them in Texas.[6]

Under the law, individuals were required to register for selective service once they reached the age of twenty-one. By August 1918, another 910,564 men had registered, 42,166 of them Texans. Another 13,395,706 nationally and 530,196 in Texas registered after Congress passed legislation in August 1918 extending ages for registration from eighteen to forty-five years. In all, 24,234,021 Americans registered for selective service during the war; 990,522 of them were Texans.[7]

From the pool of registrants, each state was required to provide for induction to the new national Army a number of men based upon the state's percentage of population in the national total. In determining the number of men to be provided, each state was given credit for the number of men from the state serving as volunteers in the regular Army, National Guard, Navy, and Marine Corps. This number was deducted from the state's quota of men selected for service in the national Army.[8]

During most of 1917, individuals could still volunteer for service and thus avoid conscription. In December 1917, the regular Army stopped taking volunteers who were registered for selective service. In August 1918, the Navy and Marine Corps also ceased accepting volunteers.[9]

Administration of the process by which registered individuals were selected for military service was placed in civilian hands. A local selection (or draft) board was created in every subdivision of approximately 30,000 persons—in all, 4,545 boards, 279 in Texas. Each board consisted of three members, all white males, appointed by the president upon the recommendation of state governors. These board members, who served without pay, were assisted by a small, paid clerical staff.[10]

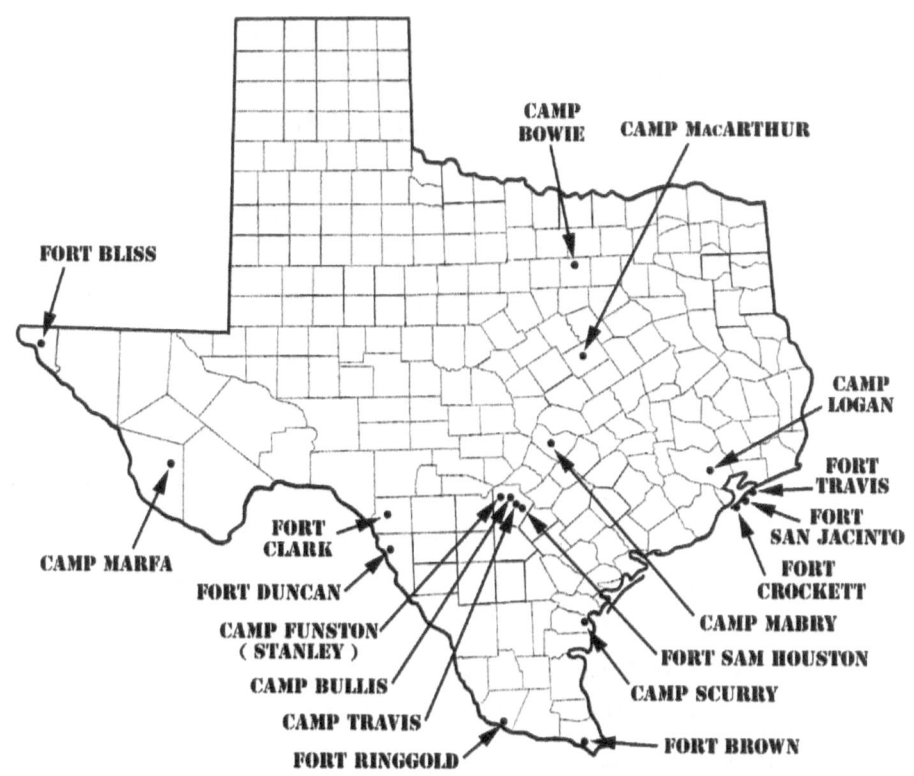

MILITARY POSTS & TRAINING CAMPS IN TEXAS, WORLD WAR I

In determining the order in which individuals would be called for induction, the local boards were guided by a series of national lotteries in which registration numbers were called.

A number of individuals were exempted from military service by law or presidential decree. These included federal and state legislators; federal, state, and local governmental officials; clergymen and students preparing for the ministry or priesthood; policemen, firemen, and sailors; and religious pacifists. Individuals who were physically, mentally, or morally deficient were also exempt from induction. In addition, the staff of the Selective Service System developed a classification system whereby husbands and fathers as well as industrial and agricultural workers could be deferred. Considerable discretion was given to the local boards in granting deferments. Some boards granted deferments to virtually all husbands and fathers. Other boards were more rigorous in determining dependency, examining such factors as the wife's employment, family assets, and support to the family from relatives. Nearly half of all Texans registered between June 1917 and September 1918 were married; three-fourths of them were deferred.[11]

In Texas and other Southern states, African-American registrants were more likely to be inducted than whites. Thirty-seven percent of black Texas registrants were drafted into the national Army; only 22 percent of white Texas registrants were inducted. This was due in part to the limited number of blacks who were allowed to volunteer for service in the regular Army or Navy, leaving a large pool of able-bodied black men relatively undepleted by voluntary enlistment. But it also reflected discrimination by some draft boards. Seventeen percent of all Texans—31,506—who served in the military in the First World War were black; blacks formed 16 percent of the state's population.[12]

According to the final report of Provost General Enoch Crowder, the officer in charge of selective service, 127,797 Texans were inducted into the national Army by conscription. In addition, another 37,704 regular Army and National Guard volunteers, 16,889 Navy volunteers, and 2,073 Marines were Texans, making a grand total of 184,463 Texans in military service during the First World War.[13]

At the same time that local boards were selecting the first men to be inducted into the new national Army, the various National Guards were federalized. In 1916, the government had federalized the Texas and Oklahoma guards as part of the buildup along the Mexican border. Both were being deactivated in March 1917 as the threat from Mexican bandits eased when orders were received suspending further deactivation and recalling partially demobilized units into federal service.[14]

Under the new mobilization plans, the Texas Guard and the smaller Oklahoma Guard formed the 36th Division. The new division, one of seventeen formed from National Guard units, included two infantry brigades of two regiments each, one separate infantry regiment, one cavalry regiment, two artillery regiments, one engineer battalion, one signal battalion, a supply train, and various service units. The Table of Organization provided for 991 officers and 27,114 men.[15]

Recruitment efforts increased the number of men in the Texas Guard before federalization as the 36th Division on August 5, 1917. The initial efforts in June produced fewer than 3,000 new recruits. A second effort was made in July. Gov. Ferguson declared the week of July 7 to be Texas Enlistment Week and appealed to newspapers, local government, and civic organizations. This drive was more successful. By August, the Texas Guard had grown from 194 officers and 5,097 men to 611 officers and 19,154 men. A similar drive brought the smaller Oklahoma Guard up to 2,576 men.[16]

Because of favorable climate, open space, and political influence, several military training facilities were located in Texas even before the war. These included Fort Sam Houston in San Antonio, Fort Bliss in El Paso, Fort Clark near Brackettville, Fort Duncan near Eagle Pass, Fort Ringgold at Rio Grande City, Camp Scurry in Corpus Christi, and Fort Brown in Brownsville.[17]

As volunteers, draftees, and guardsmen enrolled in the growing American military force, the War Department took steps to provide additional training facilities in Texas and elsewhere. Construction of thirty-two new training camps—sixteen for National Guard divisions and sixteen for national Army divisions, each capable of housing 40,000 men—was authorized. Wooden barracks would be built for national Army units; because of continued increments of draftees, they would be used for some time. On the assumption that National Guard divisions could be brought up to federal standards quickly, canvas tents were used for National Guard camps, all located in the South because of its milder weather.¹⁸

Many city officials and chambers of commerce moved quickly to persuade the War Department to locate these new training camps—or "cantonments," as they were called—in their communities. Houston, Dallas, Fort Worth, Waco, and El Paso all made contacts with Washington sources to point out their cities' advantages. Historian Lonnie White notes that San Antonio leaders were so confident that their city would be chosen they made little effort at first to convince Washington. After all, the Alamo City was an old Army town with a climate suitable for year-round training. It already had a facility—Camp Wilson, five miles northeast of downtown San Antonio adjacent to Fort Sam Houston—that could easily be expanded.¹⁹

Many believed that San Antonio would be awarded a new cantonment with no effort on the part of local officials. However, the War Department announced on June 1 that it was investigating vice conditions in all proposed camp locations. When it was learned that the secretary of war was concerned about allegedly bad moral conditions in San Antonio, local civic leaders moved quickly to clean up the area. Gambling and prostitution houses were closed, and individuals selling liquor to soldiers were arrested. The effort was successful. On June 11, the War Department announced that Camp Wilson—soon renamed Camp Travis in honor of William B. Travis, the commander of the Alamo garrison—would be the site for a national Army division composed primarily of Texas and Oklahoma draftees. When completed at the cost of $8.3 million, Camp Travis on 18,290 acres would have a troop capacity of 42,809 men.²⁰

The War Department selected Fort Worth as the location of the training camp for the Texas-Oklahoma National Guard. Work began on the newly designated Camp Bowie located about three miles north of downtown Fort Worth in July. Four troops of the 1st Texas Cavalry, which had been stationed in the Big Bend region, arrived in late July to serve as camp guards during construction. Engineer and infantry units began arriving in August. On August 5, Major General Edwin St. John Greble, a West Point graduate and veteran of the Spanish-American War, arrived to take command of the newly federalized 36th Division. Construction of the base hospital was completed in October. The 756-acre rifle range was opened in late November. The tent camp, supplemented by 316 temporary buildings, had a troop capacity of 41,879. Construction of the camp, completed in 1918, cost $3.77 million.[21]

Waco and Houston were the other Texas cities chosen for National Guard training camps. Both had aggressively pursued selection, utilizing city leaders, chamber of commerce officials, and area congressmen to convince the War Department of their merits. The War Department designated the proposed Waco facility as Camp MacArthur, in honor of General Arthur MacArthur. The Houston cantonment was named Camp Logan, for Union Civil War general and congressman John A. Logan. The War Department assigned men of the Michigan and Wisconsin Guards (federalized as the 32nd Division) to Camp MacArthur. Troops of the Illinois National Guard (federalized as the 33rd Division) were ordered to Camp Logan for training.[22]

The War Department assigned the 1st and 3rd Battalions of the 24th Infantry Regiment, each approximately 600 men, to guard the construction sites at Waco and Houston. The 24th, an all-black regular Army regiment except for white officers, had extensive experience in Indian campaigns, the Spanish-American War, and the Philippine insurrection. The regiment, currently in New Mexico, had just returned from service with John J. Pershing's "Punitive Expedition" in Mexico.[23]

Officials in Houston and Waco were apprehensive that the presence of armed black troops in their cities might lead to violence, but they were assured that strict military discipline would prevent any disorders. It was also pointed out that these two battalions were the only troops available for what would be a brief assignment of less than two months.[24]

Officers and men of the 24th Infantry were also concerned about the Texas assignment. African-American troops had had trouble in Texas before. The 1st Battalion had difficulties in a brief tour of duty in Del Rio in 1916; the 25th Infantry, the Army's other black regiment, had been involved in a serious 1906 incident in Brownsville. Too, the state had a bad record of racial violence. Brutal lynchings occurred in Temple in 1915, Waco in 1916, and Galveston in 1917.[25]

The two black battalions arrived in Waco and Houston by train on July 28. Disturbances occurred almost immediately. When black enlisted men went into Houston that evening, several incidents took place when soldiers refused to accept segregated seating on streetcars and tore down "white" and "colored" signs. Additional incidents occurred the next night in Houston, but military and civil authorities took steps to cool the tensions momentarily.[26]

In Waco, similar incidents involving black soldiers and local police occurred that first evening. Several soldiers returned to camp, armed themselves, and headed back toward town. They were cut off by a white officer and a detail of provost guards. An exchange of gunfire took place in an alley, but no one was injured. The rebellious soldiers escaped into the night but were later arrested by military authorities. After an investigation, six soldiers were found guilty of felonious assault and were sentenced to dishonorable discharge, forfeiture of pay and allowances, and five years' imprisonment.[27]

The July 28 incidents were the only serious disturbances during the 1st Battalion's duty assignment in Waco, as an uneasy truce prevailed between soldiers and civilians until the battalion departed and Michigan and Wisconsin guardsmen arrived.[28]

Unfortunately, relations between the 24th Regiment's 3rd Battalion and Houstonians took a more serious—and deadly—turn. Tensions in that city had grown steadily since the first arrival of the battalion. After nearly a month of enduring racial insults, humiliating encounters, and physical insults by police officers, black troops—led by Sergeant Vida Henry—decided to settle grievances against Houston police on the evening of August 23. Dozens of black soldiers marched into town armed with loaded rifles and bayonets. In an exchange of fire with police and civilians, the black troops killed fifteen whites—including four police officers and two white soldiers (one an officer) mistaken for police—and wounded twelve others. Two black soldiers were killed during the disturbance; two others died a few days later.[29]

The death of a white Army officer in the affair shocked some of the mutineers. They began quarreling among themselves and decided to return to camp. Henry, who had been the leader in the march, stayed behind and apparently committed suicide.[30]

Local authorities and troops from the 5th Illinois National Guard who had recently arrived in Houston slowly restored order. Gov. Ferguson, who at the time was involved in a political battle leading to his impeachment, proclaimed martial law. Companies of the Texas National Guard from Galveston and San Antonio were ordered to the area.[31]

The morning after the night of violence, military authorities collected all weapons of the 3rd Battalion, placed in custody those suspected of participating in the mutiny, and took steps to get the entire battalion out of town as soon as possible. The next morning, trains carrying the men and their equipment departed for New Mexico.[32]

In the several weeks that followed, rumors spread that local African-Americans were planning an armed uprising. Uneasiness prevailed in both the white and black communities as charges and countercharges were made. Houston congressman Joe Eagle requested that all black troops, including members of Company C, 8th Illinois, assigned to Camp Logan for training, be removed from the state. Fellow congressmen Jeff McLemore demanded that soldiers involved in the mutiny be returned to Houston to stand trial. A local board of inquiry appointed by the mayor exonerated the police department in causing the riot but agreed that the police chief should be replaced.[33]

The Army, meanwhile, conducted its own investigations. Sixty-three mutiny suspects charged with disobeying orders, murdering fourteen individuals, and feloniously assaulting eight others were brought before a court-martial board in San Antonio. On November 27, the court found fifty-four of the defendants guilty. Thirteen were sentenced to be hanged; the other forty-one were sentenced to life imprisonment.[34]

After additional evidence was gathered, the Army held two other courts-martial. At the first of these, forty soldiers were charged with crimes similar to those that drew convictions earlier. Twenty-three defendants were found guilty; eleven were sentenced to death and twelve to life imprisonment. In the third and last court-martial, fifteen soldiers were charged with murder and destruction of property. All were found guilty; five were sentenced to hanging, three to ten years' imprisonment, and seven to five years' imprisonment.[35]

In spite of the racial episodes during construction, work on Camp MacArthur and Camp Logan continued. When completed, MacArthur was a tent city supplemented by 1,234 temporary wooden buildings on a 10,000-acre tract. The facility's capacity was 47,074, but the highest number of troops at one time was 27,294 in October 1917. After the departure of the 32nd Division for overseas duty in February 1918, the number of trainees dropped, but it rose to 23,158 as draftees in the national Army arrived for training.[36]

Camp Logan received 20,000 Illinois National Guardsmen during September 1917 as the tent city was being completed. Built at a construction cost of approximately $4 million, the camp had a 44,899-man capacity, but the largest number of troops at one time was in December 1917, when 33,346 men were in training. The number dropped when the 33rd Division departed for France in the late spring of 1918. By June, only 3,500 men were at the camp, but the number rose to 17,586 in November as national Army trainees arrived.[37]

The enlargement and upgrading of existing army posts such as Fort Clark, Fort Sam Houston, Camp Bullis, Camp Funston, Camp Mabry, and Camp Marfa brought thousands of additional jobs and millions of dollars in construction money to Texas during World War I. El Paso officials hoped that a new training facility would be located there to complement Fort Bliss. Congress appropriated money for such a project, but the work was held up by Secretary of War Newton Baker, who was concerned about poor moral conditions in the border city. To satisfy the secretary's concerns, civic leaders inaugurated a concerted effort to drive out liquor and vice. In addition, measures were taken to provide Fort Bliss soldiers with wholesome recreation. Even so, the proposed new camp was not built. Historian Garna L. Christian concludes that although "it was never clear that Secretary Baker withheld the training camp solely because of moral conditions at the Pass, it was abundantly clear that he held out the cantonment as a means of reforming moral conditions there."[38]

In addition to the camps built for training ground troops in Texas, a dozen flying fields were constructed in the state for the aviation section of the Army. Texas was the location for some of the earliest experiments in U.S. military aviation. In 1910, Benjamin Foulois—the only officer in what was then the Aeronautical Section—was ordered to San Antonio, where he learned to fly and later conducted flights along the Mexican border. In 1915, the 1st Aero Squadron—which had been assigned previously to Texas City and San Diego, California—was reassigned to San Antonio. The army created the San Antonio Air Center, which was later renamed Kelly Field in honor of a pilot killed in 1911. From this field, the 1st Aero Squadron participated in the 1916 Pershing expedition.[39]

Although the National Defense Act of 1916 allocated $13 million for military aeronautics, flying schools, and new aero squadrons, little had been expended when the United States entered the war. The Army operated only two flying schools. The Aviation Section, as it was called, included 131 officers and 1,087 enlisted men and had only fifty-five trainers, most of them obsolete.[40]

With the entry into the war, the U.S. government, influenced by an appeal to President Wilson from French Premier Alexandre Ribot, launched a major program to produce thousands of aircraft and train pilots, observers, and ground personnel to man them. Believing that the quickest and easiest method of handling the ground phase of the training was to work with colleges and universities, the government contracted with six institutions—the universities of California, Texas, Illinois, Ohio State, and Cornell, and the Massachusetts Institute of Technology—to provide basic training of air cadets.[41]

At the same time that ground school training began, the construction of flying fields for primary flight training and servicing aircraft was pushed forward. Kelly Field—built in San Antonio and named for Lieutenant George E. Kelly, one of Foulois's students killed in a 1911 crash at Fort Sam Houston—was officially opened for primary flight instruction on August 11, 1917. A second field, known as Kelly No. 2 and later Duncan Field, was opened later that year for maintenance and supply functions. By November 1918, Kelly was the largest flying school in the world. By that time, more than 1,000 officers and 31,000 enlisted men were assigned to the field.[42]

Brooks Field, on a 1,300-acre site southeast of San Antonio, was opened for primary flight training in December 1917 when it became apparent that Kelly could not handle all the pilots needed. The army initially established Brooks, originally known as Gosport Field, to train flight instructors in the "Gosport system" developed by the Royal Air Force. In this system, instructors spoke to student pilots in flight through a tube. Gosport Field—or Kelly No. 5, as it was briefly known—was

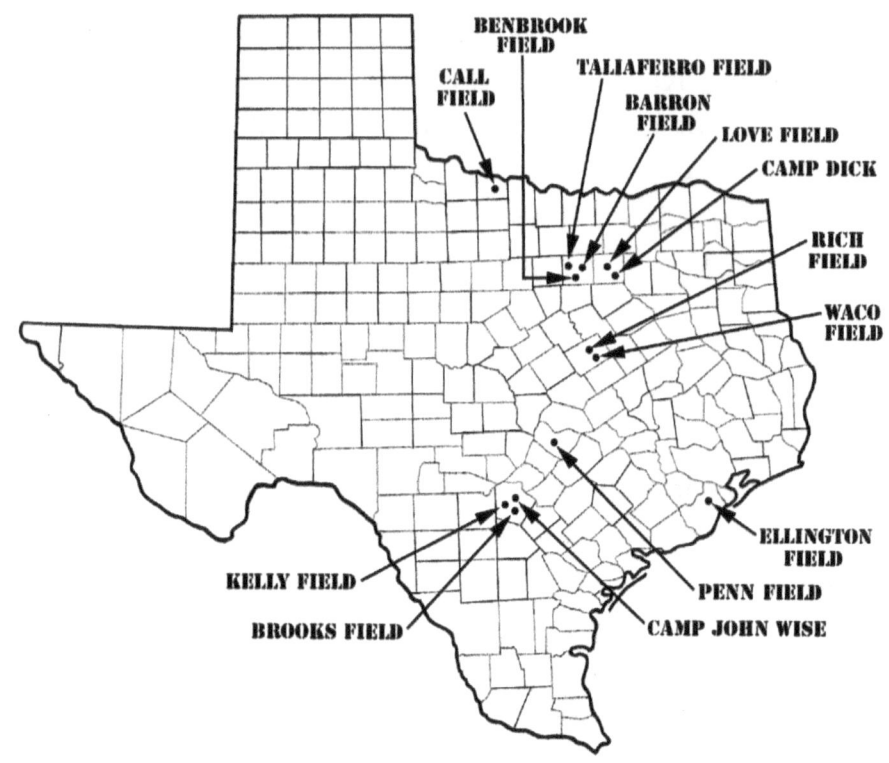

MILITARY AIRFIELDS IN TEXAS WORLD WAR I

renamed Brooks Field in February 1918 after the death of Cadet Sidney Johnson Brooks Jr. in a training accident.[43]

Three airfields were located in the Fort Worth area. Taliaferro Field, northwest of Fort Worth, was used by Canadian Royal Flying Corps for pilot training before the United States entered the war. During 1917, the U.S. Army took over the facility, which was renamed Hicks Field. Benbrook Field, known initially as Taliaferro No. 2 and sometimes as Carruthers Field, was located east of Hicks. It was used by American and Canadian students for primary training. Barron Field, to the east of Benbrook and Hicks and known at first as Taliaferro No. 3, was constructed in the autumn of 1917 for pilot training.[44]

Construction work on Call Field, five miles southwest of Wichita Falls, began on September 4, 1917. The first Army cadets arrived in late November, and flight training began in early December. The camp—named for Lieutenant Loren H. Call, who was killed in a 1913 air accident—had forty-six buildings, including twelve hangars, a base hospital, and six barracks. In May 1918, four additional hangars and lofts to hold carrier pigeons were built. During its operation, 3,000 officers and men were stationed there. Five hundred officers received their wings at the field.[45]

Ellington Field, on 1,280 acres of prairie southeast of Houston, was constructed at the same time as Call Field. Building began on September 18, 1917, with work completed two and a half months later. Named for Lieutenant Eric L. Ellington, killed in a California air crash in 1913, Ellington was a large installation consisting of twenty-four hangars, twelve barracks, four warehouses, two school buildings, a hospital, an officers' club, service clubs, and motion picture theaters. Both pilots and bombardiers were trained at Ellington. An aerial gunnery school for bombing graduates was established at nearby San Leon.[46]

Rich Field at Waco was built the same time as Call and Ellington. Construction began on September 11, 1917; flying began on December 1. Named for Lieutenant Percy L. Rich, who was killed in a November 1913 flying accident in the Philippine Islands, the facility was constructed at a cost of $1,151,792 and provided an eight-week primary flight course.[47]

Work on Love Field in Dallas—named for Lieutenant Moss L. Love, killed in a 1913 training flight in San Diego—began on September 26, 1917. When completed in early December at the cost of $1,261,402, the 710-acre field provided advanced flight training for pilots and bombers (later called bombardiers). An eleven-week course was provided for pilots; bombers were trained in eight weeks.[48]

In addition to these major flying fields, the Army constructed several specialized facilities in Texas for the air service. Because of the cold weather in Nebraska, the United States Balloon School was moved from Omaha to San Antonio. Camp John Wise, named for a pioneer American balloonist, was opened in January; balloon training began shortly thereafter. By the summer of 1918, the base had a maximum strength of thirty-three officers, 1,800 enlisted men, and four balloons.[49]

Penn Field, a small flying facility, was opened near Austin in March 1918, primarily for training enlisted men in the use of radio. Camp Dick, officially the Camp John Dick Aviation Concentration Camp, was established on the state fairgrounds in Dallas as a personnel holding pool for graduates of ground training programs. A similar facility, Camp Waco, or the Aviation Concentration Camp, was established at Waco to relieve congestion at Kelly Field. An aviation repair depot opened adjacent to Love Field in March 1918 for the repairing of airplane engines. An aviation general supply depot was opened near Ellington Field at Houston.[50]

As the nation was mobilizing manpower, efforts were being made to mobilize the economy. In some ways, this was a more difficult task, with several factors contributing to the problem. President Wilson resisted full-scale mobilization planning prior to the war because he believed this might undermine his diplomatic efforts to broker an end to the European conflict. Business leaders supported preparedness but resisted any governmental direction of their operations. Rivalries and competitions among Army bureau heads further complicated efforts at coordination.[51]

A year before the United States entered the war, Congress created the Council of National Defense. Consisting of the secretaries of war, agriculture, commerce, labor, interior and the Navy, the council was given the task of supervising and coordinating industrial mobilization in the event of war. A Civilian Advisory Commission made up of business, labor, industrial, and medical leaders was created to assist the defense council.[52]

The Civilian Advisory Commission worked diligently during late 1916 and early 1917 to prepare an inventory of military needs in the event of war. As part of these efforts, dozens of committees of businessmen and civic leaders were formed. Shortly after the United States entered the war, state defense councils were also created to assist in national mobilization. The Texas State Council of Defense, composed of thirty-eight members appointed by Gov. Ferguson, had its first meeting on May 10, 1917, in Dallas. O. E. Dunlap of Waxahachie was chosen chairman, Thomas H. Ball of Houston vice chairman, J. F. Carl of San Antonio secretary, and Royal A. Ferris of Dallas treasurer.[53]

The Texas council was divided into ten committees: finance, publicity, legal, transportation, coordination, sanitation and medicine, labor, food supply and conservation, military affairs, and state protection. Like many other state councils, the Texas council organized local groups to support the war effort. Eventually, 240 county councils and 15,000 community councils were created in Texas. These local groups worked to sell government war bonds and stamps, support conservation of food and materials needed for the war effort, and generate patriotism and support for the war effort.[54]

Although the national and state defense councils gathered much information concerning military needs and resources, they were not effective in mobilizing production for the war effort. In an effort to provide greater coordination, Congress in July 1917 created the War Industries Board as a subordinate part of the Council of National Defense. Robert S. Lovett of Houston, president of the Union Pacific Railroad, was one of seven individuals whom President Wilson appointed to the new board. Lovett was also named chairman of the Priorities Committee of the board. Under his direction, the War Industries Board took steps to ease a bottleneck in the transportation of coal, a resource vital to the nation's war efforts. When Lovett later resigned from the board to accept a post in the new Railroad

Administration, he was replaced by a longtime associate from Houston, Judge Edwin B. Parker.[55]

The War Industries Board encountered many of the same problems as its parent organization, the Council of National Defense. Secretary of War Newton Baker, who headed the national council and helped create the War Industries Board, continued to believe that the government should coordinate rather than direct the nation's industrial efforts. The board was reorganized in March 1918, with Bernard M. Baruch becoming chairman, but the board continued to have only the power to recommend, cajole, and publicize rather than order industry to devote itself fully to the war effort. For example, as chairman of the Priorities Committee, Parker attempted to limit production of civilian automobiles to 25 percent of prewar production but found automobile manufacturers opposed. He finally had to accept a compromise in which the industry agreed to a 50 percent figure. Similar compromises occurred in other areas.[56]

Still primarily an agricultural state, Texas made modest contributions to the nation's efforts to manufacture guns, ammunition, and aircraft needed by the military. Texas and Texans did contribute to one area of great need: the building of additional ships necessary to carry the goods and men of war. The United States had lagged behind in shipbuilding since the middle of the nineteenth century. This and the destruction of ships by German U-boats made it imperative that more vessels be built if the United States intended to support her European allies with men, food, and supplies.[57]

In January 1917, Congress created the United States Shipping Board with general authority over procurement of ships. In an effort to build as many vessels as possible, the Emergency Fleet Corporation, a subsidiary of the shipping board, authorized the construction of steel, wood, and concrete ships. Wooden ships were not suited for the oceanic trade but could be used for the coastal trade carrying materials in the Gulf of Mexico and Caribbean and along the East Coast, thus freeing steel vessels for the Atlantic.[58]

Four Texas ports—Houston, Beaumont, Orange, and Rockport—participated in building wooden steamships for the Emergency Fleet Corporation. Shipyards in Houston, Beaumont, and Orange had been building wooden sailing vessels for the lumber trade before the war. The *City of Orange*, built of yellow pine by Captain Fred Swailes and Company of Orange, was laid down in the summer of 1916 and launched in November of that year. Two others vessels, the *City of Houston* and the *City of Pensacola*, were nearing completion at the same yard when the United States declared war on Germany.[59]

With the outbreak of war, nine shipyards along the Texas coast received contracts to build wooden steamships for the Emergency Fleet Corp. The ships were to be built of yellow pine to a standard design. Two of the shipyards, the National Shipbuilding Company and the Southern Drydock and Shipbuilding Company, were located in Orange. Four yards building wooden steamships were in Beaumont: McBride and Law, the Lone Star Shipbuilding Company, the Beaumont Shipbuilding and Drydock Company, and J. N. McCammon. Houston was the home of the Universal Shipbuilding Company and the Midland Bridge Company. The shipyard built by Fred and Carl Heldenfels at Rockport, on the middle Texas coast, was the ninth facility contracted to build wooden vessels.[60]

Although none of the Texas yards completed wooden steamships in 1917, more than twenty were launched in 1918. To meet construction deadlines, Texas yards had to compete with other war needs for labor and materials. To speed the flow of lumber to the shipyards, the chairman of the United States Shipping Board, Edward N. Hurley, appointed Texas timber baron John Henry Kirby as lumber administrator for the South. Kirby, past president of the National Lumber Manufacturers Association, had considerable success in facilitating production and delivery of timber to Gulf Coast shipyards.[61]

When the war ended in November 1918, fourteen ships were being built at Houston shipyards, sixteen at Orange, twenty at Beaumont, and four at Rockport. These, and others contracted for, were completed in 1919. In all, more than 120 wooden steamships were built in Texas for the national war effort. In addition, fourteen wooden sailing vessels were built in Texas yards during the World War I era.[62]

Although shipping and manufacturing still depended upon the coal production of the Northeast, civilians and the military were making increased use of petroleum to move their automobiles, trucks, and aircraft in 1917. Here Texas played an increasingly significant role. Oil production in Texas, which reached 28 million barrels in 1905, dropped in the five years that followed as Oklahoma became the leading producer. New discoveries at Electra (1913), Barbers' Hill (1916), Ranger (1917), Hull (1917), Burkburnett (1918), Desdemona (1918), and Breckenridge (1918) increased the flow of Texas oil from 24 million barrels in 1915 to 38 million barrels in 1918 and 79 million barrels in 1919. The price of crude oil rose from 61 cents a barrel in 1910 to $2 a barrel in 1919. The total value of Texas oil production increased from slightly less than $15 million in 1914 to more than $75 million in 1918 and $157 million in 1919.[63]

As the need for refined oil grew during the war, the Houston Ship Channel became the center of oil refining. Several refineries, including those of the Texas Company, the Farmers' Petroleum Company, and Merchants & Planters Oil, were built before the war. Between 1915 and 1918, Gulf Oil, Galena-Signal Oil, and Sinclair Oil located along the channel. Several others—Humble, Crown, Deep Water, and Kern and Wolfe—completed plants between 1918 and 1921. Magnolia Petroleum, Gulf Oil, and the Texas Company built refineries at nearby Beaumont and Port Arthur.[64]

Production of sulfur, a necessary ingredient in the making of explosives, fertilizers, and other chemical products, was another Texas contribution to war mobilization. In the early twentieth century, Texas and Louisiana were the nation's major producers of sulfur. Most of the Texas sulfur was extracted from the Bryan Mound Dome near the mouth of the Brazos River by the Freeport Sulphur Company. With the outbreak of war in Europe, increased amounts of the yellow mineral were required by the United States and its European allies. Production at Bryan Mound rose from a modest 10,500 tons in 1913 to a thousand tons a day by the war's end.[65]

Another Texas firm, the Texas Gulf Sulphur Company, was organized by Texans and Easterners in 1918 to develop resources at Big Hill Dome in Matagorda County, sixty miles southwest of Bryan Mound. However, production did not begin at Big Hill until March 15, 1919—four months after the war ended.[66]

Mercury, or quicksilver, was another modern war ingredient produced in Texas. Used in producing fulminate of mercury—a detonating agent in cartridges, shells, and grenades and in the manufacture of cellulose acetate, with which airplane wings were painted—mercury was marketed in 75-pound flasks. In the prewar years, annual U.S. production was approximately 20,000 flasks, nearly one-fourth of which came from the Terlingua Quicksilver District in the Texas Big Bend. The largest individual Texas producer was the Chisos Mining Company, headed by Chicago industrialist Howard E. Perry.[67]

Because of increased demands by the growing American munitions industry, production of Texas mercury rose from 4,177 flasks in 1915 to 6,306 flasks in 1916 to 10,791 flasks in 1917. Annual national production increased to 36,000 flasks in 1917–18.[68]

Wartime need led to the development of the helium industry in Texas. Early German difficulties with highly combustible hydrogen in its zeppelins led the U.S. government to seek a safer gas for its balloons and airships. Research by the Bureau of Mines concluded that an abundant supply of non-explosive helium was located at the Petrolia oil field in Clay County. A helium plant was constructed at Petrolia; two others were opened in Fort Worth. Two hundred thousand cubic feet of helium was produced by the end of the war. Two small shipments reached England and France, and nearly 150,000 cubic feet was on the docks at New Orleans awaiting shipment when the war ended.[69]

Little publicity was given to Texas helium production during the war, but later Assistant Secretary of Navy Franklin D. Roosevelt (whose department was in charge of the program) told a New York reporter that if the war had lasted another year, the British and Americans would have had helium-filled rigid airships over strategic points in Germany, each capable of dropping ten or more tons of high explosives.[70]

The mobilization of agricultural commodities was another part of the nation's war effort. Not only was food needed to feed America's growing military forces, but the Allied nations also required vast amounts of grain, meat, and other farm goods. Even before the adoption of unrestricted submarine warfare, Allied food production was reduced by enemy occupation of French and Russian territory. Also, Turkish control of the Dardanelles and German dominance in the Baltic disrupted normal routes of trade. The opening of all-out submarine warfare magnified the problem.[71]

In an effort to feed the European allies and at the same time meet American needs, the Wilson administration urged both increased production and greater conservation of agricultural goods. In August 1917, Congress passed the Lever Food Control Act, which put government controls on food, fuel, fertilizer, and agricultural products. Herbert Hoover, a successful mining engineer who had earlier directed the Belgian relief program, was appointed to direct the newly created Food Administration.[72]

Hoover actually had begun work in an unofficial capacity four months earlier. During this period, he took steps to secure voluntary compliance, both in producing more food (especially wheat, which was in short supply) and cutting consumption of such items as flour, sugar, and meat. Now, as food administrator, he had authority to buy and sell food, offer price guarantees to farmers, prevent hoarding and speculation, establish trade mergers, suspend exchange trading, and eliminate waste.[73]

The Food Administration was divided into a number of separate bureaus that regulated and administered vital commodities. To assist in the work, a state administration was appointed in each of the forty-eight states. Edward Andrew Peden, a prominent and highly successful Houston businessman, was appointed state administrator for Texas. Peden was assisted by assistant administrator R. F. Crow and a staff of eighteen employees who were responsible for the work of various state committees.[74]

On October 3, 1917, Peden divided the state into three districts, each with a local administrator with headquarters in Houston, Dallas, and El Paso. A week later, he enlarged this to eight districts. In December 1917, seven additional districts were created. A final district was established in late September 1918. These state districts were subdivided into county organizations.[75]

As will be described in Chapter Four, the work of the Food Administration, both on the national and state level, was felt throughout the country as the war went on. The efforts of Hoover and his agents were generally successful, as production of food did increase and some modest reductions were made in the consumption of scarce items.[76]

Greater production of grain was a major objective of the Food Administration. Texas made substantial contributions in this area. A major increase in wheat production took place in Texas, from slightly over 2.5 million bushels in 1909 to over 36 million bushels in 1919. Oats showed equally impressive gains, from 7.5 million bushels in 1909 to nearly 64 million bushels in 1919, making Texas the fifth-largest producer of oats in the United States. The increase in corn production was less spectacular, from over 75 million bushels in 1909 to 108 million bushels in 1919. Texas was the seventh-largest corn-producing state by the end of the First World War.⁷⁷

Although Texas continued to be the nation's largest cotton-producing state, there was a slight drop in the number of bales ginned in 1917 and 1918. This was caused by one of the state's worst droughts, increased destruction by the boll weevil, and the appearance of a new pest: the cotton pink bollworm. In spite of increased demand for cotton and more acres placed in cultivation, Texas production dropped from 3.7 million bales in 1916 to 3.1 million in 1917 and 2.7 million in 1918. Increased demand for cotton and reduced production brought prices to new levels, rising to thirty cents a pound in 1918 and thirty-eight cents in 1919.⁷⁸

During the war, the Army purchased 800 million yards of cotton for khaki uniforms, work clothes, duck for tents, webbing gauze, sheets, pillow cases, towels, and other purposes. In addition, the demand for cottonseed oil and cottonseed meal to be used in lard, soap, margarine, and cattle feed increased. As the leading producer of cottonseed, with one-fourth of the nation's mills, Texas made a major contribution. A byproduct—cotton "linters," the fine cotton fiber that sticks to the rough surface of the cottonseed as it comes from the gin—was used as a base of nitrocellulose, or smokeless powder. In normal years, linters were used for stuffing mattresses, pads, celluloid, felts, and absorbent cotton, but other materials were used for these purposes during the war. The U.S. government contracted for the entire national output of linters for making smokeless powder.⁷⁹

The demand for raw wool nearly doubled during the war. The Army needed wool for winter uniforms, stockings, underwear, sweaters, and blankets for troops sent overseas. To help meet the increased demand, the War Industries Board promoted a "Raise More Sheep" campaign. Individuals were discouraged from eating lamb, and sheepmen were encouraged to raise more sheep for shearing. As a symbolic gesture, President Wilson ordered a flock of sheep placed on the White House lawn.[80]

The Texas sheep industry contributed to the government's efforts. The number of sheep raised in Texas increased slightly, from 2.2 million in 1917 to 2.6 million two years later—9 percent of the national total. Historian Paul Carlson points out that the increase probably would have been greater except for the 1917–18 droughts and the action of the Council of National Defense in setting a maximum price for raw wool—a step that pleased woolen manufacturers but angered sheepmen in Texas and elsewhere.[81]

The efforts made in Texas and elsewhere to mobilize economic resources for war in 1917–18 were less successful than the mobilization of manpower. By the end of 1917, more than a million young men were in training for overseas assignment to fight the enemy. Production of ships, guns, ammunition, airplanes, and other tools of war increased but never reached full potential. Most historians and economists believe that the Wilson administration's reluctance to impose stronger restrictions and regulations upon business interests and civilian consumers was a major factor in this failure. Even Wilson's most loyal adviser, Colonel House, in writing about industrial mobilization, concluded that "there is nothing that the Administration has done that I regret so much." House stated, "The President and Secretary Baker seem to be the only ones that think the organization is as it should be."[82]

CHAPTER THREE

TEXANS IN WARTIME NATIONAL AND STATE AFFAIRS

Texans played an active role in national and state affairs during the First World War. The state was ably represented in Washington during the conflict. Edward M. House of Austin was President Wilson's closest adviser during the war and had a leading role in the peace negotiations following the end of fighting. Fellow Austinite and former congressman Albert Sidney Burleson was not only postmaster general but also served as liaison between the Wilson administration and Congress. David F. Houston, former president of the University of Texas and Texas A&M, was secretary of agriculture and a member of the Council of National Defense. Austin attorney Thomas Watt Gregory headed the Justice Department and led the government's efforts to quash any internal criticism of administration policies during the war.

Burleson, Houston, and Gregory owed their appointments to the influence of House, who emerged as the president's confidant and close personal friend after the presidential campaign of 1912. Born in Houston in 1858, the son of wealthy Texas merchant, planter, and cotton exporter Thomas W. House, Edward Mandell House attended Cornell University for two years but returned home when his father became ill. When his father died in 1880, House decided to remain in Texas to

Colonel Edward M. House

manage the extensive family estate. After marriage and a wedding trip to Europe, House moved to Austin, where he expanded his business activities and became an adviser and confidant of Texas politicians.[1]

House was drawn into politics through his friendship with Gov. James Stephen Hogg. In 1892, House directed Hogg's successful re-election campaign. As a reward, Hogg made House an honorary lieutenant colonel on his staff. Newspapers soon shorted his title to "Colonel," a designation that remained with him throughout the rest of his life.[2]

Historian Robert C. Hilderbrand points out that the success of Hogg's 1892 campaign "drew House deeply into Texas politics for a decade." A skillful organizer and motivator, House managed the campaigns of the next three Texas governors: Charles A. Culberson, Joseph D. Sayers, and Samuel W. T. Lanham. He was also instrumental in the election of Culberson to the U.S. Senate in 1898.[3]

Eventually House tired of state politics. By 1906, he was spending less and less time in the Lone Star State. To avoid the Texas heat, he spent the summers on the Massachusetts North Shore and later established a residence in New York City. His thoughts turned more and more to national affairs, especially the election of a Democrat as president. In November 1911, he met Woodrow Wilson, then governor of New Jersey. Friendship between the two men rapidly developed. Writing to Culberson after a second meeting with Wilson, House stated that "the more I see of Governor Wilson the better I like him." Said House:

"I think he is going to be a man one can advise with some degree of satisfaction." Impressed by Wilson's progressive views, House worked among Texas Democrats to secure support for Wilson's presidential nomination in 1912.[4]

House became one of Wilson's inner circle after the election. Wilson offered House a Cabinet post, but the Texan declined, preferring to work behind the scene in advising the president. He secured Cabinet positions not only for his Texas friends but also for others he considered worthy. Mutual admiration and confidence between Wilson and House grew. Within several months, *Harper's Weekly* referred to House as the "Assistant President." *Collier's* labeled him the "Silent Partner."[5]

House was involved in planning and implementing all of Wilson's "New Freedom" reforms in the prewar years. His role as presidential adviser grew with the outbreak of war in Europe. He continued to counsel the president on domestic issues when asked, but he found foreign policy matters of much greater interest. Even though he believed that Wilson made errors in wartime mobilization, House remained silent. He preferred to concentrate on foreign policy, noting in his diary that "in foreign affairs he [Wilson] does nothing without the closest possible cooperation with me, and since I am so much more interested in that than in domestic affairs, I have been willing to accept the situation [wartime mobilization failures] as he has willed it."[6]

Prior to American entry in the war, House made three trips to Europe as Wilson's representative. On these visits, he met with and discussed international matters with European leaders including Kaiser Wilhelm II and Chancellor Theobald von Bethmann-Hollweg of Germany and Prime Minister Herbert H. Asquith and Foreign Secretary Edward Grey of Great Britain. These discussions convinced House that war between the United States and Germany was inevitable. When the German submarine campaign led to a break in diplomatic relations,

House advised the president on his message to Congress requesting a declaration of war.⁷

Wilson relied even more heavily upon House once the United States was at war. During the summer of 1917, as mobilization pushed ahead and as the first contingent of American troops commanded by John J. Pershing arrived in France, the president consistently asked House (who spent the summer in Massachusetts) for advice concerning foreign policy and relations with the European allies. When it became apparent that closer cooperation between the United States (which chose to be known as an Associated rather than an Allied power) and the Allies was necessary, Wilson selected House as head of the American War Mission to Europe. Before his departure again to Europe in October, House proposed (and the president agreed to) the creation of a commission, later named the Inquiry, to study the issues of peace and peacemaking once the war ended.⁸

The American War Mission, headed by House, sailed for Europe in late October 1917. The U.S. delegation arrived in Europe at a time of crisis. That month, the Italians (allies of the British and French) suffered a military defeat at Caporetto that threatened to destroy the Allied defense line in the Alps. Then, just as the House mission reached London, word was received that the Bolsheviks had seized power in Russia and threatened to leave the war. With House's input, the Allied and Associated Powers formed a Supreme War Council to provide closer coordination in the war effort. House attended the council's opening meeting as the president's personal representative. At House's suggestion, Wilson appointed Army Chief of Staff Tasker Bliss as U.S. military representative on the council.⁹

Although the council took steps to improve coordination and cooperation among the nations aligned against Germany and Austria-Hungary, House was discouraged by the excessive talk and lack of positive action. He was disappointed that the Allies failed to develop a statement of war aims and objectives. He was more convinced than ever that victory could be achieved only by greater American military participation. When he met with Wilson upon his return to the United States in late December, he recommended rushing more American troops to Europe. He also urged the president to develop a statement of war aims—advice that eventually led to Wilson's Fourteen Points.[10]

Albert Sidney Burleson

As noted above, House was instrumental in the appointment of three fellow Texans to Wilson's cabinet. The postmaster general, Albert Sidney Burleson, was a longtime friend. The grandson of a Republic of Texas vice president and son of a Confederate army major, Burleson had deep roots in Texas. Born in San Marcos and a graduate of Baylor and the University of Texas law school, Burleson served as assistant city attorney and district attorney in Austin during the 1890s. In 1898, he was elected to Congress, where he served for fourteen years. As a congressman, he supported most progressive legislation. He also became a leader in partisan political fights in the House and in 1910 was chosen chairman of the House Democratic caucus.[11]

Burleson was one of only four Texas congressmen who supported Wilson's nomination for president in 1912. He served as a leader of the Wilson forces during the Democratic convention and was director of the speakers' bureau during the presidential campaign.[12]

After Wilson's election, Burleson asked House to suggest his name for the position of postmaster general. House did so, but Wilson, who wished to keep Burleson as an active lieutenant in Congress, initially declined to make the appointment. Only after several prominent congressmen and party leaders endorsed Burleson did Wilson give him the job.[13]

As a Cabinet member, Burleson had a primarily three-fold role: direction of his large department, distribution of patronage, and administration liaison with Congress. The latter two roles took much of Burleson's time and energy. He worked diligently in advising the president on appointments and in helping push the president's domestic program through Congress. He was soon regarded as "the president's politician."[14]

Burleson's biographer, Adrian Anderson, notes that "Burleson's record as postmaster general would prove a mixed one." He supported the extension of segregation in governmental offices, opposed wage increases for postal employees, supported an increase in the cost of second-class mail, and fought for government ownership of telephone and telegraph. At the same time, he extended the parcel post service and introduced airmail delivery.[15]

The war placed new burdens on Burleson's post office. Anderson points out that "in addition to handling an enormous volume of mail generated by the military forces and war agencies, the Department sold savings certificates and thrift stamps, registered draftees, recruited soldiers, censored the mail, operated the telephone and telegraph systems, and assisted citizens with their income tax reports."[16]

It was in the censorship of the mail that Burleson received the greatest criticism. The Espionage Act passed by Congress in June 1917 provided severe penalties for any individual who willfully attempted to obstruct the war effort or induced others to do so. The act empowered the postmaster general to exclude from the mail any material designed to obstruct the prosecution of the war. The measure gave the postmaster general wide discretionary power; he was to determine what constituted "willful obstruction" and withhold this material from the mail. Most newspapers and periodicals at the time depended upon the mail for delivery, so this amounted to censorship.[17]

Burleson was vigorous in his enforcement of the law. The day after the Espionage Act became law, he instructed local postmasters to forward any "suspicious" material to his office for inspection. Within a month, the Post Office excluded from the mail fifteen major publications, some of them socialist. Historian Donald Johnson notes that these publications "were clearly unpatriotic and obviously antiwar; whether they constituted a willful attempt to obstruct the war is another matter."[18]

Civil libertarians immediately protested Burleson's action to the president. Wilson sent a copy of their letter to Burleson, asking for an explanation. Burleson quickly replied, arguing that he was merely enforcing the law. The president upheld Burleson's position.[19]

In the autumn of 1917, Congress gave Burleson a vote of confidence. The Trading With the Enemy Act, passed in October 1917, required foreign-language newspapers to submit to the postmaster general, in advance of publication, translations of any articles about the war. Such a procedure was costly and caused delays in publication, but Burleson "wielded this new authority with the same unremitting fierceness that he had shown to the radical press." The newspapers protested, but Burleson defended his department's enforcement of the law. While denying that he would suppress any legitimate criticism of the government, he insisted that nothing could be "said to hamper and obstruct the Government in the prosecution of the war." Despite continued objections from the press and civil libertarians, hundreds of mailings were excluded; seventy-five publications lost their second-class status.[20]

Burleson's fellow Texan, Attorney General Thomas Watt Gregory, was equally zealous in his determination to prosecute those suspected

Thomas Watt Gregory

of disloyalty. A native of Mississippi, Gregory practiced law in Austin after his graduation from the University of Texas law school in 1885. He became involved in local and state politics as a member of House's coalition of progressive reformers and conservative Democrats. As an early supporter of Wilson's candidacy, Gregory hoped for but did not receive appointment as an ambassador to Mexico. He was, however, named a special assistant to Attorney General James McReynolds in the antitrust case against the New York, New Haven, and Hartford Railroad in 1913. When McReynolds was appointed as a Supreme Court justice in 1914, Gregory was named attorney general.[21]

As attorney general, Gregory worked with Burleson to root out and punish critics of Wilson administration policies. He helped frame and enforce the Espionage Act of 1917. Under its provisions and, later, those of the Sedition Act, Gregory's Justice Department prosecuted more than 2,000 cases of individuals suspected of disloyalty and secured convictions of more than 1,000 individuals, including members of the International Workers of the World and Eugene V. Debs, leader of the Socialist Party and a frequent candidate for president.[22]

The Justice Department gave support to a quasi-vigilante organization called the American Protective League (APL), which served as a citizen's auxiliary to the department's Bureau of Investigation. By the end of the war, more than 250,000 individuals belonged to the league.

Carrying official-looking badges that read, "American Protective League-Secret Service," members spied on neighbors, fellow workers, and anyone suspected of disloyal activity. Under the guise of patriotism, they opened mail, intercepted telegrams, conducted raids against suspected draft evaders, and sometimes assaulted those suspected of not supporting the war effort.[23]

The APL's activities led to complaints from various quarters. In June 1917, Treasury Secretary William McAdoo protested to Gregory about the league, especially its use of the designation "Secret Service." Wilson, who received a copy of McAdoo's complaint, expressed his belief that it was "very dangerous to have such an organization operating in the United States." He wondered "if there was any way in which we could stop it."[24]

In response to Wilson and McAdoo, Gregory defended the APL's work, declaring that its members performed "a patriotic and effective service for the common good." His reply apparently satisfied the president, for the league continued its activities. Criticism by Republican congressmen for a series of arrests of "slackers," or draft dodgers, by APL agents in New York City in the summer of 1918 caused the president to order an investigation, but little came from it. The investigative report, written by one of Gregory's lawyers, generally commended APL members for their restraint. Gregory did apologize for any excesses that may have occurred but claimed that no individuals had been assaulted or mistreated.[25]

David F. Houston was the other member of the Wilson Cabinet with a Texas background. Born in North Carolina and reared in South Carolina, Houston came to Texas in 1894 as an adjunct professor in the newly created political science department of the University of Texas. Author of a critically acclaimed study of the South Carolina nullification movement, Houston became dean of the faculty in 1899. In 1902, he was appointed president of Texas A&M College. Three years later, he returned to the University of Texas as president. He left the state in 1908 to become chancellor of Washington University in St. Louis but retained close ties with Texas.[26]

Houston was asked to join the Cabinet by House, whom he had known for twenty years. House suggested an appointment to the Treasury, but Houston preferred the Agriculture Department, which he believed had greater developmental potential.[27]

As secretary of agriculture, Houston played a key role in the passage of agricultural legislation including the Smith-Lever Act, the Farm Loan Act, the Warehouse Act, and the Federal Road Aid Act. He also helped obtain a regional Federal Reserve Bank for Dallas.[28]

When relations with Germany deteriorated in 1916–17, Houston advocated a strong stand. He was one of the first Cabinet members to urge the president to declare war. He served as a member of the Council of National Defense throughout the war and worked with Herbert Hoover to encourage American farmers to increase productivity of the food and fiber needed to win the war. He was one of the Cabinet's most highly respected officers. House considered him the most able member. Wilson, who placed great weight upon Houston's advice, told House that he (Wilson) "found himself nearly always agreeing with what he [Houston] said."[29]

Although House, Burleson, Gregory, and Houston had the most direct contact with Wilson in managing the war effort, other Texans also occupied important administrative positions in the federal government. Former Texas House Speaker Thomas B. Love of Dallas, one of the first Texans to support Wilson's presidential nomination, was appointed assistant secretary of the treasury in November 1917. A highly capable individual with long experience in insurance and banking, Love was placed in charge of the Bureau of War Risk Insurance.[30]

Robert Lovett and Edwin Parker of Houston, mentioned earlier, performed significant service as members of the War Industries Board and other boards and commissions during the conflict. Stockton Axson, an English professor at Rice Institute and a brother-in-law of the president, served as national secretary of the American Red Cross during the war years. Houston businessman Jesse Jones was appointed by Wilson as director general of military relief for the American Red Cross in 1917 and became the chief liaison between the Red Cross and the chief executive. Sidney E. Mezes, who was married to House's sister-in-law and was president of the University of Texas in 1908–14, was appointed head of the "Inquiry," the commission that House conceived to gather information for postwar peacemaking.[31]

Most members of the Texas congressional delegation supported the Wilson administration war efforts. Although some of them criticized the administration's handling of the submarine issue, only one of the twenty Texas congressmen, Jeff McLemore, voted against the declaration of war. Several of them spoke against conscription, but only three Texans voted to recommit the selective service measure to committee.[32]

James Slayden, the senior member of the Texas delegation in years of congressional service, was one of the Texans critical of Wilson's policies. A native of Kentucky, Slayden settled in San Antonio in 1876 and became a cotton merchant and rancher. He was elected to the Legislature in 1892 and to the U.S. House four years later. Early in his political career, he became interested in the peace movement. He served as a delegate to the 1909 Hague Convention and was president of the American Peace Society for several years. He was one of the original trustees of the Carnegie Endowment for International Peace.[33]

Although Slayden backed the war effort once the United States was involved, he was not enthusiastic in supporting administration policies, especially in limiting freedom of expression. In an introduction to the published journal of Slayden's wife, Ellen Maury Slayden, historian Walter Prescott Webb notes that Slayden "refrained from war hysteria

Charles A. Culberson

and clamor for revenge." This, Webb believes, was due to Slayden's long dedication to peace and the sizable German population in his congressional district. He saw no need to harass or intimidate German-Americans or impose upon their culture and traditions. His lack of enthusiasm for programs supported by the president ultimately cost him his congressional seat.[34]

The senior U.S. senator from Texas, Charles A. Culberson, came to Congress only two years after Slayden. Culberson, who served two terms as governor before coming to Washington, was one of the administration's most loyal supporters. Always in poor health and frequently absent from the Senate during the prewar years, Culberson weathered a strong challenge from Oscar Colquitt to win a fourth term in the summer of 1916. As chairman of the Senate Judiciary Committee, Culberson worked to give the administration more power and authority in dealing with wartime critics. He introduced the legislation that became the Espionage Act of 1917 the same evening that Wilson asked for a declaration of war. When Cabinet members Burleson and Gregory advocated additional measures to control deserters, Culberson authored legislation that came to be known as the Sedition Act.[35]

Culberson's Texas colleague in the Senate, Morris Sheppard of Texarkana, came to Congress in 1903. After a ten-year career in the House, Sheppard was elected to the Senate to fill the seat vacated by Joseph W. Bailey. As senator, Sheppard consistently supported Wilson's domestic programs and foreign policy initiatives. An advocate of women's suffrage, Sheppard was also a dedicated foe of alcoholic beverages who led the fight in Congress for nationwide prohibition.[36]

TEXAS MEMBERS OF 65th CONGRESS

March 4, 1917 – March 3, 1919

Senators
  Charles Culberson, Dallas
  Morris Sheppard, Texarkana

Representatives
  Eugene Black, Clarksville
  Thomas Blanton, Abilene*
  James P. Buchanan, Brenham
  Thomas T. Connally, Marlin*
  Martin Dies, Beaumont
  Joseph Eagle, Houston
  John Nance Garner, Uvalde
  Daniel E. Garrett, Houston (at large)
  Alexander Gregg, Palestine
  Rufus Hardy, Corsicana
  Marvin Jones, Amarillo*
  A. Jeff McLemore, Houston (at large)
  J. J. Mansfield, Columbus*
  Sam Rayburn, Bonham
  James L. Slayden, San Antonio
  Hatton W. Sumners, Dallas
  James C. Wilson, Fort Worth*
  James Young, Kaufman

* New members

Source: *Biographical Directory of the American Congress, 1774-1949* (Washington: Government Printing Office, 1950).

Morris Sheppard

John Nance Garner of Uvalde and Alexander W. Gregg of Palestine, two other congressional veterans in the Texas wartime delegation, came to the House of Representatives the same year as Sheppard. Gregg, a lawyer and former member of the Texas Senate, was critical of the president's preparedness campaign in 1914–16 but gradually came to support administration measures during the war. Garner, on the other hand, backed the Wilson administration from the beginning. His biographer, Lionel V. Patenaude, notes that although Garner took little initiative in introducing bills, he had considerable influence in the passage of legislation. Chosen as Democratic party whip in 1909, he became a member of the powerful Ways and Means Committee in 1913. Wilson did not particularly like Garner at first but soon became fond of him. During the war, Garner often acted as liaison between the lower chamber and the president. At Wilson's request, he visited the White House twice a week to discuss legislative matters.[37]

Martin Dies, a former district attorney, county judge, and Spanish-American War veteran, was serving his fifth and final term in the 1917–19 Congress. A staunch foe of immigration, high tariffs, and imperialism, the East Texas congressman opposed many of Wilson's foreign policy initiatives. Although he criticized increased military expenditures, he voted for the National Defense Act of 1916 and the declaration of war with Germany, both measures highly popular in his southeast Texas district.[38]

Dies often supported fellow Texas congressman Jeff McLemore in his attacks on Wilson's wartime measures. The only Texan to vote against the declaration of war, McLemore was the maverick of the Texas delegation. A former cowboy, printer, newspaper reporter, and state legislator, McLemore was elected as a member-at-large in 1914 and reelected in 1916. As co-author of the prewar resolution warning Americans against traveling on belligerent ships, McLemore roused the ire of the Wilson administration and would, like Slayden, be marked for defeat in 1918.[39]

The other Texans who served in the wartime Congress generally supported the administration in its conduct of the war. Rufus Hardy of Corsicana, first elected in 1906, and James Young of Kaufman, chosen in 1910, were serving in Congress before Wilson became president. Both represented rural districts and were primarily concerned with agricultural matters. According to a colleague, Young had "cotton on his mind all the time." He led the House fight to prevent administration efforts to fix the price on cotton during the war.[40]

Five Texas members of the wartime Congress—James Buchanan of Brenham, Joe Eagle and David E. Garrett of Houston, Sam Rayburn of Bonham, and Hatton Sumners of Dallas—took office the same year as Wilson. They were joined by Eugene Black of Clarksville in 1915 and Tom Blanton of Abilene, Tom Connally of Marlin, Marvin Jones of Amarillo, Joe Mansfield of Columbus, and James C. Wilson of Fort Worth in 1917. Of this group, Sumners and Blanton were the most conservative and most prone to question administration policies. Connally and Jones served briefly in the Army before the war ended—Connally as a captain and adjutant at Camp Meade, Maryland, and Jones as a private in the tank corps in North Carolina.[41]

Texas congressmen supported the Wilson administration's measures to finance the war. The so-called Liberty Loan bill, which authorized the Treasury to borrow up to $5 billion through the sale of bonds and stamps, passed Congress quickly with no dissenting vote in late April 1917. Passage of a revenue bill designed to raise additional money to finance the war effort through taxation was a more difficult task. Texas congressmen joined with other Southern Democrats to defeat a proposal to impose a cotton tax of $2.50 per bale. With the support of Texas Democrats (particularly Garner and Rayburn on the Ways and Means committee), the War Revenue Act—which sought to raise $1.8 billion by reducing the exemptions on the income tax, increasing tax rates on incomes over $3,000 from 2 percent to 4 percent, doubling the excess profits tax, and imposing new luxury taxes—passed the House in May. A longer debate occurred in the Senate, where some Republican leaders attempted to reduce the excess profits tax. When these efforts failed, the Senate passed the Revenue Act in September by a 69–4 vote. A month elapsed before differences could be resolved by Senate and House conferees. Final agreement was secured on October 3, 1917.[42]

Although Texas congressmen were in general agreement on wartime taxation and revenue, they were divided on two major domestic issues that confronted Congress: prohibition and women's suffrage.

By 1917, all the Southern states except Texas, Louisiana, and Florida had adopted statewide prohibition. In Texas, a state constitutional amendment was defeated by a narrow margin in 1911, but advocates of prohibition, the "drys," were gaining momentum. The outbreak of war gave drys new hope for statewide as well as national prohibition. The need to conserve grain and sugar for wartime needs provided prohibitionists with an additional weapon. Too, the knowledge that Germans dominated the American brewing industry worked to the advantage of the drys in an atmosphere in which all things German were considered evil.[43]

The Texas delegation in Congress reflected divisions within the state on the issue. In general, congressmen from rural West and East Texas counties with Protestant constituencies supported prohibition; those from South and Central Texas with Mexican and German voters and those representing large urban areas opposed prohibition.[44]

Morris Sheppard, a Yale-educated Methodist from East Texas, was leader of the prohibitionists in the U.S. Senate. A son of a former Texas congressman, the forty-two-year-old Sheppard was a supporter of progressive domestic reforms and the Wilson foreign policy. But his great interest was prohibition. In 1913 and 1914, he failed in his attempt to ban the sale of liquor in the District of Columbia. On the day that war was declared, he wrote to the president to urge national prohibition. At the same time, Sheppard introduced a constitutional amendment for national prohibition.[45]

In the late summer of 1917, the Senate debated Sheppard's amendment. Opposition came largely from East Coast senators who had large constituencies of foreign extraction for whom drinking beer or wine was part of their culture. A few Southern senators, including Sheppard's Texas colleague, Charles A. Culberson (himself a heavy drinker), opposed the bill. Sheppard led the speakers supporting the measure, citing statistics showing the relationship between alcohol and crime, the waste of grain and labor devoted to the manufacture of alcohol, and work time lost due to drunkenness. Sheppard pointed out that one of America's greatest presidents, Abraham Lincoln, had opposed alcohol as a young man.[46]

The resolution for a prohibition amendment passed the Senate by a 65–20 vote on August 1, 1917. It was taken up in the House in the second session of the 65th Congress in December. On December 17, 1917, the House voted 282–128 in favor of passage. The Texas delegation was evenly divided—eight voted in favor, eight were opposed, and two did not vote.[47]

The issue of women's suffrage, like prohibition, gained momentum in the pre-World War I decade. By the outbreak of war, all Western states except Texas, Oklahoma, New Mexico, Nebraska, and North

Dakota had given women the franchise; Oklahoma did so in 1918. As will be discussed in the next chapter, the Texas Woman Suffrage Association, led by Mary Eleanor Brackenridge and Minnie Fisher Cunningham, worked energetically for suffrage but failed in 1917 to secure the two-thirds majority in the Texas Legislature that was necessary for a statewide referendum on the subject.[48]

While suffragists were fighting for political rights in the Texas Legislature, the National American Woman Suffrage Association was working for an amendment to the U.S. Constitution giving women the right to vote. In 1914, such an amendment was voted down in the House of Representatives, with not a single Texan voting for passage; indeed, veteran congressman Robert L. Henry of Waco, chairman of the House Rules Committee, led the fight against the proposal. By 1917, however, the drive for an amendment was gaining ground. Some of the leading opponents—such as Henry, who ran unsuccessfully for Culberson's Senate seat—were no longer in Congress. More importantly, President Wilson, who had argued previously that the issue should be left to the states, now supported suffrage. Influenced in part by the contribution of the women to the war effort and in part by the need for additional support for party candidates in the 1918 elections, Wilson persuaded House leaders to create a special committee to study suffrage.[49]

In January 1918, the special committee, by a split vote, agreed to send a resolution to the full House calling for a women's suffrage amendment. Tom Blanton of Abilene, a fiscal conservative and critic of organized labor, was the only Southerner on the committee to vote in favor of the resolution.[50]

On January 10, the House voted 274–136—one vote over the required two-thirds majority—in favor of submitting a constitutional amendment to the states. Twelve of the House members from Texas joined the majority of their Southern colleagues in voting against the suffrage resolution. Six Texans—Blanton, Connally, Garrett, Gregg, Jones, and Sumners—voted in favor of passage.[51]

Opposition to suffrage was stronger in the Southern-controlled Senate. In an effort to win over some of their colleagues, supporters delayed a vote until autumn. When the issue was brought up, Sheppard was one of only a handful of Southern Democrats supporting suffrage. Using the states' rights argument, Sheppard urged fellow senators not to deprive the states of the right to consider the issue. As historian Richard L. Watson notes, Sheppard's was "a lonely southern voice." Most Southern senators, including Texan Charles Culberson, opposed the amendment. The amendment failed by two votes to secure the necessary two-thirds approval. The nation would wait until after the war to send a constitutional amendment for suffrage to the states for their consideration.[52]

While Texans in Washington were debating such issues as conscription, civil liberties, taxation, prohibition, and suffrage during 1917, Texans in Austin were voting to remove James E. Ferguson as governor.

As noted earlier, Ferguson, a relative newcomer to politics, was elected governor just as the war in Europe was beginning in 1914. During his first term as the state's chief executive, Ferguson, who was a charismatic public speaker, worked with the Legislature to pass a bill that limited the amount of rent that landlords could charge tenants; legislation granting $1 million to rural schools; and a measure requiring compulsory school attendance. Three new "normal" schools were authorized, a school for students with mental retardation was created, and the Department of Forestry was established.[53]

Ferguson was easily re-elected in 1916, once again defeating a prohibitionist candidate in the Democratic primary. He was in the fourth month of his second term when the United States went to war with Germany. Although he criticized Wilson's policies earlier, he supported the president in most issues once war was declared. However, disagreements between Ferguson and the University of Texas soon absorbed much of his attention and led to his removal as governor in September 1917.

Ferguson's fight with the university began in 1915, when the governor quarreled with the university's acting president, William J. Battle, about the school's budget. The conflict continued in 1916 when the board of regents, without consulting the governor, named Robert E. Vinson, head of the Austin Presbyterian Seminary, as the university's new president. Unhappy that he had not been consulted, Ferguson became even angrier when Vinson refused to fire six faculty members whom the governor wanted dismissed. At an October 1916 meeting with the regents, Ferguson repeated his demands that the faculty members (who had been critical of the governor) be fired, but the regents declined to do so.[54]

When Ferguson began his second term in January 1917, the fight spilled over into the Legislature. Lawmakers held up the confirmation of three new regents appointed by Ferguson pending a committee investigation. In the meantime, old allegations that Ferguson had committed misdeeds in handling personal and official finances led to another investigation. This inquiry found some questionable financial transactions but concluded that they did not constitute an impeachable offense. The Senate confirmed the Ferguson appointments to the board, and the issue appeared to be closed.[55]

As the Legislature failed to adopt an appropriation bill during the regular session, a special session was called in April 1917. The Legislature gave the University of Texas a sizable increase in the appropriation bill, which was sent to the governor at the end of the special session in May. The governor, still angry at the university, vetoed the school's appropriation.[56]

Ferguson's veto set off a wave of protest, particularly among the university's faculty, students, and ex-students. It also gave old critics of the governor, including prohibitionists and suffragists, additional incentive to seek Ferguson's removal. As criticism of the governor mounted, Texas House Speaker Francis O. Fuller, a prohibitionist and political foe of the governor, called a special session of the Legislature to consider impeachment. There was some question about the legality of the speaker's action, but on July 31, Ferguson himself issued a call for a special session, ostensibly to consider the university appropriation.[57]

After taking care of the university appropriation, the special session turned to considering charges against the governor. After hearing testimony from Fuller, Vinson, and Ferguson, the Texas House voted a twenty-one-article bill of impeachment against Ferguson. Fourteen of the articles dealt with the governor's finances; one of these charged the governor with contempt for failing to answer questions about a $156,000 loan he had received. Five articles related to the fight with the university, and two to disputes involving the governor, the courts, and the Legislature.[58]

Sitting as a high court of impeachment, the Texas Senate heard testimony in September. Ferguson again defended himself but still refused to answer questions concerning the $156,000 loan. On September 22, the Senate by the required two-thirds vote found the governor guilty of ten charges, seven of them involving the governor's finances and three concerning his relations with the university.[59]

In an effort to avoid removal, Ferguson resigned before the Senate determined the penalty for his actions. The Senate ignored the resignation and on September 25 voted to remove him from office and disqualify him from holding public office in Texas again. Predictably, Ferguson denounced the Legislature's actions and promised to run for governor again in 1918.[60]

William P. Hobby, a Houston and Beaumont newspaper editor and publisher who was elected lieutenant governor in 1914 and re-elected in 1916, was now governor of Texas. He faced the challenge of directing state affairs during the last year of the war and defeating Ferguson's efforts to regain the governor's office in 1918.[61]

CHAPTER FOUR

LIFE ON THE TEXAS HOME FRONT

William P. Hobby became governor as the First World War was having a real effect upon the lives of most Texans. The month before Hobby succeeded Jim Ferguson, the Texas National Guard was federalized as the 36th Infantry Division, Camp Bowie was opened at Fort Worth for the new division, Kelly Field at San Antonio began pilot training, and the first draftees arrived at Camp Travis in the Alamo City. Dozens of additional airfields and Army camps were hurriedly being built for thousands of young men to be trained in the skills of warfare. The Texas Food Administration had completed its organization and was beginning to encourage Texans to conserve food for the war effort.[1]

Hobby, only thirty-nine when he succeeded Ferguson, served as the state's chief executive during the thirteen most difficult months of the war. A son of a former state senator and district judge, Hobby was born in rural Polk County but spent much of his young adult life in Beaumont and Houston as a newspaper reporter, editor, and publisher. Active in state Democratic party affairs, he was elected lieutenant governor in 1914, defeating prohibitionist candidate B. B. Sturgeon of Paris. Hobby ran on a platform emphasizing educational improvements, minimum rental rates for tenant farmers, and a runoff system in party primary elections. Like his unofficial running mate, Ferguson, Hobby argued that there were more important issues than the consumption of

William P. Hobby

alcoholic beverages, a position that caused prohibitionists to regard him as a "wet."[2]

Easily re-elected lieutenant governor in 1916, Hobby became governor when the impeached Ferguson was found guilty by the state Senate. Elated over the removal of their old foe, prohibitionists began to press the new governor. At first, Hobby attempted to ignore the alcohol question; war-related issues appeared more pressing. The U.S. Treasury Department launched its second Liberty Loan drive in October. The governor was expected to help promote the sale of Liberty bonds. Hobby was also called upon to host governors from Illinois and Oklahoma who were visiting troops from their states who were being trained in Texas. The new governor also met with state officers of the Council of National Defense and the Food Administration in efforts to promote mobilization and conservation.[3]

Other problems confronted Hobby. The state was being asked to produce more wheat, cotton, and cattle during one of the worst droughts in its history. The year 1917 was the driest on record in the state. Rainfall was far below average in every section of the state, particularly West Texas. Farmers were asking for federal assistance. Hobby, realizing that the national government with its large war budget could not provide direct financial aid, called upon President Wilson to direct large federal bank deposits in the most drought-stricken counties so that farmers could borrow money to see them through the drought.[4]

Prohibitionists continued to pressure Hobby to take action on alcoholic beverages. In late 1917, the anti-prohibition Ferguson announced that he would be a candidate in the 1918 Democratic primary in a bid to regain the governorship. To counter Ferguson and his wet supporters, Railroad Commissioner Earle Mayfield, a prohibitionist, announced that he would run for governor unless Hobby called a special session of the Legislature to consider the issue. Passage of the national prohibition amendment by Congress in December added weight to the growing demands for legislative action.[5]

In February 1918, Hobby, bowing to growing pressure and political realities, called a special legislative session. In response to concern about vice and excessive alcoholism near Texas training camps, Hobby recommended legislation creating a ten-mile zone around military camps in which alcoholic beverages could not be sold. Hobby included with his message to the Legislature a telegram from Secretary of War Newton Baker supporting such legislation.[6]

The Legislature, which convened on February 26, 1918, was quick to tackle the prohibition issue. On February 28, the Texas House voted 73–36 to ratify the national prohibition amendment. Senate action came four days later by a 15–7 margin. The ten-mile zone legislation cleared the House by a 108–10 vote on March 4. The Senate followed with a 22–1 favorable vote three days later. The legislation became effective at the close of business on April 15, 1918. Practically every large city had some type of military training facility, so the act, which closed 1,800 of Texas' 2,550 saloons, made much of the state dry.[7]

The national prohibition amendment would not take effect until ratified by three-fourths of the states, and the ten-mile zone legislation left some saloons open, so prohibitionists were eager to adopt measures to make the state totally dry in the meantime. State constitutional amendments could not be proposed in a special session, and prohibitionists decided to press for a statewide prohibition law as a "war measure" to protect the health of soldiers and industrial workers. Such a measure passed the House by a 103–21 vote and the Senate by a 18–9 tally. Although Hobby still had some misgivings about the legislation, he signed the bill late in the special session.[8]

The new statewide prohibition law was immediately challenged in court. The section prohibiting the sale of alcoholic beverages was ruled unconstitutional, but the courts upheld the sections banning the transportation and manufacture of liquor.[9]

The 1918 special session also passed laws prohibiting prostitution near military camps, providing for runoff elections when a majority was not secured in party primary elections, giving counties the task of registering motor vehicles and collecting license fees, appropriating $2 million for the purchase of feed and seed in drought-stricken counties, and prohibiting criticism of the government in wartime.[10]

The session's most heated debate involved women's suffrage. Attempts to grant the vote to women by constitutional amendment had failed in 1915 and 1917. Unlike a constitutional amendment, a bill giving women suffrage in party primaries could be considered during a special session. Accordingly, suffrage advocates introduced such legislation.

The war added support for the suffragists who pointed out that their disfranchisement contradicted the democratic principles for which Americans were fighting and dying. They noted that women had demonstrated their patriotism and support of the war effort through Red Cross service, Liberty Loan drives, food conservation programs, and war industries work.[11]

Historian Judith N. McArthur points out that although these arguments helped the cause, "political exigency and a split in the Democratic party put suffrage across in Texas." Ferguson, who had announced his plans to regain his office in the 1918 election, was opposed to both prohibition and suffrage. Minnie Fisher Cunningham, leader of the Texas Equal Suffrage Association, pointed out to progressives and prohibitionists that if women were allowed to vote in the Democratic primary, their numbers would defeat Ferguson and keep Hobby in office as governor.[12]

The prospect of enlisting female voters to defeat Ferguson appealed to longtime foes of the former governor. In the special session, state Rep. Charles B. Metcalf of San Angelo introduced a bill permitting women to vote in political primaries. Although there was opposition from Ferguson supporters and the Texas Association Opposed to Woman Suffrage, the measure passed the House by an 84–34 vote and the Senate by 18–4. When signed by Hobby on March 26, the measure was almost equivalent to full enfranchisement, given that Democratic primary winners of that era were always victorious in the general election.[13]

Minnie Fisher Cunningham

The bill permitting Texas women to vote was passed just as campaigning for the July Democratic primary was getting under way. Since the Metcalf bill waived the poll tax requirement for voting in the 1918 primary, women were eligible to vote in this election. Although some contests for legislative and congressional posts attracted interest, most of the attention focused upon the governor's race. In office for only seven months, Hobby was attempting to direct the state's contribution to the war effort while campaigning against the formidable Ferguson for election to a full two-year term.

At one time, it appeared that the governor's race would have several candidates. Railroad Commissioner Earle Mayfield, a prohibitionist, had indicated earlier that he might run but, satisfied that Hobby had taken the necessary steps against the liquor industry, he then announced he would not oppose the incumbent. State Attorney General Ben F. Looney, who led the fight in the courts against the brewing industry, withdrew his candidacy in early April after praising the work of Hobby and the fourth special legislative session. With the withdrawal of Mayfield and Looney, the contest was between Hobby and Ferguson.[14]

Ferguson had indicated his intention to run for his former office almost immediately after his impeachment. Although the Senate had stipulated that he could not hold office in Texas again, Ferguson argued that the measure was void because he had resigned before the final Senate vote. The Texas Democratic Executive Committee, still controlled by Ferguson supporters, put his name on the primary ballot. Hobby's friends urged him to take court action to block the Ferguson candidacy, but he declined to do so.[15]

Ferguson formally opened his campaign at Mount Pleasant on April 6. Denouncing those who had removed him from office, he contended that he had been impeached because of his fight to provide better opportunities for the poor. He ridiculed the University of Texas for extravagance and corruption, charging that the school carried dead men on its payroll and wasted research money on projects such as proving "you cannot grow wool on the back of the armadillo." He declared that the 35th Legislature was "crooked," that Hobby was a drunkard, that two University of Texas regents owned large blocks of brewery stock, and that former Govs. Thomas Campbell and Oscar Colquitt (who supported Hobby) were "arrogant" and "ignorant fools."[16]

Hobby did not open his election campaign until after he had completed his work in promoting the third Liberty Loan drive in early May. Already his friends and supporters were organizing for what would be a bitter contest. Prohibitionists led by Dr. A. J. Barton, head of the Anti-Saloon League, Methodist Bishop E. D. Mouzon, and former Gov. Tom Campbell endorsed and campaigned for Hobby. Even anti-prohibitionists such as Colquitt and lawyer-soldier Jacob Wolters, whom Hobby named as brigadier general in the Texas National Guard, worked in the Hobby campaign. As promised, Minnie Fisher Cunningham organized women to work for Hobby's election.[17]

Hobby himself began active campaigning in mid-May. He skillfully counterattacked Ferguson by reminding voters of the former governor's misuse and misapplication of public funds. At the same time, Hobby emphasized his own record on domestic issues and support for the war effort. He cited his role in cooperating with the national government in the administration of selective service, conservation of food, and assistance in the sale of Liberty bonds and stamps.[18]

Historian Lewis Gould notes that Hobby "proved much more adept on the platform than anyone anticipated." When Ferguson, referring to Hobby's short stature and big ears, described the governor as a "misfit," Hobby responded that although the Supreme Being failed to favor him with pleasing physical attributes, "at least he gave me the intelligence to know the difference between my own money and that which belongs to the state." Later, when Ferguson remarked that there was an autocracy in Texas as vicious as flourished under Germany's ruler, Hobby countered that "nothing ever existed in Texas or anywhere else as vicious as the autocracy of the Kaiser."[19]

In the closing days of the campaign for the Democratic nomination, the Hobby organization emphasized patriotism. Ferguson's early opposition to the draft and his strong backing by German Texas voters in earlier elections caused many to question his loyalty. Ferguson's refusal to reveal the source of a $156,000 loan led to rumors that the money came from the Kaiser. Although Ferguson repeatedly denied the allegation, the issue would not go away.[20]

With support from prohibitionists, reformers, friends of the University of Texas, and many of the 310,00 newly registered female voters, Hobby swept the state, receiving 461,479 votes compared to 207,072 for Ferguson. Hobby carried the northern and western counties, the overwhelming majority of female voters, and all the largest cities except San Antonio.[21]

Ferguson led in only twenty-two of the state's 254 counties. These were clustered in three areas: San Antonio and the German counties in Central Texas; Duval and McMullen counties in South Texas (controlled by Ferguson's friend, political boss Archie Parr); and seven timber counties in southeastern Texas where Ferguson's fight with lumber baron John Henry Kirby appealed to populists and disgruntled timber workers.[22]

As Hobby won renomination and virtual election, Annie Webb Blanton, a member of the English faculty at North Texas State Normal College (now the University of North Texas), won nomination for the state superintendent of public instruction. The sister of Texas congressman Tom Blanton, Annie Blanton was the first woman to serve as president of the Texas State Teachers Association. Encouraged by suffragist leaders to seek state office, she defeated incumbent Walter F. Doughty, a close associate of Ferguson, to win the Democratic nomination. When elected in November, she became the first woman in Texas to hold a statewide office.[23]

Thirteen of the eighteen Texas congressmen were renominated in the 1918 Democratic primaries. Two veteran members, Alexander Gregg of Palestine and Martin Dies of Beaumont, did not seek renomination and retired from politics. Gregg, a seventy-three-year-old lawyer, was in failing health and died the following year. Dies, who was only forty-eight, decided not to seek a sixth term. Some speculated that, having been renominated by a close vote in 1916 because of his criticism of Wilson's foreign policy, he feared defeat; however, biographer Dennis K. McDaniel argues that no evidence supports this view. Dies moved to Kerrville after retirement from Congress but died after an emergency operation in July 1922. His son Martin Dies Jr. later served in his father's old seat in Congress in 1931–45. The younger Dies is best known for his chairmanship of the House Un-American Activities Committee.[24]

Three Texans who served in the wartime Congress, 1917–19, were not renominated in the primaries. James L. Slayden, dean of the Texas House delegation and a critic of Wilson policies, withdrew from the race after his opponents obtained a telegram from the president stating that Slayden had not supported the administration. When the Wilson message was made public, Slayden announced his withdrawal, declaring that "no matter how false the statements made to the President to secure this telegram, my continued candidacy for Congress in view of it will appear to put me in opposition to those charged with the prosecution of the war." Slayden's seat was taken by Carlos Bee, a longtime Democratic party activist and brother-in-law of Slayden's political rival, Postmaster General Albert Sidney Burleson.[25]

Annie Webb Blanton

Neither Daniel Garrett nor Jeff McLemore, who held at-large seats in the 65th Congress, were re-elected in 1918. Forced to run in Houston's 8th Congressional District because of redistricting, Garrett—who had served as chairman of the House subcommittee on war expenditures—was unable to unseat veteran incumbent Joe Eagle. Both Garrett and Eagle had supported the president, but Garrett was a prohibitionist and Eagle a foe of prohibition running in a wet district. McLemore, the other former at-large congressman and an outspoken critic of the Wilson administration, was defeated in a contest in the 7th Congressional District by Clay Stone Briggs, a Galveston district judge.[26]

By the time of the Democratic primaries in July, Texans were feeling the real effects of the war. The 32nd Infantry Division, made up primarily of National Guardsmen from Wisconsin and Michigan, completed its training at Waco's Camp MacArthur in late January and departed for overseas assignment. By May, the men of the 32nd were on the line in France. The Illinois National Guard, now the 33rd Division, finished its training at Houston's Camp Logan in April. By late May, the division was in France. After additional training in France, the 33rd took its place on the line in September 1918.[27]

In late May, units of the 90th Division, the National Army division made up of draftees primarily from Texas and Oklahoma, began departing from San Antonio's Camp Travis for overseas duty. The division sailed for England in June. By July, the "Alamos," as men in the division were called, were in France. The Texas-Oklahoma National Guard, now the 36th Infantry Division, ended its training at Fort Worth's Camp Bowie in July and headed for embarkation ports in New York and New Jersey. By mid-August, the division was in France.[28]

Those Texans not in the military worked to support the troops overseas in various ways. Three Liberty loan drives to encourage Americans to buy bonds to finance the war effort were conducted in May and October 1917 and May 1918. A fourth drive was held in September 1918. A final "Victory Loan" subscription took place in April 1919. In each of these campaigns, Texans were urged by governmental officials, newspaper editorials, community organizations, patriotic speakers, and entertainment celebrities to purchase bonds. The response to the campaigns was impressive; in each instance,

Texans and the nation oversubscribed, raising almost $20 billion nationally.[29]

In addition to the sale of interest-bearing bonds, the smallest denomination of which was $50, the Treasury Department in December 1917 began a program to reach investors in the lower income brackets through the sale of war savings certificates (in denominations as small as $5), war savings stamps (ranging from $4.12 to $4.23) and war thrift stamps (25 cents). These could be purchased at post offices, banks, and public schools.[30]

Three-fourths of the money required to finance the American effort was raised by borrowing; the other fourth came through higher taxation. Prior to the war, nearly half the federal government's revenue came from excise taxes, with another fourth derived from customs duties. This changed dramatically during the war as Congress enacted legislation raising income and excess profits taxes. By the last year of the war, more than two-thirds of federal revenue came from these sources.[31]

During the war, the bulk of federal income taxes was paid by individuals with incomes exceeding $3,000. Representing only 22.3 percent of taxpayers, these individuals paid 96.4 percent of all income and excess profits taxes. Although the income tax rate set at 1 percent by the Revenue Act of 1913 (passed after the ratification of the 16th Amendment) was doubled by the Revenue Act of 1916, the $1,000 exemption for single persons and $2,000 for married couples meant that the majority of citizens paid only modest ($20 to $40) or no income taxes.[32]

Treasury Secretary William Gibbs McAdoo hoped that the sale of bonds and increased taxation on higher income would eliminate inflation, but prices for goods continued to rise. The cost of living doubled during the war years. The table that follows shows increases for various commodities during this period.

PERCENT CHANGE *

Item	1914–16	1917–20
Food	+20.0	+ 73.8
Clothing	+18.8	+139.6
Housing	+ 2.3	+ 31.8
Fuel and Light	+ 7.3	+ 58.6
Furniture and Furnishings	+22.9	+129.0
Miscellaneous	+10.0	+ 77.8
All Items	+14.8	+ 83.0

* **Source:** Gilbert, *American Financing of World War I*, **214.**

The higher cost of goods was caused in large measure by the increased demands brought about by the war. Herbert Hoover's Federal Food Administration attempted to control food prices through voluntary agreements and public pressure, but with only limited success. To encourage greater productivity, the Food Administration often pegged agricultural prices at higher levels than some consumers, including Allied purchasing commissions, believed necessary.[33]

Hoover rejected the idea of food rationing and attempted to persuade Americans to conserve foods through voluntary means. As described earlier, the Texas division of the Food Administration, headed by Houston businessman E. A. Peden, had offices throughout the state. In October 1917, as part of a national effort, the Texas division attempted to get housewives to sign food conservation pledge cards. Hobby issued a proclamation designating the week beginning October 28 as "Food Conservation Week" and called upon Texas housewives to sign the cards. Hundreds of volunteer workers spread out across the state visiting homes to get signatures.[34]

Although the volunteers secured more than 300,000 pledges, the Texas drive was only partially successful—pledges were secured from only 35 percent of the homes, below the national average of 47 percent.[35]

The Food Administration in Texas conducted a vigorous educational program. Newspaper advertisements, posters, placards, and films stressed the importance of food in the war effort. Citizens were encouraged to observe meatless Tuesdays, wheatless Mondays and Wednesdays, and porkless Thursdays and Saturdays. At the same time, Texans were urged to save surplus garden and orchard produce by canning and drying. Canning demonstrations were given throughout the state, with "victory kitchens" set up in public schools where women learned to can fruits and vegetables.[36]

Emphasis was placed on the conservation of sugar. Cooks were urged to bake without sugar, recipes were distributed showing how to prepare dishes without sugar, and people were asked to eliminate sweet foods, candies, and sweetened coffee and tea. The Food Administration distributed posters showing the importance of sugar to the war effort and issued "teaspoonful rules" urging people not to use more than one teaspoon of sugar in their coffee and tea.[37]

Crop failures in drought-stricken West Texas and other Plains states in 1917 led to an all-out effort to conserve wheat. Wholesalers, millers, and retailers were required to conform to a 50-50 rule that the sale of wheat be accompanied by an equal sale of wheat substitutes: cornmeal, corn flour, hominy, corn grits, barley flour, sweet potato flour, rice, and oat mash. This was followed by a statewide wheat fast from April 15 to June 15, 1918. During this period, no wheat flour was shipped into the state. At the same time, stacks of flour were shipped out of the state for exportation to Allied countries.[38]

As Texans were asked to make sacrifices for the war effort, criticism of anyone who opposed the government's policies grew. As noted above, officeholders who failed to show total support for the administration were defeated in the 1918 elections. Anyone speaking out against the war effort or suspected of disloyalty was dealt with quickly.

Tom Hickey, an Irish immigrant long active in the Socialist Party, was one of the first to feel the effects of Postmaster General Albert Burleson's crackdown on political dissent. A fiery speaker and tireless organizer, Hickey had an active career in socialist-labor circles before coming to Texas in 1907. Settling in Hallettsville in South Texas, Hickey—labeled by some as "Red Tom" because of his radical political views as well as his ruddy complexion—became editor of a weekly newspaper, *The Rebel*. By 1917, *The Rebel*, which was the official organ of the Socialist Party in Texas, had a circulation of more than 20,000.[39]

Hickey emphasized the growing plight of tenant farmers in Texas and elsewhere, but he was also increasingly critical of Wilson's foreign policy. When authorities learned of a possible armed uprising to prevent selective service registration in June 1917, Hickey was arrested along with leaders of another radical group, the Farmers' and Laborers' Protective Association. Although he was held for several days, Hickey was released later. At the same time, *The Rebel* became the first victim of Burleson's crackdown when the Post Office refused to accept it in the mail, effectively suppressing the paper.[40]

In a flier sent to subscribers, Hickey stated that his arrest and the suppression of *The Rebel* was the result of wartime hysteria. He noted that he had been singled out because he had exposed the mistreatment of tenants on Burleson's plantation. He further charged that Burleson, Edward M. House, Morris Sheppard, and other politicians were taking "advantage of a national crisis to crucify a political opponent they could not bribe or control."[41]

In their study of American opposition to the war historians, H. C. Peterson and Gilbert L. Fite cite numerous examples of Texans who were punished for failure to support the war effort. They point out that twenty-four men were arrested in Rains Country in northeastern Texas on charges of organizing resistance to the draft. In West Texas, fifty-five men attending a meeting of the Farmers' and Laborers' Protective Association were arrested on similar charges. In both instances, most of the accused were later released, but four were found guilty and sentenced to prison.[42]

When the San Antonio *Inquirer*, an African-American newspaper, carried an article criticizing the execution of black soldiers for their involvement in the Camp Logan affair, editor C. W. Bouldin was indicted and found guilty of "attempting to cause insubordination, disloyalty, mutiny, and refusal of duty." Although he was out of the state and claimed to know nothing about the article, Bouldin was sentenced to two years in the Leavenworth prison.[43]

The Nonpartisan League, a militant Midwestern farmers' organization critical of governmental policies, was dealt with rudely when it attempted to organize in Texas. In the northeastern Texas town of Mineola, organizers were arrested and jailed. When M. M. Offset, the state office manager, protested, his hair and beard were shaved off with sharp shears before he was driven out of town. Three other league organizers were taken by a mob and whipped. The nearby Greenville *Banner* cited this as evidence that "Americanism is not to be tampered with around Mineola."[44]

In the town of Electra in Wichita County, George Geanapolis, a local confectioner suspected of disloyalty, was tarred and feathered and driven out of town. In another instance, a Texan was sent to prison for saying: "Wilson is a wooden-head son of a bitch. I wish Wilson was in hell, and if I had the power I would put him there." In Brenham, several townsmen flogged a man who reportedly said "to Hell with the Red Cross" after refusing to support a local membership drive.[45]

Peterson and Fite point to federal Judge Waller T. Burns of the Texas Southern District as an example of the rabid intolerance of the period.

Burns, a former Republican state senator, declared that "traitors" in Congress should be shot. Although he declared that the law should be administered fairly, he stated his belief that "this country should stand them up against an adobe wall tomorrow and give them what they deserve."[46]

Various committees and councils promoted patriotism and support for the war effort. The Texas State Council of Defense used its 240 county councils and 15,000 community councils to support Liberty Loan and Red Cross drives. A national organization, the Committee on Public Information, headed by journalist George Creel, printed and distributed millions of copies of pamphlets explaining that this was a "War to Save Democracy" and "A War to End All Wars." Hundreds of Texans served as part of the committee's 75,000 Four-Minute Men, who gave brief patriotic speeches to civic groups, clubs, and schools.[47]

Public schools and colleges were enlisted for the war effort. The Texas Legislature stipulated that all public schools devote at least ten minutes a day to teaching patriotism. Colleges offered special "war education" classes, welcomed Student Army Training Groups on campus, and invested in Liberty bonds. Professors at several colleges edited pamphlets for patriotic programs, including a collection called "War Songs for Community Meetings." Frederic Duncalf, a professor of medieval history at the University of Texas, wrote a war pamphlet that described Germany as "barbarous, brutal, and destructive beyond all belief." A colleague in the history department, Eugene C. Barker, gave lectures in American history and "Americanism" at military installations in Central Texas.[48]

Professors who questioned American policies during the war were dismissed. The most celebrated Texas case was that of Lindley M. Keasbey, a brilliant scholar and stimulating teacher at the University of Texas. A graduate of Columbia University who had done advanced study at Berlin and Strasbourg, Keasbey came to the University of Texas in 1905 as head of the political science department. His allegedly socialist leanings brought criticism from university regents, but the popular instructor was defended by President David Houston, who appointed him head of the newly created Institutional History Department. It was in this role that Keasbey came into contact with a young student, Walter Prescott Webb, who later in his inaugural address as president of the American Historical Association described Keasbey as his most influential teacher.[49]

Lindley M. Keasbey

During the prewar years, Keasbey joined several pacifist groups that opposed American involvement in the European war. He helped organize the People's Council of America, a radical antiwar group, in the summer of 1917 and spoke at its rallies. The regents, under pressure from various quarters and involved at the time in the Ferguson controversy, asked Keasbey to defend himself before the board, but he refused. On July 19, 1918, the regents voted unanimously to remove him from the faculty in "the best interests of the University."[50]

Another University of Texas faculty member, Eduard Prokosch, professor of Germanic languages and a native of Austria, was the subject of a loyalty probe. A former American ambassador to Germany, James W. Gerard, accused him of being pro-German in his textbooks used in American secondary schools. Prokosch was initially defended by university administrators, but the regents dismissed him in July 1919.[51]

Rice Institute, a private college in Houston, faced some of the same pressures as the public universities. Lyford C. Edwards, a sociology professor, was under fire for making favorable comments about the new Soviet leader, Vladimir I. Lenin. The board of trustees dismissed him in 1919.[52]

Texans of German descent were suspect during the war. A young nurse at Camp Bowie, Ella Behrens, a daughter of German immigrants, became the subject of local gossip when she was heard singing a German song and conversing with a fellow nurse in German. More rumors spread when the influenza epidemic of 1918 hit Camp Bowie. It was alleged that she had slipped influenza germs into the food of camp patients.[53]

Behrens was arrested and held incommunicado for eight days. When she was released, she was told by men who identified themselves as federal agents to go home and remain quiet. She later received a letter from the War Department informing her that she had been dishonorably discharged. She appealed the decision but was told she had been discharged because she had been absent without leave for eight days—the time she was in jail.[54]

For thirty years, Behrens lived with the stigma of her imprisonment and dishonorable discharge. With the aid of a local congressman, she finally secured a hearing. In January 1949, a military review board cleared her of the charges and changed her military discharge to honorable.[55]

Some German Texans were physically attacked by zealous patriots. In his book *Bonds of Loyalty: German-Americans and World War I*, historian Frederick C. Luebke states that a German Lutheran pastor in Corpus Christi was whipped because he preached in German after the county council of defense had forbidden it. In the town of Bishop in the same county (Nueces), another German Texan was publically flogged for his comments concerning the local war committee.[56]

Although few Texas Germans suffered physical abuse, they were often the objects of suspicion and distrust. Lola Bracht Woellert, a member of a German family in Aransas County, later recalled that "during the war we didn't want to be known as German." A neighboring family changed its name from "Klaeser" to "Glass" in an effort to avoid suspicion, although the Brachts kept their name. Lola's brother Fred Bracht volunteered for active duty and served in the Navy, as did many German Texans.[57]

Playing German music and reading German prose and poetry were discouraged. The Texas Legislature required all classes in public school to be taught in English. One legislative committee recommended that all books extolling the greatness of Germany be destroyed or locked away. King William Street in San Antonio's German district was renamed (temporarily) Pershing Avenue. The small town of Brandenburg in Stonewall County changed its name to Old Glory. Familiar food items such as hamburgers became "liberty sandwiches." Frankfurters were "liberty pups," and sauerkraut was "liberty cabbage." Efforts were made to put German newspapers out of business, although exceptions were made. Some, such as *Das Wochenblatt*, a German-language weekly published by William Trenckmann, received permits allowing them to continue publication.[58]

The war also affected Texas women. Although they were not called upon to enter the industrial sector or the military in great numbers, as in the Second World War, they played a major role in home-front activities in the First War. As they were gaining the right to vote (at least in the Democratic primaries) and helping to close saloons in the state, Texas women were conserving food, improving working conditions in industry, selling Liberty bonds and war stamps, supporting the Red Cross, and providing wholesome recreation and entertainment for troops in military training camps.[59]

In a weeklong conference billed as the "War College for Women" held in June 1918 at the University of Texas, nearly 100 participants representing various voluntary associations met with state and federal officials to discuss ways in which Texas women could aid the war effort. Chaired by Mary Dearing, head of the University of Texas School of Domestic Economy, the conference covered all aspects of women's wartime service.⁶⁰

Although the overall number of women who entered the labor market did not increase dramatically in World War I (less than 500,000 nationally), there was a shift in the type of employment. Many women who had earned a livelihood as charwomen, cleaners, laundresses, dressmakers, seamstresses, and servants found new opportunities as stenographers, typists, bookkeepers, cashiers, accountants, teachers, telephone operators, and nurses. The number of women employed by railroads rose sharply, from 37,400 nationally in 1917 to more than 100,000 by October 1918.⁶¹

Some Texas women attempted to enlist in the army during World War I but were turned away. When the Army asked for volunteer pilots for the air service, Katherine Stinson of San Antonio, one of the first American women to earn a pilot's license and the first woman to be commissioned a mail pilot, applied but was rejected. She later volunteered to be and was accepted as an ambulance driver in France.⁶²

Although overseas commanders repeatedly asked for women to handle clerical duties so that men could be released for front-line duty, the Army never sanctioned enlistment of women (other than as nurses) in the First World War. The American Expeditionary Force did "borrow" hundreds of British servicewomen for clerical duties at its headquarters in France. The Signal Corps recruited more than 200 French-speaking American women to serve as telephone operators in France. Similarly, the Medical Corps employed 200 American women to work as civilian rehabilitation aides in overseas base hospitals.⁶³

The Navy accepted women for military service from the beginning of the war. Secretary Josephus Daniels, discovering that no law prevented it, authorized the enlistment of female yeomen for clerical work.

By the end of the war, 11,274 women served in this capacity, most of them in the United States.⁶⁴

Later in the war (August 1918), the Marine Corps opened its ranks to a limited number of women. Some 350 women—including at least one Texan, Teresa Lake—signed up as Marines before the end of the war.⁶⁵

Among the Army and Navy nurses who served during the war were 449 Texas women. At least seven Army nurses from Texas died during the great influenza epidemic of late 1918.⁶⁶

The Army excluded women from serving overseas in the Army Medical Corps. However, several female physicians served in France as a part of the American Red Cross. May Agness Hopkins of Dallas was the only Texas female physician in France. A native of Austin, Hopkins received her medical degree from the University of Texas Medical Branch at Galveston in 1911. After internship and residency in Massachusetts and Pennsylvania, she opened practice in Dallas. She volunteered in 1918 to work with refugee children in France but was later assigned to treating American battlefield casualties at Chateau-Thierry. She worked close to the front lines, treating more than 1,000 casualties a day for several weeks. Later she was transferred to the south of France, where she took charge of children's medicine in departments along the Mediterranean.⁶⁷

Henrietta Goodnough Deuell, a Texas woman who wrote under the pseudonym Peggy Hull, went to France as a reporter for her newspaper, the *El Paso Morning Times*. A native of Kansas, Hull came to Texas in 1916 to report on Pershing's expedition into Mexico. In June 1917, she persuaded her editor to send her to France, even though the War Department did not accredit female reporters at the time. Her acquaintance with Pershing enabled her to spend six weeks at the artillery training camp at Le Valdron, France. Her articles for the *Morning Times* and the Army edition of the *Chicago Tribune* made accredited male correspondents jealous. They succeeded in getting her recalled.

In the summer of 1918, Deuell journeyed to Washington, where she obtained accreditation from Army Chief of Staff Peyton C. Marsh, whom she knew from El Paso days. As an accredited correspondent, she went to Siberia in the autumn of 1918 to report on the American intervention in Russia.[68]

For the 700,000 African-American Texans living in a segregated society, the First World War was a period of hope and frustration: hope that "the war to make the world safe for democracy" fought abroad might bring equality and social justice at home, and frustration that African-American support for the war at home and on the war front did not achieve that goal.[69]

In their belief that victory in the war might lead to improvements at home, most Texas African-Americans supported the war effort. They purchased Liberty bonds and war stamps, participated in Red Cross drives, and had patriotic rallies in various cities including Austin, Cleburne, Dallas, Ennis, Mexia, and Houston. Black speakers such as political activist William M. McDonald toured the state, urging support for African-American soldiers. More than 5,000 African-Americans paraded in a two-day celebration in Dallas sponsored by the Negro Business League to support the war effort.[70]

African-American Texans were called upon to assist in the conservation of food. The Federal Food Administration established a Negro Division with subdivisions in each state. Black deputy directors were appointed in each Texas county with large African-American populations. Ernest T. Atwell, a purchasing agent for the Tuskegee Institute, was sent to Texas as a special organizer and speaker on food conservation. He was assisted in the Texas campaign by Clifford Richardson, editor of the *Houston Observer*; William L. Davis, a Houston black newspaper editor and secretary of the Negro Division of the Federal Food Administration; and William M. McDonald. Mary Evelyn V. Hunter of the Cooperative Extension Service at Prairie View State Normal School and

Industrial College for Negroes was the state director of Colored Women's Work of the Food Administration.[71]

Many African-Americans saw the war as an opportunity to improve their economic status and escape the segregated South by migrating. This movement was strongest in the Deep South; indeed, in the prewar decade, Texas experienced a net migratory gain in its number of African-Americans as blacks moved to the state from the older South. This changed as a result of the onset of the war and the demand for workers in Northern factories. In 1910, about 6,000 African-Americans from Texas lived in the North; by 1920 there were approximately 17,000.[72]

This movement north was encouraged by black newspapers such as the *Chicago Defender*, which had wide circulation in Texas. Letters to the *Defender* from these prospective migrants reveal the determination of some African-American Texans to improve themselves and escape the social injustices in the state. "[I] would like Chicago or Philadelphia," wrote a Texas freight handler, "But I don't Care where so long as I Go where a man is a man."[73]

More than 31,000 African-American Texans served in the Army during the First World War. The vast majority were conscripted, as enlistment of blacks in the prewar Army was limited. Most of the Texas inductees were sent to Camp Bowie in Fort Worth or Camp Travis in San Antonio for basic training. Here they were segregated in facilities with high fences. After basic training, most black Texas soldiers were assigned to labor battalions, pioneer regiments, depot brigades, stevedore regiments, ambulance corps, and supply battalions. Some Texas African-Americans did serve with the 92nd Division, an infantry unit made up of black enlisted men and junior officers under the overall command of white generals and colonels.[74]

Most of the black officers, captains, and lieutenants of the 92nd Division were graduates of the officer training camp at Fort Des Moines, Iowa, the only black officer training camp in the United States. The Des

Moines camp was established as a result of pressure from the National Association for the Advancement of Colored People. A single class of 639 officers graduated from the camp in October 1917. Twenty-four members of the class were Texans; all were commissioned lieutenants with the exception of Aaron Day Jr. of Austin, who was commissioned captain. Other black Texans received commissions as a result of examination. In all, sixty-eight Texas African-Americans (out of 31,506 black Texans in the Army) were officers during World War I—four as captains, thirty-two as first lieutenants, and thirty-two as second lieutenants.[75]

The large number of African-American soldiers training in Texas caused tension. As noted earlier, this was heightened by incidents at Camp MacArthur in Waco and the riot and mutiny at Camp Logan in Houston during the early summer of 1917. As a result of mounting concern about the treatment of black soldiers, particularly in the segregated South, Secretary of War Newton Baker appointed Houstonian Emmett Jay Scott—an African-American author, editor, and chief adviser to Booker T. Washington—as his special assistant to investigate racial incidents and charges of abuse of black servicemen. As a result of Scott's efforts, some modest improvements in the treatment of African-American troops training in the South occurred.[76]

Twelve thousand Texas African-Americans served overseas in World War I, the majority in the Service of Supply. At least 240 Texas African-Americans saw combat, most with regiments of the 92nd Division. Charles G. Young, a black lieutenant from Austin in the 366th Infantry, was awarded the Distinguished Service Cross for extraordinary heroism while leading his scout patrol near Binarville, France, in September 1918. Twice wounded, he refused medical aid and held his position, protecting the exposed right flank of his battalion. Another Texas African-American, Corporal Russell Pollard from Weatherford, serving in the 365th Infantry, received the Distinguished Service Cross for action at Bois Frehaut, France, on the last day of the war. Captain William B. Crawford from Denison, a member of the 370th Regiment brigaded with the French 73rd Division, was awarded the Distinguished Service Cross and the French Croix de Guerre for heroism in action on September 30, 1918.[77]

African-Americans in uniform suffered various forms of discrimination while in the states but little while in France. Walter E. Pitts, a black farmer from Denison who served in the 360th Infantry, recalled "no prejudice at all" while serving with French troops. Another black Texan wrote that he had one desire: "to be able to go over our land and tell of my experiences in the democratic France."[78]

African-Americans at home who failed to support the war effort were sometimes treated harshly. George Cabiness, an African-American who failed to register for selective service, was fatally shot by whites near Huntsville. The next day, six other members of his family were killed when they attempted to defend themselves against a white mob.[79]

Lynching continued to be used to punish and intimidate African-Americans. Sixty lynchings were recorded in Texas during 1914–18. The most vicious of these was the brutal 1916 lynching of Jesse Washington by a Waco mob. Convicted of murdering a white woman, Washington was beaten, stabbed, mutilated, hanged, and burned. After his death, some of his personal possessions were sold to onlookers as souvenirs.[80]

But African-Americans were not the only victims of lynching in the First World War era. Twenty-nine Mexicans were lynched in Texas during 1910–16. Twenty-six of these were lynched in 1915 during the swift retribution after the discovery of the Plan of San Diego. As tensions eased and the need for Mexican labor increased, the number of lynchings dropped. There were no reports of Mexican-Americans lynched in Texas during 1917–19.[81]

Historian Carole Christian believes that World War I "represented a crucial stage in the assimilation of Hispanics into the political and social life of Texas and the nation." She notes that prior to the war, most Texas Mexicans, or Tejanos, lived isolated lives as tenants or peons on South Texas ranches and farms. The war and the government regulations that accompanied it brought more Mexican Texans into the whole of society. It also brought them into the interior of Texas in greater numbers than ever before.[82]

During the war, the demand for Mexican labor, both resident and migratory, to fill new industrial jobs and replace the thousands of men called into military service was greater than ever. The flow of Mexican immigrants was temporarily reduced by the passage of the Immigration Act of 1917, which imposed literacy requirements and an $8 head tax on new immigrants. The law, however, permitted the secretary of labor to set aside the restrictions if convinced of a labor shortage. Under pressure from farmers and ranchers in Texas and elsewhere in the Southwest, Secretary William B. Wilson in early 1918 exempted agricultural workers from Mexico from all of the requirements of the new law. In the summer of 1918, he extended the waiver to include non-agricultural workers. Under these exemptions, more than 250,000 Mexicans entered the United States as temporary workers.[83]

Spanish-language newspapers—especially San Antonio's *La Prensa* and Laredo's *Evolucion* and *El Democrata Fronterizo*—and Texas leaders encouraged Mexican Texans to register for selective service, purchase Liberty bonds and stamps, conserve food, and donate time to the Red Cross, YMCA, and other civilian agencies. While advising Mexican citizens in the state that they were exempt from the draft, they urged Tejanos who were citizens to demonstrate their patriotism and not evade the draft.[84]

Hundreds of Tejanos served in the armed forces during the First World War. Unlike African-Americans, Mexican-Americans were not placed in segregated units. They were permitted to volunteer and were trained and assigned to military units with other Americans. Although some discrimination occurred, Mexican-Americans were not perceived as a threat to social order and stability.[85]

Mexican Texans fought in France with various units, particularly the 36th and 90th Divisions. Many distinguished themselves in combat. David Bennes Barkley of Laredo, serving in the 89th Division, was awarded the Medal of Honor posthumously for courageous action in fighting along the Meuse River. Marcus B. Armijo, a former employee of an El Paso printing shop who rescued an American nurse from downing on the torpedoed *Tuscany* and later served courageously in France, received the Distinguished Service Cross posthumously. Conception Ortiz, a private from Eagle Pass assigned to Company I, 125th Infantry Regiment, was awarded the Distinguished Service Cross posthumously for his role in delivering messages across a valley swept by enemy machine gun fire. Marcelino Serra from El Paso received the Distinguished Service Cross, two Purple Hearts, the French Croix de Guerre, the Italian Cross of Merit, and the British Medal of Bravery for capturing twenty-four enemy prisoners. Another Tejano, Graviel Garcia, was awarded a Distinguished Service Cross for giving first aid to the wounded in No-Man's-Land.[86]

As historian Carole Christian notes, this military service accelerated the assimilation of Mexican Texans into the mainstream of American society. The wartime experience, Christian believes, "was the first step for many Texas Hispanics in thinking of themselves as American citizens rather than outsiders."[87]

The expansion of the construction, manufacturing, shipbuilding, and oil industries during the war provided new employment opportunities for many Texans, whether they were black, Anglo, or Mexican. Although Texas workers received higher wages in these industries, they often found that prices for food, housing, clothing, and other commodities rose more rapidly than their wages. They also disliked the long hours, poor working conditions, and paternalistic management policies that prevailed in much of industry.[88]

Several labor stoppages occurred in Texas during the war, but most were brief. Dallas carpenters seeking higher pay went on strike in July 1918 on work projects at the American Exchange National Bank and the Texas & Pacific and Goldsmith buildings. They agreed to continue working on an aviation repair depot project while negotiations for pay increases continued. Settlement was reached after nine days, with the carpenters receiving a boost in wages.

Similarly, shipyard workers in Orange went on strike in January 1918, but appeals to their patriotism and a promise to negotiate in good faith brought them back to work after several days.[89]

The November 1917 strike by Texas-Louisiana oil field workers was much larger and more serious. Early in the year, local unions invited oil producers to meet with them in Houston to consider grievances including hours and wages. When the producers—led by Ross Sterling, head of Humble Oil & Refining—refused to meet with them, the oil field workers voted to strike. On November 1, 1917, approximately 10,000 oil field workers went on strike.[90]

After the strike was a month old, Vernon S. Reid, President Wilson's personal representative and chairman of the President's Mediation Committee, was given the task of negotiating a settlement. After meeting with workers and producers, Reid issued a report agreeing with most of the strikers' demands, including an eight-hour day, a minimum daily wage of $4, revision of the bonus system, and union recognition. The workers were pleased with Reid's report, but the producers were not. At a meeting in Houston on January 2, 1918, more than 240 producers, representing 95 percent of the area's production, rejected Reid's findings.[91]

The strike went on several more weeks. The availability of strikebreakers looking for work because of the West Texas drought and the $3.50 daily wage gave the producers the upper hand. Newspapers, refinery workers, and the general public supported the producers, who cleverly used stories and rumors that the workers were unpatriotic radicals.⁹²

In late January 1918, representatives of the workers and producers met with Labor Department officials and struck an agreement that was a complete victory for the producers. The settlement rejected the eight-hour day, immediate wage increases, and other union demands.⁹³

Approximately one-fourth of the strikers, including R. E. Evans, president of the Goose Creek local, lost their jobs. The failure convinced oil field workers that they needed to form a national union. In June 1918, the American Federation of Labor issued a charter to the International Association of Oil Field, Gas Well, and Refinery Workers of America. The new organization faced problems similar to those of the locals, however, and had little success until the advent of Franklin D. Roosevelt's New Deal.⁹⁴

As noted earlier, the war affected Texas schools and colleges. Public schools were expected to contribute to wartime morale and spirit. The Legislature stipulated that a patriotic lesson be taught each day, a flagpole be set up in each school yard, and Texas history be included in the course of instruction. Teachers were expected to inform their pupils of the causes of the war and its progress, and to inspire them to "do their bit" to bring about victory. The schools were to encourage the purchase of war stamps and Liberty bonds and participation in Red Cross drives, food conservation programs, and war garden cultivation.⁹⁵

The war years saw some improvement in state support for public education. Gov. Jim Ferguson convinced the 1915 Legislature to give additional financial assistance to rural schools and to pass a compulsory attendance law. The 1915 Legislature also adopted a measure authorizing free textbooks, but this did not become a reality until the passage of a state constitutional amendment in 1918 providing a state tax for the purpose.⁹⁶

The 35th Legislature, which met in early 1917, authorized new four-year colleges in Commerce (East Texas), Alpine (Sul Ross),

Kingsville (South Texas Normal—later Texas Arts and Industries), Nacogdoches (Stephen F. Austin), and Abilene (West Texas A&M). The outbreak of war caused legislators to have second thoughts. Noting that enrollment would probably decline during the war and that the state needed additional money because of the war effort and the West Texas drought, the third special session of the Legislature in August 1917 postponed the opening of the Alpine, Nacogdoches, and Kingsville schools and repealed the law authorizing West Texas A&M at Abilene.[97]

The war had an impact upon Texas higher education. Young men under age 21 were not liable for the draft until August 1918, so the issue of college deferments did not come up. Colleges and universities did play a major role in the training of military personnel. Under the National Defense Act of 1916, Reserve Officer Training programs were established at the major Texas schools. In addition, special programs such as the School of Military Aeronautics at the University of Texas and the schools of Radio Mechanics, Auto Mechanics, and Meteorology at Texas A&M were established.[98]

Texas A&M, at that time an all-male college, went on a war status almost the moment that hostilities were declared. College administrators canceled the 1917 commencement and released all seniors for military duty. Members of the Class of 1917 received their diplomas in a special off-campus ceremony at Camp Funston in Leon Springs, where most members of the class had gone for additional training. During the war, 1,233 Aggies served as commissioned officers. Included were two general officers, seven colonels, twelve lieutenant colonels, fifty-two majors, 173 captains, and 986 lieutenants. Six were awarded the Distinguished Service Cross, and four received the French Croix de Guerre. Forty-nine Aggies died in service.[99]

Nearly 5,000 students or former students of the University of Texas saw military service in World War I—1,768 as officers and 3,062 as enlisted men. Seventy-seven died in service; 157 were wounded. Colonels Ward Dabney of Fannin County, Arthur R. Sholars of Orange County, and Edwin Roberts of Williamson County were the highest-ranking University of Texas students who served in the war. Five other Texas alums, including future Railroad Commissioner Ernest O. Thompson of Amarillo, held the rank of lieutenant colonel.[100]

Rice Institute, a private college in Houston that opened in 1912 as a result of an endowment by wealthy businessman William Marsh Rice, made its contribution to the war effort. Thirty-four of the fifty-two graduates of the Class of 1917 left campus before commencement for officer training at Camp Funston. President Edgar O. Lovett confirmed degrees upon the graduates at a special ceremony on the Funston drill field. Twenty-five Rice faculty members served in the military during the war.[101]

The war had an impact upon sports and entertainment. The Texas League, the only professional sports organization in the state at the time, cut short its 1918 baseball schedule. Attendance had dropped already, causing the Beaumont and Galveston clubs not to field teams in 1918. The other six clubs continued to play, but a government announcement that the sport was not essential to the war effort and that players would be subject to the draft persuaded owners to end the season early. League officials halted play on July 7 with the Dallas Submarines, with a 52-37 record, in first place. For the second year, the Fort Worth Panthers finished in second place to the Submarines.[102]

College and high school football continued during the war, although many college players and coaches were in military service. Texas A&M won the 1917 championship of the young Southwest Intercollegiate Athletic Conference (a name soon shortened to the Southwest Conference) with an undefeated and unscored-on team. Even without their coach, Dana X. Bible, and much of the squad who were in military service, the Aggies won their first six games in 1918 but lost in the season finale to rival University of Texas, 7-0. The Longhorns won all of their nine games and the conference title in 1918 in a schedule that included Penn Radio School (twice), Reams Flying Field, and the Auto Mechanics School.[103]

Texas high school football was still in its infancy in the World War I era. In the prewar decade, teams were assembled and games played with little regard for participants' age, academic status, or school attendance. The Texas Interscholastic Athletic Association (which later became the Interscholastic League) was formed in 1913, with member schools agreeing that high school athletes must be amateurs, not over 21 years of age, and have a three-month record of attending and passing courses in the school represented. It was not until January 8, 1921, that the first state championship game was played, a scoreless tie between Cleburne and Houston Heights.[104]

In addition to sporting events, Texans found various ways to entertain themselves in the midst of war. Traditional entertainments such as hunting, fishing, dancing, masquerade parties, "tacky" parties, dominoes, and bridge continued to be popular. A new family pleasure, taking an afternoon or Sunday automobile drive, was becoming fashionable, although the government encouraged conservation of (but did not ration) oil and gasoline.[105]

American entry in the war ushered in an era of community singing, not heard previously in most of Texas. At the same time, the German singing societies, so much a part of German culture in Central Texas, were being disbanded or silenced. Other communities were encouraging public singing. Songs such as "Smiles," "Pack Up Your Troubles," and "There's a Long, Long Trail A-Winding" were quite popular. George M. Cohan's rousing "Over There" became almost a national anthem during the war.[106]

Motion pictures became increasingly popular in Texas. The uncomfortable nickelodeons were replaced in several cities by the larger "deluxe" theaters such as the Iris and Queen in Houston, the Iris in Fort Worth, and the Alhambra in El Paso. Too, the product on the screen improved as feature films made more serious efforts at storytelling. Animated cartoons and newsreels were added features. As film historian Richard Schroeder points out, " 'Going to the pictures' in a deluxe theater became a family activity."[107]

The movies were used to promote the war effort. Hollywood films such as *To Hell With the Kaiser*, *The Kaiser's Finish*, *The Woman the Germans Shot*, and *The Kaiser, the Beast of Berlin* depicted the brutality and cruelty of the enemy. Others such as *The Eagle's Wings*, *The Slacker*, and *The Little American* praised Americans in military service. Popular film stars Charlie Chaplain, Douglas Fairbanks, and Mary Pickford promoted the sale of Liberty bonds and encouraged patriotism.[108]

Texas churches, with nearly 1.8 million members, played their part in the war effort. With few exceptions, they backed the war to save democracy by sending their ministers abroad as chaplains or YMCA workers, encouraging young members to enlist and fight, and participating in numerous federal, state, and local activities to win the war. Few voices of dissent were heard, as ministers in their sermons depicted the righteousness of the Allied cause. The journals of the state's largest Protestant religious bodies, the *Baptist Standard* and the Methodist *Christian Advocate*, endorsed the war effort and called upon their members to rally behind the president's crusade "to save democracy." Texas Catholics, under the leadership of the National Catholic War Council, likewise flocked to the colors as soldiers and chaplains and contributed to fund raising drives to sell Liberty bonds and support the Red Cross. They also provided service to the troops through the Knights of Columbus, which maintained recreation and worship centers at military installations.[109]

In a recent study of the rural South during the First World War, historian Jeanette Keith points out that in some areas, leaders of the conservative Churches of Christ were pacifists. They attempted unsuccessfully to get their members exemptions from military service. Keith notes, however, that the group's leaders in the Southwest, including Texas, generally supported the war. Abilene Christian College, a small Church of Christ institution opened in 1906, established a student officer training corps during the war.[110]

Dr. George W. Truett, pastor of the First Baptist Church of Dallas and probably the most prominent Protestant minister in Texas, was one of twenty ministers invited by President Wilson to go overseas to deliver religious and patriotic message to Allied troops.[111]

Officially, Truett went overseas under the auspices of the YMCA, thus avoiding any question of separation of church and state. He arrived in England in August 1918. Here he spoke to thousands of troops in training camps and hospitals, delivering as many as six sermons in one day. In late October, Truett went to France and ministered to the needs of American servicemen during the closing days of the war. After the armistice, Truett preached to occupation troops in Germany.[112]

In their churches, theaters, clubs, and schools, Texans were enlisted in the national struggle to defeat the enemy and save democracy. Pride in America was greatly enhanced by support for and participation in the Great War. For five decades following the Civil War, most Texans thought of themselves first as Southerners and then as Americans. At most public occasions, "Dixie," not "The Star-Spangled Banner," was played, as audiences stood and removed their hats in tribute to the fallen sons of the old Confederacy. Monuments and statues were erected to honor heroes of the Lost Cause.

The First World War, with its emphasis upon nationalism and the virtues of American democracy, marked a change in Texas life. As Walter Buenger observes in his study of socioeconomic changes in northeastern Texas during these years, the "First World War helped Texans think like Americans instead of southerners." Respect for the Old South and the Confederacy remained, but a new pride in being American took its place in the front rank.[113]

CHAPTER FIVE

OVER THERE: TEXANS IN FRANCE

As Texans at home were choosing candidates for governor in the July 1918 Democratic primary, hundreds of other Texans were arriving in France with the 36th and 90th Divisions. A few Texans, including Beaumont Bonaparate Buck, commander of the 28th Infantry of the lst Infantry Division; John W. Thomason Jr., a platoon leader with the 5th Marines; Warren R. Jackson, a private with the 6th Marines; Clyde Balsley, a fighter pilot with the famed Lafayette Escadrille; and Robert A. Lovett, commander of a naval bombing squadron, were already serving in Europe. However, the majority of Texans arrived during the summer and autumn of 1918.[1]

The decision to send American troops to France was made soon after the declaration of war against Germany. The hope of some leaders in Congress that America's role would be primarily economic and financial was quickly dashed. Allied officials made it clear that American troops in great numbers were needed to support the war-weary British and French forces. Within a month after the declaration of war, President Wilson promised to send an American Expeditionary Force to France. On May 18, Congress passed the selective service legislation under which a large citizen army would be created to fulfill that commitment. That same day, the president appointed Major General John J. Pershing to command the American soldiers who would be sent to France.[2]

The appointment of Pershing—a West Point graduate and veteran of thirty years' service, including the Spanish-American War and the Philippine insurrection—was based largely upon his recent experience in commanding the "Punitive Expedition" into Mexico. Although the Mexican revolutionary leader Pancho Villa had not been captured, Pershing displayed considerable military and logistical skill in leading the expedition. In excellent physical condition, a stern disciplinarian, and a capable organizer and administrator, Pershing had the qualities of leadership believed necessary to command a large American force overseas.[3]

Even before he received official notification of his appointment, Pershing was instructed by the War Department to choose four infantry regiments and one field artillery regiment to make up the first contingent of American troops to be sent to France. Pershing selected the 16th, 18th, 26th, and 28th Infantry and the 6th Field Artillery—all regular Army units. Placed under the command of an old friend, Major General William Sibert, these units formed the 1st Division, later to be known as the "Big Red One" because of its insignia: a large red numeral on a brown background.[4]

Pershing and his staff departed for Europe on May 28, 1917. After a brief stopover in England, Pershing arrived in Paris on June 13. After visiting with French and British dignitaries, he began seeking training areas for his troops. Advance parties of the 1st Division arrived in France two weeks later. By the end of the year, four other divisions—the 2nd Division (made up of two regular Army regiments, the 9th and 23rd, and two Marine regiments, the 5th and 6th) and three National Guard divisions (the 26th, 41st, and 42nd)—were in France, bringing the total number of American troops up to 175,000 men.[5]

Although the majority of Texans came later, some Lone Star natives were among the first Americans in France. Beaumont Bonaparte Buck commanded the 28th Infantry of the 1st Division, John W. Thomason Jr.

was a lieutenant in the 5th Marines, and Warren R. Jackson and William L. Speaker were enlisted men in the 6th Marines—all part of the 2nd Division. Several hundred Texans were in the 42nd Division, the "Rainbow Division" made up of national guardsmen from twenty-six states and the District of Columbia. Texas provided the 117th Texas Supply Train, consisting of six motor truck companies from Dallas, Houston, Austin, and Big Spring.[6]

Buck was the highest-ranking Texan in France during the summer of 1917. Born in Mississippi in 1860, Buck came to Texas with his parents in 1872, attended school in Dallas, and joined the state militia in 1878. He obtained an appointment to West Point, graduated thirtieth in his class of thirty-nine in 1885, and served in the regular Army in frontier duty, the Spanish-American War, and the Philippines. He became commander of the 28th Infantry with the outbreak of war and led the regiment when it came to France. On August 2, 1917, he was promoted to brigadier general and assumed command of the 2nd Brigade, consisting of the 26th and 28th Regiments.[7]

Some Texans were in France fully a year before the arrival of Buck and the 1st Division. In 1915, Clyde Balsley, a tall, handsome youth, left his mother's bakery in San Antonio to serve in France. He enlisted as an ambulance driver in the American Field Service. After four months as a driver on the front line, rescuing wounded French troops, he enlisted in the French Flying Service. After completing flight training, he joined the Lafayette Escadrille, a group of young Americans who volunteered for flying duty with the French Foreign Legion.[8]

On June 18, 1916, Balsley made his first and only patrol over the German lines. Flying French Nieuports, Balsley and three other pilots were covering French observation planes when sighted by a larger formation of German fighters. In the ensuing air battle, Balsley's machine gun jammed. He managed to avoid enemy fire for a few moments but was hit in the hip by an explosive bullet. Although badly wounded and in terrible pain, Balsley managed to pull away from his attackers. He brought his plane back to friendly lines but when attempting to land struck an obstacle on the ground. His plane flipped on its back, and Balsley was thrown from the cockpit. Although nearly unconscious, he dragged himself into an old shell hole. He lay there for an hour while under heavy enemy artillery fire. Finally, some French soldiers managed to rescue him.[9]

Balsley was taken to a French hospital. During the next twelve months, he underwent six operations to remove bullet splinters. In late 1917, nearly eighteen months after his aerial encounter, Balsley was well enough to return to Texas. He was decorated with the French Medaille Militarie and Croix de Guerre and finished the war in Washington, D.C., as a captain in the U.S. air service.[10]

Balsley was the first American pilot in the Lafayette Escadrille to be seriously wounded. He was also the first American to be hit by an explosive bullet, which had been outlawed by the Hague Convention.[11]

Weston Bert Hall was another pilot, possibly born in Texas and certainly a resident there, who served with the Lafayette Escadrille before the United States entered the war. Hall came to Paris in 1912 as a chauffeur for a Fort Worth cotton broker. When the war in Europe began, Hall joined the French army and later transferred to the French air service. One of the first Americans in the French service, he transferred to the Lafayette squadron when it was formed. He shot down two enemy aircraft but was disliked by fellow airmen, who claimed he lied and cheated at cards. In anger, he left the American squadron and joined French Escadrille No. 130. He shot down another enemy plane but still had personal problems. He deserted and fled to the United States, abandoning his wife and two children in Paris. He was later convicted in an American court in Shanghai of swindling the Chinese government out of $10,000 and sentenced to two and a half years in federal prison.[12]

Hall and Balsley were no longer with the Lafayette Escadrille when its members transferred to the American air service after the United States entered the war. Many of its pilots became members of the 103rd Squadron, the first American pursuit squadron in France. Some were assigned to command other American squadrons that arrived in France during 1917.[13]

By the end of 1917, ten American Army squadrons, seven of which were organized and trained at San Antonio's Kelly Field, were in France. Among the squadrons trained in San Antonio, the 94th, later known as the "Hat in the Ring" Squadron, became the most famous. Its pilots shot down more enemy aircraft (seventy) than any other squadron; one of its airmen, Captain Eddie Rickenbacker, destroyed more enemy aircraft (twenty-two planes and four observation balloons) than any other American pilot.[14]

Lieutenant Edgar C. Tobin, a native Texan and a graduate of the San Antonio Military Academy, was a member of the 94th Squadron when it arrived in France but was later transferred to the 103rd Squadron. Tobin became one of the early American aces, shooting down six enemy aircraft—five in one month. At the time of his sixth aerial victory (September 1918), he was the leading American ace still flying, the four American pilots with more victories having been killed in action.[15]

Two other Texans, Henry R. Clay of Fort Worth and Byrne V. Baucom of Milford, were among the eighty Americans who qualified as "aces" by shooting down five or more enemy planes or balloons. Clay, a pilot in the 148th Squadron, had the highest number of victories (eight) of any Texan. He served briefly with the 43rd Squadron of the Royal Air Force before joining the 148th. This squadron, which flew on the British front in 1918, had a total of sixty-four aerial victories, second only to the "Hat in the Ring" Squadron. With eight enemy aircraft destroyed, Clay was one of the leading American aces when he was transferred to command a newly created squadron late in the war. Only thirteen Americans shot down more planes in the First World War than Clay.[16]

Lieutenant Baucom became the third Texas ace during 1918. As an aerial observer whose main tasks were to operate a camera, observe the tactical situation on the ground, take notes, and adjust artillery fire, Baucom shot down six enemy pursuit planes with his Lewis machine gun. He was awarded the Distinguished Service Cross in October and received an Oak Leaf Cluster in November for action against the enemy. He was one of only three American observers to earn the title "ace" during the war.[17]

Not all Texans with the Army air service in France were pilots or observers. Hundreds performed vital duty as part of the squadron ground crews. William Shelton Leslie, son of a Texas Baptist preacher, was one such individual. Only nineteen years of age, he enlisted at Dallas in December 1917 and was assigned to the 169th Aero Squadron at Love Field. In March 1918, Leslie accompanied the squadron as it traveled overseas to England, where it spent several months training pilots and ferrying planes to France. The squadron was transferred to France in August 1918, assigned to the U.S. 1st Army. It was cited for meritorious service during the St. Mihiel and Argonne Forest campaigns.[18]

Nearly 19,000 Texans served in the naval forces of the United States during the war. Some, such as James O. Richardson from Paris, Texas, and Chester W. Nimitz from Fredericksburg, both future commanders of the Pacific Fleet, were career officers and graduates of the U.S. Naval Academy at Annapolis. Richardson spent seventeen months of the war serving on the U.S.S. *Nevada*, a battleship that joined the British Grand Fleet, protecting troop convoys off the coast of Ireland. Nimitz, regarded as an expert on submarine warfare, served as chief of staff for Admiral Samuel S. Robison, commander of the Atlantic Submarine Force.[19]

The majority of Texas seamen spent the war serving on one of the 373 American naval vessels in European waters, convoying troop ships and searching for enemy submarines. Some served on the five American battleships, including the U.S.S. *Texas*, that formed a squadron in the British Grand Fleet maintaining a naval blockade of Germany in the North Sea.[20]

Some Texans, including Robert A. Lovett—a son of Robert Scott Lovett, head of Union Pacific and a member of the War Industries Board—served in the Naval Air Service, attacking enemy submarines in the North Sea. Young Lovett, who later became assistant secretary of war during the Second World War and secretary of defense in the Cold War, was one of a group of Yale University students who qualified as naval pilots in 1917. Lovett became commander of a night bomber wing of the Northern Bombing Group. By late summer, Lovett was commanding 1,500 men in bombing operations. For his wartime service in France, Lovett later received the Navy Cross.[21]

More than 200 Texas bluejackets lost their lives during the war. More than half of these died from disease—in most instances influenza or pneumonia. Forty-two enlisted Texans died at the Great Lakes Naval Training Station, thirty-five of them before the major influenza epidemic in the autumn of 1918. The majority of Texas deaths occurred in autumn, however. Eleven of the sixteen Texas seamen who died on the cruiser U.S.S. *Pittsburgh* expired in a ten-day period—October 15–24, 1918—during the peak of the epidemic.[22]

The largest single loss of Texas seamen from non-disease-related causes occurred in the late spring of 1918, when the armed collier *Cyclops* was lost somewhere in the Atlantic. Assigned to duty fueling British vessels in the south Atlantic, the *Cyclops* disappeared in the so-called Bermuda Triangle after leaving Barbados on March 3. Twelve Texans were among the fatalities when the *Cyclops* was listed missing on June 14, 1918. According to the Navy Department "her loss without trace is one of the sea's unsolved mysteries."[23]

Three Texas seamen—Paul Dickerson, fireman third class, Riveria; Oscar Wesley Gideon, fireman second class, Granbury; and Willis Earl Patton, water tender, Petrolla—were among the 204 Americans killed when the transport vessel *Ticonderoga* was attacked and sunk by a German submarine. The *Ticonderoga* (originally a German steamer taken over by the U.S. Navy) had been transporting trucks, automobiles, supplies, and animals to Europe. In September 1918, she dropped behind her convoy after developing engine trouble. She was attacked by the German U-boat U-152. Her crew fought a two-hour gun battle with the enemy, but the *Ticonderoga* eventually was sunk by a torpedo. Only twenty-five crewmen were saved, and this after four days of incredible hardship.[24]

By the late spring of 1918, the American and British navies had the upper hand on the German submarines. Each week, convoys from the United States arrived in England and France, bringing more troops and equipment for Pershing's American Expeditionary Force. The 32nd Division—the old National Guard division from Wisconsin and Michigan that trained at Camp MacArthur near Waco—arrived in March and by late May was in the line of the war zone. The 33rd Division, the Illinois National Guard, and the 5th Division, a regular Army division augmented by draftees, both trained at Houston's Camp Logan, arrived in May. After additional training, they entered the line shortly thereafter.[25]

The two divisions with the greatest number of Texans, the 36th and 90th, arrived in France during the summer of 1918. The 90th, a National Army division made up primarily of draftees from Texas and Oklahoma, left its training cantonment at Camp Travis in San Antonio in early June. Commanded by Major General Henry T. Allen of Kentucky (a West Point graduate and former aide to General Nelson Miles), the 90th, known at the time as the "Alamo Division," was processed for overseas duty at Camp Mills on Long Island. The first units sailed for Europe on June 13; by July 6, all were under way.[26]

The 90th Division landed at various points in England. From there the division was transported by channel boat to Le Havre and Cherbourg. Most of the division traveled by rail to the 14th Training Area at Aignay-le-Duc, south of Dijon. For the next six weeks, the 26,000 Texans and Oklahomans were engaged in strenuous advanced training. Pershing was convinced that stateside units had spent sufficient training in trench warfare but not enough in open maneuver. Believing that an aggressive offensive would be necessary to win the war, Pershing wanted his troops to have more experience in open warfare tactics before entering combat.[27]

Edwin St. John Greble

The 36th Division, generally called the "Panther Division" because it had trained at Fort Worth (known at the time as "Panther City"), left Texas a month after the 90th. The division was joined at Camp Mills on Long Island by its new commander, Major General William R. Smith. Smith succeeded Major General Edwin St. John Greble, who had commanded the division since its formation in August 1917. Although the fifty-eight-year-old Greble, a West Point career soldier, had done a satisfactory job in training the Texans and Oklahomans, he failed to meet Pershing's high physical standards for overseas division command. Smith, a Tennessean and West Point graduate, was eight years younger than Greble and possessed robust health and physical stamina.[28]

At the same time that Greble was relieved of command, two other senior officers of the division were replaced. Brigadier General George

Blakely, commander of division artillery, was transferred after receiving poor efficiency evaluations. His place was taken by Brigadier General John E. Stephens—a native of Tennessee, West Point graduate Class of 1898 and former member of the War Department General Staff. Colonel Jules Muchert of Sherman was relieved as commander of the 144th Infantry Regiment, probably because of his German background. Muchert had served in the Prussian army before coming to Texas. Although he had been a member of the Texas National Guard for several years and his patriotism and loyalty never had been questioned, there was concern that he would not be a suitable combat commander because of his German background. He was replaced by Colonel James S. Parker, a West Pointer.[29]

The overseas movement of the 36th Division came in July. By mid-August, most of the division had arrived at the port of Brest. From there, the Texans and Oklahomans were taken by rail to the 13th Training Area, 120 miles southeast of Paris, with division headquarters established at Bar-sur-Aube. For the next month, the 36th, like the 90th, underwent intensive training in open terrain warfare. The 36th lost a number of its original contingent when several hundred men who had trained with them at Camp Bowie were transferred to the 42nd (Rainbow) Division, a composite division made up of troops from twenty-six states.[30]

The American Expeditionary Force was already engaged in combat when the 36th and 90th Divisions arrived in France. The first American divisions in France—the 1st, 2nd, 26th, and 42nd—all entered the line during the summer of 1917 and were engaged in skirmishes with the enemy. In the spring of 1918, the tempo of fighting picked up when German commander Erich Ludendorff launched a massive offensive in an attempt to break the British and French lines before the arrival of more Americans.[31]

Louis J. Jordan from Fredericksburg, a first lieutenant in the 149th Field Artillery, 42nd Division, was among the first American casualties that spring. A football star at the University of Texas, where he won All American honors, Jordan completed officer training at the Leon Springs Officers Training Camp in 1917. He was killed in the bitter fighting in Lorraine in March 1918 and was buried in France. Awarded the French Croix de Guerre posthumously, Jordan was reinterred in Fredericksburg in June 1921.[32]

The first major action of the AEF occurred in May 1918. In an effort to eliminate an enemy salient in the British sector, Pershing committed Beaumont Buck's 2nd Brigade of the 1st Division in an attack on the village of Cantigny. The brigade's 28th Infantry led the assault, forcing the enemy from the town and then repelling a fierce German counterattack.[33]

Texan Daniel R. Edwards, who was born in Mooreville and entered service at nearby Bruceville, south of Waco, received the Distinguished Service Cross for his role in the fighting at Cantigny. Edwards, a private in Company C, 3rd Machine Gun Battalion, was covering the battalion with machine gun fire when his unit was forced to give ground under enemy counterattack. Although wounded in the wrist and stomach, Edwards held his position until darkness allowed the battalion to stabilize its position.[34]

Edwards later earned the Medal of Honor in the battle of Soissons on July 18, 1918. Although still in the hospital when the campaign began, he hitched a ride to the front to rejoin his battalion. During fierce fighting, he crawled into an enemy trench, where he killed four Germans and captured four others. While escorting his prisoners to the rear, Edwards was severely wounded in the leg by an artillery shell.[35]

While Edwards and other Americans in the 1st Division were fighting at Cantigny in the British sector on the north, the Germans were pushing the French army back toward the Marne River. In an effort to stop the German advance, the U.S. 2nd Division, consisting of the 9th and 23rd Infantry in one brigade and the 5th and 6th Marines in the second brigade, was engaged in a major battle in Belleau Wood.[36]

Texans were with the Marines in the bloody struggle for Belleau Wood. Carl A. Brannen, a nineteen-year-old former student at Texas A&M, was a rifleman with the 6th Marines in the month-long battle for control of the woods. In his account written years later, Brannen noted that one day of fighting (June 6) cost the Marines 1,092 casualties. "Bodies of men," he wrote, "were scattered in all directions, lying as they fell." The German use of mustard gas in artillery shells was particularly painful. "The inside of my nostrils stayed raw several days from breathing the gas from high explosive shells," wrote Brannen. The fighting was made even more unpleasant by the lack of sleep. For fear of enemy infiltration under cover of darkness, most of the American troops stayed awake in their trenches.[37]

Warren R. Jackson, a former student at Sam Houston Normal College, was also with the 6th Marines. In his memoirs, Jackson recalled the devastating effect of German artillery: "Shell after shell dropped about us. Now one in front, another behind or one on the side, ever with that hellish scream that accompanied them."[38]

Jackson believed that trench mortars were the most fearful weapon used by the enemy. "A shell [from artillery] a man could hear coming—if it wasn't coming too fast. There was at least a faint consolation that it could be heard and a fellow could dodge. Not so with the trench mortar . . . There was no warning, just a terrifying crash."[39]

Private Herbert D. Dunlavy from Goose Creek (now Baytown), another 6th Marine enlisted man, was awarded the Distinguished Service Cross posthumously for his role in the fighting at Belleau Wood. He single-handedly captured a German machine gun in the village of Bouresches on the night of June 6. Two days later, he was killed while helping repulse an enemy counterattack.[40]

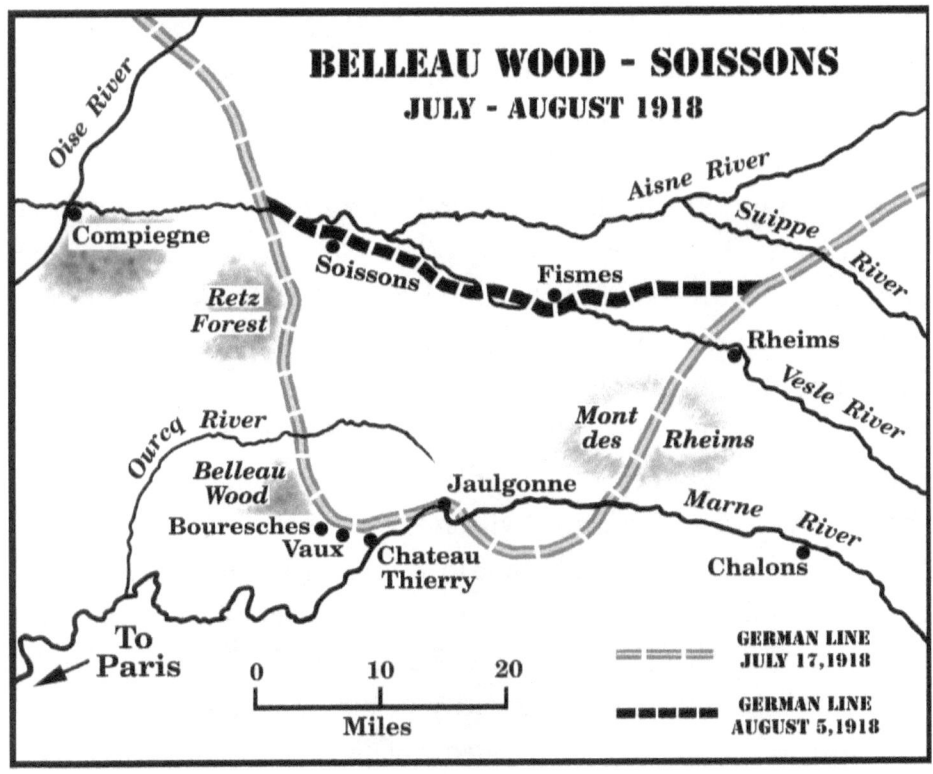

John W. Thomason Jr., later to become well known as a Marine Corps officer and writer-artist, saw his first combat with the 5th Marines in Belleau Wood. A native of Huntsville, Thomason had attended Southwestern University, Sam Houston Normal, the University of Texas, and the Art Students League in New York City. He was working as a writer for the *Houston Chronicle* when the United States entered the war. He enlisted in the Marines, received a commission, and after nine months training at Quantico, Virginia, was sent overseas. Assigned as a platoon leader in the 1st Battalion, 5th Marines, he led his men in the fighting on the left side of the division line in Belleau Wood.[41]

By the end of June, the Marines had cleared Belleau Wood of Germans. At the same time, the 9th and 23rd Infantry, which made up the 2nd Division's other brigade, pushed the Germans out of the village of Vaux southeast of Belleau Wood. In early July, another American division—the 3rd, commanded by Major General Joseph T. Dickman—stopped a German offensive at Chateau-Thierry on the Marne, earning it the sobriquet "Rock of the Marne."[42]

By mid-July 1918, the last of Ludendorff's great offensives had been halted. Marshal Ferdinand Foch, now the Allied commander-in-chief, decided to take the offensive to eliminate the German salient running from Soissons on the Aisne River to slightly east of Chateau-Thierry on the Marne. The attack would be made by General Charles Mangin's French 10th Army, which included several American divisions. The main assault would be on the north by the U.S. 1st and 2nd Divisions and the French 1st Moroccan Division.[43]

The battle of Soissons, as it came to be known, began on July 18 with a major assault by the 1st and 2nd Divisions. Before the end of battle, more than 100,000 Americans were engaged in the fighting. Many of those involved remember the ferocity in the fighting. Texan John W. Thomason of the 5th Marines recalled that "machine guns raved everywhere; there was a crackling din of rifle, and the coughing roar of handguns. Company and platoon leaders lost control—their men were committed to the fight and so thick was the going that anything like formation was impossible. It was every man for himself."[44]

Fellow Texan Carl A. Brannen of the 6th Marines described the heavy losses suffered by his regiment on July 19: "In thirty or forty minutes our regiment had been almost annihilated. The field which had been recently crossed was strewn with dead and dying."[45]

Private Warren Jackson, another Texan with the 6th Marines, recalled that "the grainfield was strewn with men who had fallen, men wounded in almost every conceivable way. . . . Along the length of the battlefield there must have been thousands of dead and wounded."[46]

The battle of Soissons officially ended on August 2 with the elimination of most of the Marne salient. Soissons was in American hands, and the enemy had been pushed back twenty miles. American casualties were high. The 1st Division lost 7,200 killed and wounded, the 2nd Division more than 5,000.[47]

Several Texans were decorated after Soissons. As mentioned earlier, Dan Edwards of Mooreville was awarded the Medal of Honor for his heroic actions on July 18. Frank Martin of Gatesville, a private in Company C, 26th Infantry, 1st Division, received the Distinguished Service Cross for capturing an enemy machine gun, making the advance of his platoon possible. John L. Taylor of Laredo, a captain in the 9th Infantry, 2nd Division, was awarded the Distinguished Service Cross posthumously. Taylor assumed command of his battalion when all senior officers were killed. Taylor himself was wounded several times and died later that day. Colonel Hamilton R. Smith of San Antonio, commanding officer of the 26th Infantry, was awarded the Distinguished Service Medal posthumously. Smith was killed while leading his regiment in an attack on an enemy machine gun emplacement. Major Andrew D. Bruce, a graduate of Texas A&M, commanding the 4th Machine Gun Battalion, 2nd Division, was awarded the Distinguished Service Cross for leading his troops through flanking machine gun fire to capture its objective near Vierzy on July 17–18, 1918.[48]

Brigadier General Beaumont B. Buck, the Texan who commanded the 2nd Brigade of the 2nd Division, received mixed marks for his conduct of the brigade. In the opening attack, Buck apparently failed to maintain contact with Colonel Smith of the 26th Infantry, leading to some confusion. Then, in the intense fighting of July 20, Buck attempted to reconnoiter the front-line positions by motorcycle sidecar but ran into the 1st Division sector, where he spent four hours out of contact with his own troops.[49]

Buck redeemed himself on July 21 when he directed the brigade in the capture of the village of Berzy-le-Sec. Modern-day scholars Douglas V. Johnson II and Rolfe L. Hillman Jr., although critical of Buck's performance in the early fighting, agree that the Texan's action at Berzy-le-Sec was "a fine example of combat leadership in the sense that there comes a time when senior commanders must move to the point of decisive action."[50]

Apparently Buck's superiors were satisfied with his overall performance, for he was promoted to major general in August 1918 and given command of the 3rd Division.[51]

With the French and American success along the Marne-Aisne line and the British victory at Amiens in July and August, the Allied forces now had the upper hand. Foch approved a series of offensive actions to drive the enemy farther back in the autumn. At Pershing's insistence, the newly formed American 1st Army was assigned the task of eliminating a large bulge in the line with the village of St. Mihiel near the point of the salient.[52]

The St. Mihiel salient had been in enemy hands since September 1914. The Germans had developed a series of carefully formed defenses consisting of barbed wire, deep trenches, concrete dugouts, and artillery and machine gun emplacements. The French had tried on several occasions to drive the Germans out, but without success.[53]

Pershing planned to use seven American divisions for the primary assault against the southern sector of the German salient. Three of these divisions, the 1st, 2nd, and 42nd, were already battle-tested. The other four, the 5th, 82nd, 89th, and 90th, had no prior experience under heavy fire. The 5th, although a regular Army division, was made up primarily of wartime volunteers and draftees. The 82nd, the "All American" Division, consisted of Southern mountaineers and Northern city dwellers; the 89th was filled with draftees from a tier of states from Missouri to Arizona; the 90th was primarily draftees from Texas and Oklahoma.[54]

The 90th Division—commanded by General Henry T. Allen, described by military historian Edward M. Coffman as "an impeccable dandy"—was on the right (or east) side of the American line when the attack on the St. Mihiel salient was launched on the morning of September 12, 1918. The two Texas regiments of the 180th brigade, the 359th and 360th, were on the division's right in the attack. The two Oklahoma regiments, the 357th and 358th, were on the division's left next to the 5th Division.[55]

The attack began after a heavy artillery bombardment by French units to the west and north of the salient. East Texan Chris Emmett, later a lawyer, historian, and author (including *Texas Camel Tales* and *Shanghai Pierce, A Fair Likeness*), was an enlisted man in Company C, 359th Infantry. In his account of his war experiences, Emmett described the assault at St. Mihiel: "Men were rising from the mud along the trenches. I looked to the left . . . . A soldier was moving from his concealment into the open. He stood erect, lined against a faint sky-line, his rifle grasped in his left hand, and without taking a step, the rifle fell. . . . Slowly he bent over. . . . Down on his face with a thud! He was dead . . . dead from a machine-gun bullet. Momentarily I could not understand what had taken place so suddenly before my eyes."[56]

Although losses in some regiments, particularly the 358th Infantry, were substantial, the Allied attack was successful. By the evening of September 12, the villages of Thiaucourt and Bouillonville to the east of St. Mihiel were in American hands. A steady advance continued for the next four days. By September 16, the St. Mihiel salient had been taken. Overall, American losses were 7,000 killed and wounded. The 90th Division reported 1,751 casualties, 231 of whom were killed.[57]

For many Texans such as Emmett, St. Mihiel was their first taste of combat. Maury Maverick of San Antonio, nephew of Texas congressman James L. Slayden and later himself a congressman, was among the Texans first under fire at St. Mihiel. A lieutenant in the 28th Infantry, Maverick encountered German soldiers for the first time. "I was scared to death, and nearly fell off my horse," wrote Maverick. "My knees banged up against the horse. I think even the horse was scared. I expected to be shot full of holes. My first day of battle would be my last." But to his amazement, Maverick found the Germans wanted to surrender. Twenty-six Germans dropped their weapons and raised their hands. They persuaded Maverick to escort them to the rear as prisoners.[58]

Another Texan, Sergeant Harry J. Adams of Sweetwater, in Company K, 353rd Infantry, 89th Division, captured an even larger number of Germans in the St. Mihiel offensive. When he saw an enemy soldier run into a house at Bouillonville, Adams followed him. Adams fired the last two rounds of his pistol at the door and demanded that the German surrender. As Adams stood waiting, more than 300 German officers and men came out. The Texan, with an empty pistol in his hand, marched the prisoners to the rear. For his action, Adams was awarded the Distinguished Service Cross.[59]

David E. Hayden, a Navy Apprentice 1st Class from Florence in Williamson County serving with the 6th Marines, was awarded the Medal of Honor for his heroism in the St. Mihiel campaign. When a Marine corporal was wounded during the advance at Thiaucourt, Hayden "disregarded his own personal safety to dress the wound under intensive machine-gun fire, and then carried the wounded man back to a place of safety."[60]

Texas airmen played their part in the St. Mihiel offensive. Byrne Baucom, mentioned earlier as one of three Allied observers to become an air ace, received the Distinguished Service Cross for the role that he and his pilot, William P. Erwin of Illinois, played in flying at extremely low altitudes to support infantry ground patrols on September 12, 1918. Another Texan, Lieutenant Hugh Brewster from Fort Worth, a member of the 49th Aero Squadron, was awarded the Distinguished Service Cross for driving off attacking German monoplanes and shooting down two of them on September 14, 1918.[61]

The American success in reducing the St. Mihiel salient was preliminary to a much larger Allied offensive against the German lines in late

September. With additional American forces pouring into France, Foch ordered an all-out assault against the enemy. Part of this offensive consisted of an attack by the American 1st Army and the French 4th Army in the Champagne region north of St. Mihiel. Like St. Mihiel, the area had been held by the Germans since 1914 and was even more heavily defended. With the heights along the Meuse River on the east and the densely wooded Argonne Forest on the west, the Germans had an ideal defensive position. Bunkers, trenches, barbed wire, observation posts, machine gun and artillery emplacements, and a series of ridges and valleys running through the area made the region appear impenetrable.[62]

The opening assault in what came to be known as the Meuse-Argonne offensive began on the morning of September 26 with nine American divisions of the U.S. 1st Army attacking from the south toward Montfaucon, and the French 4th Army with the attached American 2nd Division attacking from the southwest.

The opening drive by the 1st Army was successful. Montfaucon was taken, and American troops pushed on into the Argonne Forest.[63]

Meanwhile, the French and Americans to the west were having more difficulty in advancing. The Marine brigade assigned to the French army was finally able to push the Germans off the strongly defended Blanc Mont Ridge but took heavy casualties. By October 4, the advance had been halted.[64]

On October 5, the Marine brigade was relieved by the 36th Division, which had been brought forward as part of the army reserve. The 36th's 71st Brigade—consisting of the 141st Infantry, commanded by Colonel Will E. Jackson of Hillsboro; the 142nd Infantry, commanded by Colonel Alfred W. Bloor of Austin; and the 132nd Machine Gun Battalion, commanded by Major Preston Weathered of Waco—was ordered to attack German positions near the village of St. Etienne, north of Blanc Mont.[65]

William H. Smith

The 71st Brigade was led in the attack by a new commander, Brigadier General Pegram Whitworth, a West Point graduate from Louisiana. Whitworth replaced Henry Hutchings, the veteran National Guard officer from Austin who had headed the brigade since its formation. Hutchings was relieved of command by division commander General William H. Smith on August 31, 1918, and returned home.⁶⁶

The 71st Brigade opened its attack on German positions on October 8. Throughout the next two days, the Texans pushed the enemy slowly back in bitter fighting. Major Edwin Hutchings of Austin, son of Henry Hutchings, was killed in the initial assault. Another battalion commander and three company commanders were killed and several other officers wounded on October 8. In all, the brigade suffered 1,600 casualties in two days' combat, October 8–9.⁶⁷

On October 10, the 72nd Brigade of the 36th Division, commanded by Brigadier General John A. Hulen, a prominent railroad executive from Gainesville and a veteran of the Spanish-American War and the Philippine insurrection, relieved the 71st Brigade on the front line. During the next several days, the brigade's 143rd Infantry (commanded by Colonel John S. Hoover) and the 144th Infantry (led by Colonel James S. Parker) pushed the enemy steadily backward. Stiffening enemy resistance brought a halt for regrouping on October 14.⁶⁸

Although the division had suffered badly, the men of the 36th fought well in their first time under fire. Corporal Samuel M. Sampler, a native of Decatur who grew up in Oklahoma, received the Medal of Honor, the French Croix de Guerre, and the Italian War Cross for his actions on October 8. A member of Company H, 142nd Infantry, Sampler sprang from his trench, picked up some German grenades, and threw them into an enemy machine gun emplacement. One of the grenades killed two Germans and caused the surrender of twenty-eight men.[69]

Henry Hutchings

Several other Texans in the 142nd Infantry were awarded the Distinguished Service Cross for action in the St. Etienne campaign. Captain Thomas D. Barton of Amarillo received the DSC for leading his company against a strongly defended enemy position and capturing twenty machine guns and ninety prisoners. Private Will C. Curtis of Red River County was awarded the DSC for encouraging his comrades in Company M to follow him through a heavy enemy barrage. Though mortally wounded, he gave confidence to others in the company through his example of courage. Corporal Lonnie O. Shoemaker of Childress, a member of Company I, received his DSC for continuing the attack despite having been severely gassed. Lieutenant Roscoe R. Haley was awarded the DSC for leading his platoon forward while severely injured. Wounded in the face while cutting wire entanglements, Haley refused to go the rear, remaining with his platoon until he lost consciousness.[70]

Texans in the 141st Infantry and the 132nd Machine Gun Battalion were also decorated for their heroism. Among these were Sergeant Abner E. Lipscomb from Brenham (141st Infantry), Lieutenant John S.

Loomis from Dallas (132nd Machine Gun Battalion), Lieutenant C. H. Mason from Hillsboro (141st Infantry), Captain Willis Moore from Austin (132nd Machine Gun Battalion), Captain Ira C. Ogden from Alpine (141st Infantry), Sergeant Paul Willis from China Springs (141st Infantry), and Sergeant Sam Dreben from El Paso (141st Infantry). All received the Distinguished Service Cross for their actions at St. Etienne.[71]

After a brief rest and regrouping, the 36th Division was ordered to relieve the French XI Corps near the Aisne River. The French army commander in the region ordered General Smith and the 36th Division to assault a German defensive position along the Aisne known as Forest Farm, after a nearby abandoned farm. The French had attempted to take the position, but without success. Now it was the Texans' turn.[72]

Smith carefully planned the attack. Suspecting that the Germans might be listening in to phone communications, he arranged to use Choctaw Indians in the 142nd Infantry to transmit orders in their own language—an example of the kind of Indian "code talking" that became famous during the Second World War.[73]

The 36th Division attacked the German position at Forest Farm before dawn on October 27. Advancing behind a "creeping" barrage, the Texans and Oklahomans moved forward. In less than an hour, they overran the German trenches and forced the enemy back of the Aisne. "Admirably planned, elaborately prepared, and superbly executed, Forest Farm was, from start to finish," writes historian Lonnie J. White, "a magnificent operation."[74]

After the success at Forest Farm, the 36th Division was assigned as reserve to the I Corps, U.S. 1st Army, and dispatched to a rest area. There the men were given new clothing, additional arms, and equipment. They were preparing to re-enter the line when word of the armistice was received.[75]

According to figures given by the secretary of war in 1926, the 36th Division sustained 2,584 battle casualties in the war. Of these, 591 (26 officers and 565 enlisted men) were killed. The 142nd Infantry suffered the greatest losses: 1,007 men. The 141st Infantry had 709 casualties, the 144th 369 casualties, and the 143rd 272 casualties. The three machine gun battalions sustained 194 casualties, 148 of them in the 132nd Battalion. Engineering, signal, sanitary, and headquarters companies accounted for the other losses in the division.[76]

The other infantry division from Texas, the 90th, entered the Meuse-Argonne offensive in early October. When the operation began in late September, the men of the 90th remained in the St. Mihiel sector, where they and troops from other divisions in the area staged a diversionary attack to deceive the enemy about Pershing's main assault to the north. The action did draw some German units from the main offensive in the Argonne, but the 90th suffered heavy casualties: 1,830 men killed and wounded.[77]

In mid-October, the 90th Division was moved by truck northward to Cuisy, a war-ravaged village several miles northwest of Verdun. The Meuse-Argonne offensive, begun on September 26, drove the Germans back to a new defensive line northwest of Verdun running through the Romagne Heights. On October 21, the 90th Division relieved the 5th Division on the front line. The 179th Brigade, the so-called Oklahoma brigade consisting of the 357th Infantry (men largely from western Oklahoma) and the 358th Infantry (largely from eastern Oklahoma), moved into the forward trenches. The 180th (or Texas) Brigade consisting of the 359th and 360th Infantry regiments was placed in division reserve.[78]

On October 22, the 90th Division was ordered to eliminate a German-held pocket that ran between the Bois des Rappes and the Bois de Bantheville. The assault began the next morning, with the 357th Infantry leading the advance. In several days of fighting, the 179th Brigade

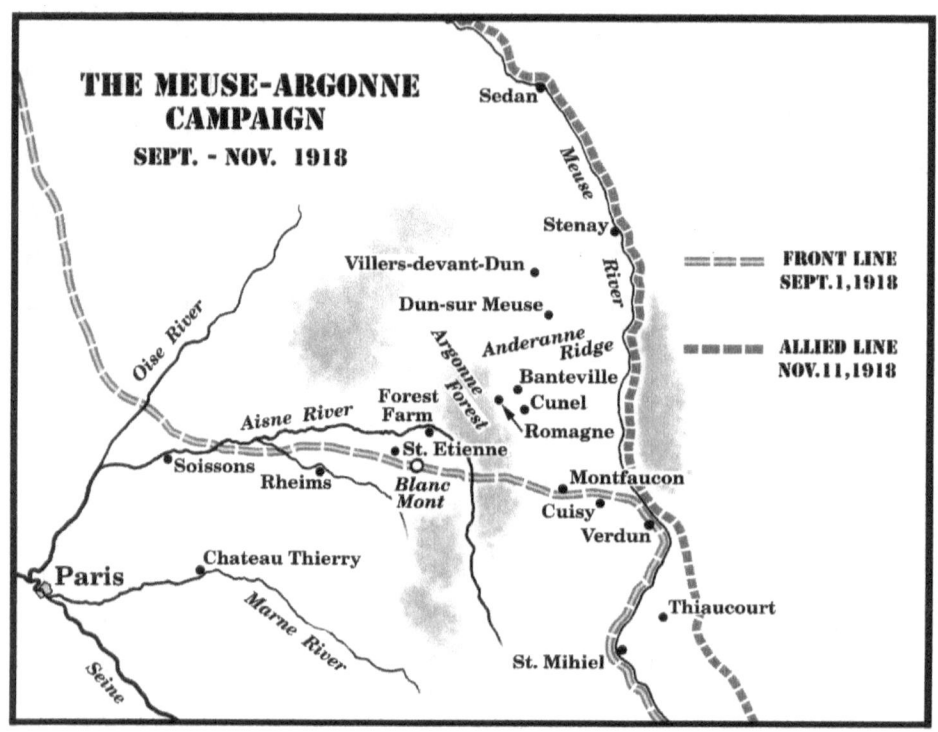

pushed the enemy out of the town of Bantheville. Stiff enemy resistance prevented the brigade from achieving all of its objectives, but it did remove the bulge in the German line.[79]

Although the 179th Brigade, which pushed through Bantheville, was largely an Oklahoma unit, a number of Texans served in the two regiments. Captain Beauford H. Jester of Corsicana, a future Texas governor, commanded Company D of the 1st Battalion, 357th Infantry. His company cleared the roads leading to Bantheville. Major Terry de la Mesa Allen of El Paso, later a World War II division commander, led the 3rd Battalion of the 358th Infantry. First Lieutenant Henry C. DeGrummond of Temple commanded Company C of the 3rd Battalion until he was hit by sniper fire in the fighting on October 24. His place was taken by 1st Lieutenant Adam B. McClanahan, also from Temple.[80]

The 179th Brigade, especially the 357th Regiment, suffered heavy casualties in the attack on the German salient at Bantheville. The 180th (or Texas) Brigade relieved the Oklahoma Brigade at the front on October 31. On the following morning, the final phase of the Argonne-Meuse offensive opened with American attacks all along the line. The 360th Infantry, commanded by Colonel Howard C. Price, a career soldier from Pennsylvania, led the assault. Massive German machine gun fire from a nearby ridge threatened to stop the advance until the 2nd Platoon of Company K, led by Sergeant Frank B. Loescher of Sealy, overran the gun emplacement, capturing seventy Germans and fourteen automatic weapons.[81]

For his leadership in the opening attack, Loescher was awarded the Distinguished Service Cross. Another member of the 360th Infantry, Corporal Fred W. Dallas of Beaumont, received the DSC for his actions during the second day of the attack. Although his arm was shattered by a machine gun bullet, Dallas refused to go to the rear. He continued to advance under heavy enemy fire until he was wounded twice more. While crawling to the rear, he helped another man to the aid station.[82]

Behind the lines of advancing infantry, members of the 315th Engineer Regiment worked to keep the muddy roads open for trucks and wagons bringing supplies and ammunition forward. At the same time, they dodged enemy machine gun fire and artillery shells, some containing poison gas. Riley Strickland, a young East Texan in the 315th, remembered the artillery fire. "Nothing more despairing than to be under heavy artillery fire," he later wrote. "On their way to their victims these shells have a sharp, shrill whistle, playing every note on both side of the G clef, except the merry ones. . . . They leave nothing but fragments and splinters of whatever they hit, whether it be man, wagons, trucks, ambulances, kitchens, tents, horses, roads, railroads, bridges, trees or what not."[83]

The 359th Infantry covered the 360th's right flank in an attack along the Andevanne ridge. Private Charles Edward Cole of Dallas, Company F, 359th Infantry, was awarded the Distinguished Service Cross for carrying front-line messages while exposed to severe artillery and machine gun fire on the first day of the attack. Corporal Thomas W. Butcher of Fort Worth, a squad leader in Company C, 359th Infantry, received his Distinguished Service Cross for leading his men through three bands of machine gun fire while wounded, capturing all three enemy guns and killing or capturing their crews.[84]

By evening of the attack's first day, the two Texas regiments had broken through the German lines on the Andevanne ridge and occupied Villers-devant-Dun several miles to the north. The Germans launched a counterattack to retake the village, but the Texans beat them off. Captain Herbert S. Hilburn of Plainview, leading Company H, 359th Infantry, was awarded the Distinguished Service Cross, the French Croix de Guerre, and the French Legion of Honor for his part in taking and defending the town.[85]

The 180th Brigade was successful in the attack but was "mauled" in the process. Because of heavy losses, it was relieved on November 3 by the division's other brigade, the 179th Oklahoma. The Oklahomans, with only three days' rest from their previous action, continued the drive north toward the Meuse. They advanced slowly the next three days, but their drive had lost its momentum by November 6. After a brief pause, the division resumed the offensive but was halted on November 10 when news was received of an impending armistice. The division was in the outskirts of Stenay on the Meuse when the war ended.[86]

The 90th Division suffered 3,596 casualties during the Meuse-Argonne campaign, 730 of whom were killed or died of wounds. Total battle casualties for the division in the war were more than 7,000 men, with approximately 1,400 battle deaths. This was nearly three times the number of total casualties suffered by the other Texas division, the 36th. Only three national Army divisions (the 77th, 82nd, and 89th) had a higher number of casualties.[87]

The men of the 90th Division spent nearly twice as much time in the active battle line as the Panthers of the Texas-Oklahoma 36th Division. Only thirteen of the twenty-nine AEF divisions to see active combat served more time in the battle line than the 90th. The Alamos, as they were then called, took more prisoners than fifteen other divisions and captured more territory than fourteen other divisions.[88]

In the American Expeditionary Force's final drive through the Argonne Forest and across the Meuse, a number of Texans in units other than the 36th and 90th Divisions were decorated for their heroism and courage. Private Conception Ortiz of El Paso, a member of Company I, 125th Infantry, 34th Division (a unit made up primarily of Midwesterners), was awarded a Distinguished Service Cross posthumously for action near Romagne. Ortiz was killed while carrying messages across a valley swept by enemy machine gun fire. Max Shoemacher of Gray Hill, a private in the 60th Infantry, 5th Division, received the Distinguished Service Cross for action near Clergy-le-Petit on November 5, 1918. When the advance of his company was halted by machine gun fire, Shoemacher and two comrades moved across an open field, attacked the machine gun nest, killed two enemy gunners, and captured eight others.[89]

David Bennes Barkley of Laredo (mentioned earlier) was awarded the Medal of Honor posthumously for heroic action that took his life two days before the armistice. Serving in the 356th Infantry, 89th Division, Barkley drowned in the Meuse while on a reconnaissance mission for the division. He was the first Hispanic to be awarded the Medal of Honor during the war.[90]

A number of Texans who served in France during the war received the Distinguished Service Medal, a decoration that usually was awarded

John A. Hulen

to field-grade or general officers for staff duty or logistical support not in a direct combat role. Major General Robert L. Howze, a West Point graduate from Rusk County who commanded the 38th Division in the Meuse-Argonne offensive and later commanded the 3rd Division in occupation duty, was the best-known Texan to receive the Distinguished Service Medal. Howze, who had been awarded the Medal of Honor for gallantry in the campaign against the Sioux in 1891, was a veteran soldier who served in the Indian wars, the Spanish-American War, the Philippine insurrection, and Pershing's Punitive Expedition. In addition to the Distinguished Service Medal, he received the French Croix de Guerre and the French Legion of Honor. Camp Howze, a major World War II training camp at Gainesville, was named in his honor.[91]

Brigadier General John A. Hulen of Gainesville, who commanded the 72nd Brigade of the 36th Division throughout the war, was awarded the Distinguished Service Medal and the Croix de Guerre for exceptional service in leading the brigade through the Meuse-Argonne offensive of 1918. Camp Hulen, near Palacios, the training camp for the 36th Division during the period between the two world wars, was named for him.[92]

Several Texans were awarded the Distinguished Service Medal for service in providing logistical support for the AEF. Jesse R. Holman of Comanche, a colonel in the Corps of Engineers, received the Distinguished Service Medal for displaying "unusual judgment and great executive ability" while in charge of construction in the vicinity of Bordeaux. Another Texan, Lieutenant Colonel Hugh B. Moore of Texas City, was awarded the Distinguished Service Medal for his role in the Quartermaster Corps while superintendent of the Army Transportation Service at Brest and later as director of the Army Transport Service. Colonel Charles T. Harris Jr., an ordnance officer and West Point graduate, was given the Distinguished Service Medal for his work as chief of the American Mission of Powder and Explosive Manufacturers in Great Britain during the war. Another ordnance officer and West Point graduate, Colonel James K. Crain, received the Distinguished Service Medal for exceptional ability in organization and administration while serving in the 42nd "Rainbow" Division.[93]

CHAPTER SIX

VICTORY AND PEACE

At 11 a.m. November 11, 1918, the fighting in the First World War—the "Great War," as contemporaries called it—officially came to an end. The armistice came with a suddenness for most American doughboys, who had no knowledge of the negotiations between the Allied and German governments that had been going on for several weeks.

Corporal Warren R. Jackson, the young Texan who had been with the 6th Marines at Belleau Wood, Soissons, and the Meuse-Argonne, found it difficult to believe that the fighting had ended. "We of course knew that the war could not last always," he later wrote. Although there had been talk among the troops that the war could end any time, Jackson was surprised to learn that it was over. "When I was waked on that morning of 11 November, 1918, to be told that the war would cease that day, the thought was inconceivable," Jackson recalled. "To be told that someone was flying to the moon would have been easier to believe."[1]

In cities and towns in the United States and the Allied nations, people greeted the news with joy. Special editions of local newspapers ("extra" editions, as they were then called) were printed with bold headlines proclaiming the armistice. Automobile and truck drivers honked their horns; factories and locomotives blew their whistles. In many communities, church bells rang to celebrate the event. That evening, public gatherings were held across Texas to give thanks and to celebrate the glorious victory. Parades were hurriedly organized, and fireworks displays marked the occasion.²

The mood among the front-line troops in the AEF was more subdued. In some sectors, the fighting went on for several hours after the cease-fire time. All were pleased when the fighting did end, but many agreed with General John J. Pershing that unconditional surrender rather than a negotiated settlement should have ended the conflict. Many spent the afternoon and evening of November 11 sleeping or moving about without fear of enemy shelling. Texas Marine Carl A. Brannen recalled that on the evening of the armistice, "you could see fires up and down the front where men were warming and sleeping that would have been unthinkable before."³

Neither Brannen, Jackson nor the thousands of other Texans in France realized that serious talks had been taking place for several weeks. Nor did they know that a fellow Texan, Colonel Edward House, played a major role in arranging the armistice. In early October, under pressure from advancing Allied armies on the war front and growing discontent at home, the German government sent a note to President Wilson requesting an end to military hostilities. After an exchange of messages concerning an armistice, Wilson dispatched House to Europe to discuss terms for a cease-fire.⁴

House landed at Brest, France, on October 25. During the next several days, he discussed cease-fire terms with Allied leaders. He quickly discovered that the Europeans had reservations concerning Wilson's views for an armistice and lasting peace, as expressed in his "Fourteen Points" message to Congress in January 1918. The British did not agree with Wilson's declaration for freedom of the seas; the French were concerned about reparations payments; the Italians demanded territorial concessions on the eastern shore of the Adriatic. Although House was forced to yield on matters relating to German troop withdrawal and arms reduction, he was able to get

Allied acceptance of most of the Fourteen Points as the basis for an armistice.[5]

At the time of the cease-fire in France, American troops, including the Texas-Oklahoma 90th Division, had crossed the Meuse River and were pushing the Germans back toward their prewar boundaries. At the same time, other American troops were holding a bridgehead in northern Russia and occupying outposts in Siberia. In both instances, Texans commanded American forces in these operations.

The decision to send American troops to Russia was the result of Allied pressure on Wilson. The Bolsheviks seized power in Russia in November 1917 and quickly took steps to withdraw their nation from the war. In a treaty signed with the Germans at Brest-Litovsk in March 1918, the Russians dropped out of the war. This caused great concern among the Allies. In an effort to keep valuable war supplies from the enemy and at the same time help 60,000 Czech troops escape in order to fight on the western front, Allied governments agreed to land troops in Russia and Siberia.[6]

A British Expeditionary Force commanded by Major General Frederick C. Poole set up headquarters in Archangel and Murmansk, Russia, in May 1918. In August, approximately 5,000 American troops, mainly from the 339th Infantry Regiment, commanded by Colonel George Stewart, landed at Archangel. The majority of these Americans were recent draftees from Michigan, a number of whom spoke Russian. Many were suffering from the influenza epidemic that was then raging in America, Asia, and Europe. During the winter of 1918–19, these American troops—along with British, French, Canadians, and White Russians—fought a number of engagements with the Bolsheviks for control of the area.[7]

In April 1919, Brigadier General Wilds Preston Richardson, a native of Hunt, Texas, and a 1884 graduate of West Point, assumed command of American forces in north Russia. A veteran of service in Alaska,

William Sidney Graves

Richardson commanded the 78th Infantry Brigade of the 39th Division in the closing days of fighting in France. Because of his extensive experience in Alaskan cold weather, he was chosen by Pershing to command the north Russia operation.⁸

Although overall command in north Russia remained in British hands, Richardson played a significant role in bringing some order to the confused state of affairs in the region. His service there was comparatively brief, however. In August 1919, American troops were withdrawn from Russia. Richardson returned home and retired in October 1920. He was awarded the Distinguished Service Medal for his wartime service.⁹

American troops were still in Siberia when the AEF withdrew from north Russia. They had been there since September 1918. The American forces in Siberia—consisting of more than 8,000 troops, seventeen female nurses, and seventeen field clerks—had come from the 8th Infantry Division at Camp Fremont, California, and the 27th and 31st Infantry regiments in the Philippines. Brigadier General William Sidney Graves, a tall, fifty-three-year-old West Point graduate from Mount Calm, was commander of the American Siberian Expedition throughout its entire existence, August 1918–December 1919.¹⁰

Graves, a soft-spoken, well-trained, experienced officer who had served in Indian campaigns and the Philippine insurrection, did not seek the Siberian command. After serving as secretary to the Army general staff in Washington for several years, he had been given command of the 8th Division training in California. He hoped, and expected, to take the division to France.[11]

Graves received his orders to command the Siberian expedition in an unusual fashion. On August 2, 1918, he received a coded telegram from the War Department instructing him "to take the first and fastest train out of San Francisco and to proceed to Kansas City," where he would meet Secretary of War Newton Baker. The message gave no information as to why Graves was being summoned to Kansas City or what he would learn from the secretary.[12]

When Graves arrived in Kansas City, Baker met him at the railroad station. The secretary handed him a sealed copy of an aide-mémoire written by Wilson, outlining American policy in Siberia. These instructions committed the United States to assist the Czech troops attempting to withdraw from Siberia, protect stockpiles of Allied military supplies on the docks of Vladivostok, and keep open the Trans-Siberian Railway. The memo cautioned Graves against interfering in purely internal political affairs.[13]

Baker told Graves that "this contains the policy of the United States in Russia which you are to follow. Watch your step; you will be walking on eggs loaded with dynamite. God bless you and good-bye." With this admonition, Baker boarded the train and returned to Washington. Graves returned to California.[14]

In mid-August 1918, Graves and approximately 5,000 troops from the 8th Division sailed from California to the Far East. On September 1, they landed at Vladivostok on the Siberian coast. The 27th and 31st Infantry regiments had already arrived from the Philippines. On September 3, Graves set up headquarters at Vladivostok.[15]

Graves soon discovered the reasons for Baker's warning. British and French representatives in the area, as well as U.S. State Department officials, wanted Graves to provide active support for the efforts of White

Russian elements led by Admiral Aleksandr V. Kolchak to overthrow the Bolshevik government. In addition, a large Japanese expeditionary force of more than 70,000 men seemed determined to establish a permanent foothold in the region.[16]

For the next sixteen months, Graves commanded American Siberian expedition forces under the most difficult circumstances. As a professional soldier and man of high integrity, the Texan carried out Wilson's orders as outlined in the aide-mémoire. Although the British and French representatives and American consul general Ernest L. Harris were convinced that Graves was obstinate and too rigid in interpreting his orders, Graves refused to use American troops to support the Kolchak regime. Fortunately, Wilson and Baker continued to back Graves.[17]

In December 1919, the American government ordered an end to the Siberian intervention. The Kolchak regime had collapsed, the Czechs had control of the railway leading to the coast, and the Bolsheviks had established order in the region. On December 31, 1919, Graves received orders for the withdrawal. Departures began shortly thereafter. On April 1, 1920, the last American units cleared the port. The Siberian intervention was over.[18]

Graves was not the only Texan involved in the Siberian intervention. Lieutenant Kearie Lee Berry of Denton, a University of Texas athlete who received a commission in 1917, spent seventeen months in Siberia. Dr. Josef H. Kopecky, a Texas Czech from Rutersville who joined the Army Medical Corps in 1918, headed an army hospital during the Siberian intervention. Peggy Hull of El Paso, by now an accredited war correspondent, reported on the intervention. (She also quarreled with Graves, who would not let her use his bathtub—one of the few in Vladivostok.[19])

Many of the troops who served with Richardson in north Russia and Graves in Siberia suffered from the great influenza epidemic that swept across the world in 1918. The epidemic's first wave occurred in the spring of that year. In early March, more than 1,000 soldiers at Camp Funston, Kansas, one of the nation's largest training facilities, were admitted to the post hospital suffering from influenza. Thousands more received treatment at camp infirmaries. Pneumonia developed in 237 men; thirty-eight died from the disease.[20]

The influenza epidemic that began at Funston spread to other military installations. In early April, the first major outbreak occurred in Brest, France, where American troops disembarked. The epidemic spread through France, England, and Germany in May. Under wartime conditions, the governments of these nations limited newspaper reporting of the epidemic, but in neutral Spain newspapers carried full accounts when the disease struck there. As a result, the virus was soon referred to as the "Spanish influenza" or "Spanish flu."[21]

Although thousands suffered from the virus in the spring and early summer of 1918, the death rate in this first wave was not high. Of more than 600 American servicemen admitted to a French hospital during one outbreak, only one patient died. In the British fleet, only four of more than 10,000 ill sailors died.[22]

The first wave ended suddenly in early August. Unfortunately, the illness reappeared late that month in Boston. Two sailors with influenza reported to sick bay on August 27. The disease, this time in a more deadly form, quickly spread through the naval district and on to nearby Camp Devens. By late September, more than 9,000 troops were on sick report, most with influenza. Although medical practitioners labored to confine the highly contagious virus, the disease spread rapidly. By late September, flu had spread throughout the country and overseas. By early October, flu had been reported in almost every part of the world.[23]

The influenza epidemic had a devastating effect in the United States and abroad. Thousands died in the big cities, especially Chicago, New York, Philadelphia, and San Francisco. Hundreds of deaths from influenza and pneumonia occurred in Texas. El Paso was particularly hard hit. By October 8, the border city had 1,800 cases of flu, about half of them at Fort Bliss. Although the post was placed under quarantine and public gatherings were banned, the disease spread. The number of cases on the south side of the city, where many immigrants from Chihuahua lived, was especially high. On October 23, city health officials reported more than 5,000 cases of flu and at least 400 deaths. The death toll exceeded 500 by early November, when the disease abated. A brief lull led city officials to lift restrictions on public gatherings in time for a large parade to celebrate the end of the war. Several new cases of flu were reported soon after, but the number declined in December.[24]

Other areas of Texas were affected by the epidemic. San Antonio, like El Paso, had thousands of cases of influenza, but the death rate was not as high. All military posts in the area were placed under quarantine; churches, schools, theaters, lodges, and other public gathering places were closed. Even so, the disease spread, with more than 10,000 cases reported in October. Hospitals were overcrowded; shortages of physicians and nurses made it difficult to provide adequate medical care. At Camp Travis, barracks were converted into temporary wards to house patients. Nearly 600 San Antonians died from influenza in 1918; another 543 died from pneumonia.[25]

Few Texas communities escaped the disease. Almost half the residents of Houston were stricken; 377 Houstonians died from influenza complications in 1918. Dallas reported 375 deaths from influenza in 1918; Galveston listed 118 influenza deaths. More than 100 people in Beaumont died that year from flu; another seventy-five residents died from pneumonia. In Nacogdoches County, more than 100 people died from influenza. In Jasper, the local newspaper reported "a considerable number of cases" and on October 17 announced that schools would remain closed until October 18. Sixty-four residents of Cleburne died from influenza in 1918. Numerous deaths from flu were reported at Camp Logan (Houston), Camp Bowie (Fort Worth), and Camp MacArthur (Waco).[26]

DEATHS IN TEXAS CITIES, 1918–19*

	Influenza		Pneumonia	
Reporting City	**1918**	**1919**	**1918**	**1919**
Beaumont	139	57	75	46
Cleburne	64	10	47	12
Dallas	375	136	411	132
El Paso	507	174	297	164
Galveston	118	16	99	5
Houston	377	165	257	113
San Antonio	571	116	543	150

* Texas was one of twenty-three states (mainly in the South) that did not report mortality figures in the national registry. The Texas cities listed here did report mortalities for the registry. These are given in the Bureau of Census, *Mortality Statistics, 1918* and *1919* (Washington: Government Printing Office, 1920-1921).

The flu epidemic also hit small towns in South and West Texas. The disease almost wiped out the youth at the small Macie community in southwestern Kinney County. Ten of the seventeen school pupils in the town died from influenza. Many adults also contracted the disease and died. The community never recovered. The post office closed in 1926; a school continued to operate on a nearby ranch until 1928. The community was abandoned shortly after.[27]

The disease that killed hundreds of thousands of Americans in 1918 took a heavy toll on soldiers and sailors. More than half the complement of the U.S.S. *Pittsburgh* patrolling Brazilian waters was stricken with influenza. Fifty-eight crew members, eleven of them Texans, died within a ten-day period in late October. Thousands of cases were reported at the Great Lakes Training Station north of Chicago and at the Philadelphia Naval Yard. The Navy estimated that 40 percent of all naval personnel had flu in 1918.[28]

More than 4,000 American soldiers died in transit from the United States to Europe in the last two months of the war. The AEF reported 37,000 men with influenza in September 1918 and another 3,560 with pneumonia. That month, 2,500 doughboys died from flu and pneumonia. In October, more than 38,000 cases of flu and 7,008 cases of pneumonia were reported. That month, 5,092 American soldiers in France died from flu and pneumonia.[29]

The diseases let up somewhat in early 1919 but continued to take lives. Historian Alfred W. Crosby estimates that 479,000 Americans (civilian and military) died in 1918 and 189,000 died in 1919. The Bureau of Census reported 165 influenza deaths in Houston, 174 in El Paso, 136 in Dallas, and 116 in San Antonio in 1919. Most scholars agree that 21 million people worldwide died in the great epidemic.[30]

Katherine Ann Porter, born in Indian Creek in Central Texas and later one of the nation's leading writers, was one of thousands of Americans who nearly died from influenza during the epidemic. After a brief time of teaching and a divorce from an early marriage, Porter left Texas in 1918 to become a reporter for Denver's *Rocky Mountain News*. She and a young Army officer with whom she was in love fell ill with flu. The officer died, and death appeared imminent for Porter. She ran extremely an high fever and her hair turned white, but after six months she recovered.[31]

The memory of the young officer and the time in which he lived and died led Porter many years later to write *Pale Horse, Pale Rider*, which historian Alfred W. Crosby has described as "the most accurate depiction of American society in the fall of 1918 in literature."[32]

The 1918 national and state elections took place during the peak of the epidemic. What effect the pandemic had on the elections is uncertain. It is clear that it affected campaigning in many locales. The normal torchlight parades and massive pre-election political rallies were canceled or reduced in size and number. In Texas, the major campaigning took place during the summer months before the onset of the most serious phases of the epidemic. Because of the participation of large numbers of female voters and the spirited campaign between Jim Ferguson and William P. Hobby for the Democratic gubernatorial nomination, turnout was heavy. Hobby and all the Democratic congressional nominees were easily elected in November, defeating token Republican opposition.[33]

Nationally, the 1918 voter turnout was less than that of two years earlier, but this is normal in non-presidential election years. The results were a rebuke for President Wilson, who on October 25 called upon voters to return a Democratic Congress. Republicans won thirty-seven of the fifty contested House seats for a comfortable margin. In the Senate, where Democrats had held a ten-seat edge, the Republicans now had a two-seat margin.[34]

Both Wilson and his closest adviser, Colonel House, had influenza during the peace talks at Paris that followed the German defeat. House, next to Wilson the most influential of the five American commissioners at the conference, was ill for ten days in late November and early December. In January 1919, he was stricken with a gallstone infection so serious that reports of his death were circulated. This illness probably prevented House from getting a seat on the Council of Ten (or Supreme Council), a body made up of Wilson, the prime ministers or premiers of France, Great Britain, Italy, and Japan, and their chief advisers. House ultimately recovered but never had the influence or prominence he held earlier.[35]

Wilson, who arrived in France on December 13, 1918, was in poor health for much of the conference. He returned to the United States in mid-February and went back to France three weeks later. He became quite ill on April 3, 1919. His temperature rose to 103 and was accompanied by severe diarrhea. His personal physician, Admiral Cary T. Grayson, diagnosed the illness as influenza. The president was bedridden for several days.[36]

During his illness in April, Wilson designated House as his representative to the "Big Four" meetings in which vital peace discussions were being held by Wilson and Allied leaders Georges Clemenceau of France, Lloyd George of Britain, and Vittorio Orlando of Italy. In earlier days, this would have been expected because of the close relationship between the president and the Texan. However, during the three weeks in February-March when Wilson was away from Paris, House made concessions to the French regarding a Rhineland republic and excluding Wilson's beloved League of Nations from the preliminary treaty. This angered Wilson. Upon his return from America, he repudiated practically everything done in his absence. From that time forward, the relationship between the president and the colonel was never the same.[37]

The last meeting between Wilson and House took place on the way to the rail station after the signing of the Treaty of Versailles on June 28, 1919. House urged the president to meet with the U.S. Senate in a conciliatory spirit upon his return to the states. Wilson replied that he found he never got anything worthwhile without fighting for it. The president then said goodbye and boarded the train to Brest, where he was to embark for home. The two men never met again.[38]

Historian Robert Hilderbrand believes that House never understood the reason for the break with Wilson, which House described as a "tragic mystery." The colonel remained in Europe after Wilson's departure and participated in conferences relating to the mandate system of the League of Nations. He wrote letters to Wilson during the Senate fight over the treaty, but they were never answered. Nor was House invited to Wilson's funeral when the president died in 1924.[39]

By the time of Wilson's departure from France, most American troops had returned home. The old Texas-Oklahoma National Guard, the 36th Division, sailed for the United States in May 1919. The other division with a large number of Texans, the 90th, left Europe two weeks later. By late June, most of the men in these divisions were home.[40]

The 36th Division was in the Triaucourt-Bar-le-Duc region when the war ended. After the armistice, the division was assigned to the 16th Training Area at Tannerre, France, to await orders for the movement home. Before departing for Tannerre, the 36th, like all divisions in the AEF, was required to design an insignia to be worn on the left shoulder. The first design, chosen by a committee, consisted of a star and the state flowers of Texas (bluebonnet) and Oklahoma (mistletoe), but this was rejected by higher command because it resembled the star with Indian head already chosen by the 2nd Division. The committee then came up with the T-arrowhead design that became the division insignia for the next thirty years.[41]

During the next six months, the 36th Division remained at Tannerre while awaiting orders for the movement home. During this time, the "Arrowheads" (as they were now called) marked time with training exercises, recreation, entertainment, and educational activities. The 36th Division football team won the 1st Army Championship in 1919. The Arrowheads then defeated the 2nd Army champions, the 78th Division, but lost to the 3rd Army champions, the 89th Division, 14-6, in the AEF "Superbowl" game.[42]

In late April 1919, the Arrowheads received orders to prepare for the return home. In May, units of the division were on the ocean heading for the states. The largest number disembarked at Hoboken, New Jersey, and Newport News, Virginia. From there they proceeded by rail to their home base, Camp Bowie, for demobilization, with the first units arriving on June 11. Before leaving France, the men of the division had received 475 decorations, including two Medals of Honor, thirty Distinguished Service Crosses, and 129 French Croix de Guerre.[43]

The other Texas division, the 90th, returned home shortly after the 36th. Like the 36th, the 90th was required to adopt a shoulder patch at the time of armistice. Although the 90th had been known as the "Alamo Division" throughout most of its existence, General Henry T. Allen, the division commander, selected a red "TO" emblem (standing for Texas and Oklahoma) as the division insignia. Hereafter, members of the division were referred to as the "TOs," and later as the "Tough 'Ombres."[44]

The 90th Division was one of eight AEF divisions chosen to serve in the occupation of Germany. The movement eastward to Germany began on November 17, in unison with other Allied forces assigned to occupation duty. The move was made under a new commander. Allen, who had led the TOs throughout the war, was given a new assignment, first to command the VIII Corps and later the Army of Occupation. Brigadier General Joseph P. O'Neil, commander of the division's 179th Brigade, took command until relieved by the new division commander, Major General Charles G. Martin, on December 30.[45]

The 90th Division was assigned territory along the Moselle River (southwest of Coblenz and northeast of Treves) for occupation duty. For the first several weeks, the division was subject to a heavy training schedule imposed by AEF command. In January 1919, Pershing modified the schedule to allow more recreation and entertainment. Soon athletic competition including football, baseball, boxing, track and field, gymnastics, and soccer took place on a regular basis. In addition, educational programs, theatrical productions, and religious activities helped the troops pass the time.[46]

Although the Texans and Oklahomans in the division found occupation duty more pleasant than combat assignments, they remained anxious to return home. On May 17, 1919, the first trainload of wildly cheering TOs boarded the train at Wengerohr headed for the French port of St. Nazaire. Other units followed the next week. The TOs were routed to various U.S. East Coast ports for debarkation. From there they were transported to demobilization camps near their homes. The majority were discharged at Camp Bowie and Camp Travis.[47]

Like its National Guard counterpart, the 36th Division, the 90th Division distinguished itself during the war. Eighty-eight members (twenty of whom were Texans) received the Distinguished Service Cross; three of its officers were awarded the Distinguished Service Medal. Historian Lonnie J. White, who has written detailed studies of the 36th and 90th Divisions, believes that "the 90th Division was one of the best in the American Expeditionary Forces." The division commander, Allen, was convinced that it was one of the six best divisions in the AEF.[48]

The 36th and 90th Divisions suffered heavy casualties during the war: 2,584 battle casualties for the 36th and more than 7,000 for the 90th. The 36th reported 591 battle deaths, the 90th approximately 1,400. These were not all Texans, nor do they represent the total number of Texans who died in the war. Ralph W. Steen, working with records in the Texas adjutant general's office, listed 5,171 Texans who died while in military service in the First World War. The great majority of these, more than 4,700, were in the U.S. Army.[49]

Although the fighting on the battlefield ended with the November 1918 armistice, the United States was technically at war with Germany until the Senate ratified a treaty. President Wilson submitted the Treaty of Versailles to the Senate immediately after his return from Paris in early July. Senate hearings began almost at once. It was soon apparent that there was considerable opposition to the treaty, especially to American participation in the League of Nations. Most Texas public officials, including Sens. Charles Culberson and Morris Sheppard, voiced support for the treaty and the league. A poll by the magazine *Literary Digest* in April 1919 showed strong support among the state's newspapers. However, Senate Republicans, led by Foreign Relations Chairman Henry Cabot Lodge, voiced major reservations to the treaty.[50]

As criticism of the treaty mounted in the Senate, Wilson, in spite of advice from Democratic leaders including Postmaster General Albert Burleson, decided to take the issue directly to the American people. Although still weak from his illness in France, the president left Washington on September 3 on a speaking tour of the Western states. He traveled more than 8,000 miles and delivered thirty-two major addresses and eight minor ones in twenty-three days. In these speeches, he answered critics of the treaty and warned that American failure to join the League of Nations would threaten world peace.[51]

The tour totally exhausted Wilson. After a September 25 address at Pueblo, Colorado, Wilson collapsed. His wife and his physician, Admiral Cary Grayson, ordered additional engagements canceled, and the presidential train returned to Washington. A week later, on October 2, Wilson suffered a severe stroke that paralyzed the left side of his face and body. Despite a partial recovery, Wilson never fully regained his physical and mental capacities.[52]

Diplomatic historian Thomas A. Bailey believes that it was a tragedy " that Colonel House was not available to Wilson during these crucial hours." Bailey points out that for more than six years, the Texan's talents as adviser and compromiser had complemented and smoothed the president's stubborn traits. But the two men had drifted apart at the Paris peace conference, and the gap widened when Wilson returned home. House, who had remained in Europe working on implementation of the Paris agreements, returned to America ten days after Wilson's stroke. Although he was ill himself with gallstones, House attempted to work out an understanding between Lodge and Wilson, but his overtures to the White House went unanswered.[53]

Meanwhile, efforts by Wilson supporters in the Senate to secure ratification of the Treaty of Versailles failed. On November 6, the Foreign Relations Committee recommended ratification, but with fourteen reservations proposed by Lodge. During the next two weeks, the Senate voted on the reservations. Although most Southern senators, including Texans Culberson and Sheppard, opposed the reservations, each was approved by a narrow margin. When Lodge brought up the whole treaty with reservations for a vote, however, those senators opposed to any treaty (the "irreconcilables") joined Wilson Democrats in rejecting the treaty, 39–55. The Democratic leadership, hoping now to attract some "mild reservations" (who favored the treaty even if they could not secure changes), then moved to vote on the treaty without reservations. This measure was defeated 38–53.[54]

Although the Senate had rejected the treaty, efforts to find some compromise between the president and league opponents continued. In late November, House sent two letters to the White House urging Wilson to allow Senate Democrats to vote for such reservations as required for passage. "To the ordinary man, the distance between the Treaty and the reservations is slight," wrote House. In a second letter, written three days later, the Texan advised Wilson that "your willingness to accept reservations rather than have the Treaty killed will be regarded as the act of a great man."[55]

Wilson never answered House. Moderate Democratic and Republican leaders continued, however, to work for passage of the treaty. In early February 1920, the Foreign Relations Committee brought the treaty to the Senate floor again, this time with fifteen reservations (a new one supporting self-determination for Ireland was added). The reservations were voted upon and approved by the Senate between February 21 and March 18.[56]

Historian Dewey Grantham notes there was an increase in support among Southern congressmen for the reservations in the February–March voting. Whereas only twenty-eight Southern votes were cast for the Lodge reservations in November, this time Southerners voted for some part of the reservations on sixty-two instances. Culberson and Sheppard, who voted against all the reservations in November, voted for the reservation concerning the league mandate system for former German colonies. Sheppard also voted for the reservation urging self-determination for Ireland.[57]

The final vote on the treaty with the Lodge reservations took place on March 19, 1920. Culberson, normally a strong supporter of the president's foreign policy, provided a bit of drama, in all probability unintentional. Three of the first senators to answer the roll call, all Democrats, deserted the president and voted in favor of the treaty with the reservations. Next came Culberson, a Wilson loyalist, who apparently had been touched by the speech of Sen. Thomas Welsh, in which the Montanan stated that in spite of his opposition to the reservations, he would reluctantly vote for passage. When it came Culberson's time to vote, he looked bewildered and hesitated. In spite of his physical difficulties and poor health, the Texan was highly respected by his colleagues. His vote for the treaty with the reservations might have touched off a Democratic stampede. But after a brief pause, Culberson voted "Nay." After that, there were no surprises. Twenty-one Democrats voted for passage, but twenty-three, including Culberson and Sheppard, voted no. The measure passed 49–35, seven votes short of the two-thirds required for ratification.[58]

The March 1920 vote was final. No effort was made to approve the treaty without reservations, as this was considered hopeless.

Wilson hoped that the election of 1920 would be a "great and solemn referendum" on the treaty and the League of Nations. The Democratic candidates for president and vice president, James M. Cox and Franklin D. Roosevelt, campaigned for the treaty and the league but were defeated by Republicans Warren G. Harding and Calvin Coolidge, both of whom were evasive on the issue.[59]

In Texas, support for the Wilson policies continued to be strong. In their state meeting in March 1920, Texas Democrats praised the president and endorsed his position on the League of Nations. In the general election of 1920, Cox and Roosevelt carried the state, 288,767 to 114,536. Democratic candidates for state and federal offices once again were elected.[60]

Although most public officials and news media in Texas favored ratification of the Treaty of Versailles, this was not a major issue in postwar Texas. Former U.S. Sen. Joe Bailey denounced the League of Nations in his campaign for governor in 1920, but other issues were of greater concern to Texans. A race riot in Longview in the summer of 1919 increased racial tensions. A prolonged dockworkers strike in Galveston in 1920 led to the imposition of martial law in the island city. The governor's race in the Democratic primary between the conservative Bailey and moderate Pat Neff focused upon domestic issues such as prohibition, women's suffrage, race relations, and labor unrest, not the League of Nations. In a bitter contest, Neff, a former speaker of the Texas House and a prominent Baptist layman, won the Democratic nomination.[61]

For the United States, World War I officially ended in 1921. In July, Congress passed a joint resolution declaring the war with Germany and Austria-Hungary at an end. On October 10, 1921, without fanfare or major debate, the United States ratified peace treaties with Germany and Austria-Hungary. The Great War was over.

The First World War brought significant changes to Texas. Nationwide prohibition of alcoholic beverages and adoption of women's suffrage might have occurred without the war, but the pace for their implementation was accelerated. The number of Texans living in urban communities rose during the war as rural Texans moved into towns and cities to build ships, refine oil, and construct training camps and air fields. By the end of the war, one of every three Texans lived in urban areas, twice the ratio that existed twenty years earlier.[62]

Industry that grew during the war continued to expand in later years. This was particularly true of the drilling and refining of oil. New discoveries in Texas during and immediately after the war placed the state in the forefront of the petroleum industry. During the 1920s, Texas passed Oklahoma as a producer of crude oil. The building of oil refineries along the Houston Ship Channel and in the Beaumont-Port Arthur region made Texas the national leader both in production and refining of petroleum.[63]

Even with the growth of industry during the war, agriculture continued to provide the livelihood of half of the Texas population in the postwar years. Although the cattle industry was growing, cotton remained the king of the economy. Production dropped slightly during the war because of bad weather and destruction by the boll weevil and the pink bollworm, but it rose to record levels in the first two years after the war. A serious drop in price in the latter half of 1920 was followed by a decline in production, but by the middle of the 1930s cotton was once again being grown at a record level.[64]

Social changes came slowly during the postwar years. Although women gained the right to vote, there were still limitations in employment opportunities as both industries limited women to clerical and housekeeping positions. Restrictions continued to exist on property ownership, particularly for married women. Public officeholding remained largely a male prerogative. With the exception of a few women such as Annie Webb Blanton (elected as state superintendent of public instruction in 1918), Miriam "Ma" Ferguson (wife of former Gov. Jim "Pa" Ferguson, elected governor in 1924 and 1932), Edith Williams (elected to the Texas House in 1922), and Margie Neal of Carthage (elected state senator in 1926), few female Texans held statewide political office during the next three decades.

The postwar years brought few changes in the lives of Texas African-Americans, many of whom had hoped that their patriotic service during the war would result in better treatment at home once the military conflict ended. Even though more than 30,000 black Texans served in the armed forces during the war (12,000 of them overseas) and several were awarded the Distinguished Service Cross for their wartime service, most white Texans continued to regard them as second-class citizens. A July 1919 race riot in Longview resulted in one death, several people injured, and the burning of homes owned by African-Americans. When the National Association for the Advancement of Colored People protested the treatment of Texas blacks, Gov. William Hobby replied that the organization should keep its representatives out of the state.[65]

Mexican Texans fared better than blacks both during and after the war. The need for wartime labor brought more Tejanos into the interior of the state to fill industrial and military needs. Thousands of Tejanos served in military units alongside other Texans during the war. Several Mexican Texans received the Distinguished Service Cross for military valor; one Tejano, David Bennes Barkley of Laredo, was one of four Texans awarded the Medal of Honor, the nation's highest military decoration. As Carole Christian has pointed out, their wartime experiences, both at home and overseas, was a major step in bringing Mexican Texans into the whole of American society.[66]

In many ways, the First World War marked the passing of the political old guard and the beginning of a new era. Several of the state's major political leaders including U.S. Sen. Joe Bailey, Reps. Martin Dies Sr. and James L. Slayden, Cabinet members Albert Sidney Burleson, Thomas Watt Gregory, and David F. Houston, and Wilson adviser Edward House—were ending their public careers. Several younger Texans in Congress—John Nance Garner, Tom Connally, and Sam Rayburn—were beginning their careers as political leaders who would play significant roles in the New Deal and the Second World War. Other Texans, including future Admirals J. O. Richardson and Chester W. Nimitz and future corps and Army commander Walton H. Walker, were beginning military careers that would lead them to the top of their profession. Robert A. Lovett, later a secretary of defense and one of the six "wise men" advising presidents during the Cold War, gained military and managerial skills commanding a naval bombing squadron during the war. Future U.S. Rep. Maury Maverick, future Gov. Beauford Jester, and future Railroad Commissioner Ernest O. Thompson received administrative experience commanding troops in the American Expeditionary Force in France.

The mobilization of the mind and spirit of Texans during the First World War kindled the growth of patriotism and Americanism. As historian Walter Buenger observed, for the first time since the Civil War, Texans thought of themselves as Americans rather than as Southerners. Pride in the Old South and the Confederacy remained, but the First World War brought Texans into the mainstream of American life, where they would remain throughout the twentieth century.[67]

ENDNOTES

CHAPTER ONE

1. Dewey Grantham Jr., "Texas Congressional Leaders and the New Freedom, 1913–1917," *Southwestern Historical Quarterly* 53 (July 1949): 35–36. See also Richard M. Adams, "Woodrow Wilson and the Southern Congressmen, 1913–1916," *Journal of Southern History* 22 (November 1956): 417–437.
2. O. Douglas Weeks, "Election Laws," in Ron Tyler, ed., *New Handbook of Texas*, 6 vols. (Austin: Texas State Historical Association, 1996) 2: 814–815; Lewis L. Gould, "Progressive Era," *ibid.*, 5: 351–352; and J. Morgan Krousser, *The Shaping of Southern Politics, Suffrage Restrictions and the Establishment of the One-Party South, 1880–1910* (New Haven: Yale University Press, 1974), 196–209.
3. Lewis L. Gould, *Progressives and Prohibitionists: Texas Democrats in the Wilson Era* (Austin: Texas State Historical Association, 1992), 120–149; *Dallas Morning News*, July 31, 1914.
4. Numerous works cover the 1914 events in Europe. See especially Barbara W. Tuchman, *The Guns of August* (New York: Macmillan Company, 1962) and David Fromkin, *Europe's Last Summer* (New York: Alfred A. Knopf, 2004).
5. Newspaper quotations taken from Ruth McCawley, "American Attitude Toward England and Germany As Reflected in the Newspapers of Texas From 1914 to 1917" (M.A. thesis, University of Texas, 1940), 1–6.
6. *Ibid.*, 10–27; "An Appeal to the American People," in Arthur S. Link, ed., *The Papers of Woodrow Wilson*, 69 vols. (Princeton: Princeton University Press, 1966–1994), 30: 393–394.
7. Thirteenth Census of United States, 1910, Vol. III, *Population* (Washington: Government Printing Office, 1913), 799; Fourteenth Census of United States, Volume I, *Population* (Washington: Government Printing Office, 1922), 6–17, 46–47, 303–306.
8. Thirteenth Census, *Population*, 799. Blacks constituted 50 percent or more of the population in Marion, Harrison, Fort Bend, Robertson, Walker, San Jacinto, Walker, and Gregg counties. By 1910, Texas had the smallest proportion of African-Americans in the eleven former Confederate states.
9. *Ibid.*, 799.
10. Thirteenth Census, Vol. VII, *Agriculture 1909 and 1910*, 619. The percentage of farmers was roughly the same among races and nationalities as in the total population. Native whites made up 76.4 percent of farm operators; foreign-born whites, 6.9 percent; and Negroes and non-whites, 16.7 percent. The number of women and children who worked on Texas farms is not known.
11. *Ibid.*, VII, 616. Texas was third (behind Illinois and Iowa) among the states in value of farm products in 1910.

12. Quote, Lewis L. Gould, "Progressive Era," *New Handbook of Texas*, 5: 347. Data on cotton production, Thirteenth Census, Vol. V, *Agriculture*, 626–628, 680–681.
13. Thirteenth Census, Vol. V, *Agriculture*, 350–433; Vol. VII, *Agriculture*, 624.
14. *Texas Almanac, 1941–1942* (Dallas: A. H. Belo Co., 1941), 229; Thirteenth Census, Vol. XI, *Mines and Quarries*, 279; Roger M. Olien, "Oil and Gas Industry," *New Handbook of Texas*, 4: 1120; Diana Davids Olien and Roger M. Olien, *Oil in Texas: The Gusher Age, 1895–1945* (Austin: University of Texas Press, 2002), 53–63; Gerald Forbes, *Flush Production: The Epic of Oil in the Gulf-Southwest* (Norman: University of Oklahoma Press, 1942), 39–45.
15. Thirteenth Census, Vol. IX, *Manufactures*, 1197–1198. The value of Texas oil production in 1910 was only $6.6 million.
16. Ralph W. Steen, *Twentieth Century Texas: An Economic and Social History* (Austin: Steck Company, 1942), 120; Gould "Progressive Era," *New Handbook of Texas*, 5: 348.
17. Steen, *Twentieth Century Texas*, 125; Gould, "Progressive Era," *New Handbook of Texas*, 5: 348; John D. Huddleston, "Highway Development: A 'Concrete' History of Twentieth-Century Texas," in Donald W. Whisenhunt, *Texas: A Sesquicentennial Celebration* (Austin: Eakin Press, 1984), 254–255.
18. David G. McComb, *Houston: The Bayou City* (Austin: University of Texas Press, 1964), 105; Robert A. Rider, "Electric Interurban Railways," *New Handbook of Texas*, 2: 817; H. Roger Grant, " 'Interurbans Are the Wave of the Future': Electric Railway Promotions in Texas," *Southwestern Historical Quarterly* 84 (July 1980): 28–49.
19. Louise C. Allen, Ernest A. Sharpe, and John R. Whitaker, "Newspapers," *New Handbook of Texas*, 4: 1000–1002.
20. Alwyn Barr, *Black Texans: A History of African Americans in Texas, 1528–1995* (second ed., Norman, OK: University of Oklahoma Press, 1996), 95; Diana J. Kleiner, "Houston Informer and the Texas Freeman," *New Handbook of Texas*, 3: 733; Glen E. Lich, *The German Texans* (San Antonio: Institute of Texan Cultures, 1981), 138; Clinton Machann, "Czechs," *New Handbook of Texas*, 2: 466; Conchita Hassell Winn, "Spanish Language Newspapers," *ibid.*, 6: 4–5.
21. Barr, *Black Texans*, 136–144; National Association for the Advancement of Colored People, *Thirty Years of Lynching in the United States, 1888–1918* (org. pub. 1919; New York: Arno Press, 1969), 31–33, 113–118; Walter Buenger, *The Path To A Modern South: Northeast Texas Between Reconstruction and the Great Depression* (Austin: University of Texas Press, 2001), 19–21; John R. Ross, "Lynching," *New Handbook of Texas*, 4: 346–347; William D. Carrigan, *Making of a Lynching Culture: Violence and Vigilantism in Central Texas, 1836–1916* (Urbana, University of Illinois Press, 2004).
22. Arnoldo De Leon, "Mexican Americans," *New Handbook of Texas*, 4: 664–670; Gould, "Progressive Era," *ibid.*, 5: 350; Buenger, *Path To A Modern South*, 21.
23. A. Elizabeth Taylor, "Woman Suffrage," *New Handbook of Texas*, 6: 1039–1041; Elizabeth York Enstam, "Women and the Law," *ibid.*, 6: 1047; Judith N. McArthur, "Women and Politics," *ibid.*, 6: 1051–1052; Fane Downs, "Texas Women At Work," Whisenhunt, *Texas: A Sesquicentennial Celebration*, 318–321.
24. Judith N. McArthur, "Woman's Christian Temperance Union," *New Handbook of Texas*, 6: 1037–1038.
25. Department of Commerce, Bureau of Census, *Religious Bodies, 1916*, two parts (Washington: Government Printing Office, 1919), Part I: 224–225; Gould, *Progressives and Prohibitionists*, 46–47; Brian Hart, "George Clark Rankin," *New Handbook of Texas*, 5: 445; John W. Storey, "Religion," *ibid.*, 5: 527–528.

26. *Religious Bodies, 1916,* Part I: 229–225; Gould, *Progressives and Prohibitionists,* 53–54.
27. Gould, *Progressives and Prohibitionists,* 120–146. Biographical accounts are Ralph W. Steen, "The Political Career of James E. Ferguson, 1914–1917" (M.A. thesis, University of Texas, 1918); George P. Huckaby, "Oscar Branch Colquitt: A Political Biography" (Ph.D. dissertation, University of Texas, 1946); Gary Price, "Thomas Henry Ball," *New Handbook of Texas,* 1: 357.
28. Theodore Saloutos, *Farmer Movements in the South, 1865–1933* (Lincoln: University of Nebraska Press, 1964), 238.
29. Colquitt quote, Gould, *Progressives and Prohibitionists,* 154–155.
30. Saloutos, *Farmer Movements in the South,* 239–241. George B. Tindall, *The Emergence of the New South, 1913–1945* (Baton Rouge: Louisiana State University Press and Littlefield Fund for Southern History of the University of Texas, 1967), 34–37, discusses various proposals to aid the cotton farmers, including the "Buy a Bale of Cotton" plan whereby citizens were asked to assist Southern farmers by purchasing bales of cotton.
31. Josephus Daniels to Wilson, October 6, 1914, and Edward Mandell House to Wilson, October 14, 1914, in Link, ed., *Papers of Woodrow Wilson,* 31: 126, 148.
32. Arthur S. Link, "The Cotton Crisis, the South, and Anglo-American Diplomacy, 1914–1916" in Link, *The Higher Realism of Woodrow Wilson and Other Essays* (Nashville: Vanderbilt University Press, 1971), 327–328; *Statistical Abstract of the United States, 1941* (Washington: Government Printing Office, 1942), 741.
33. Charles C. Cumberland, "Border Raids in the Lower Rio Grande Valley, 1915" *Southwestern Historical Quarterly* 57 (January 1954): 285–290; Patrick L. Cox, " 'An Enemy Closer to Us Than Any European Power': The Impact of Mexican Texan Public Opinion before World War I," *ibid.,* 105 (July 2001): 57–66; Robert M. Utley, *Lone Star Lawmen: The Second Century of the Texas Rangers* (New York: Oxford University Press, 2007), 8–25.
34. The literature on the Plan of San Diego is extensive and growing. Among various accounts see the works cited above and William M. Hager, "The Plan of San Diego: Unrest on the Texas Border in 1915," *Arizona and the West* 5 (Winter 1963): 327–336; Alan Gerlach, "Conditions Along the Border, 1915: The Plan de San Diego," *New Mexico Historical Review* 43 (July 1968): 195–212; James A. Sandos, "The Plan of San Diego: War & Diplomacy on the Texas Border, 1915–1916," *Arizona and the West* 14 (Spring 1972): 5–24; Charles H. Harris III and Louis R. Sadler, "The Plan of San Diego and the Mexican-United States Crisis of 1916: A Reexamination," *Hispanic American Historical Review* 58 (August 1978): 381–408); Rodolfo Rocha, "The Influence of the Mexican Revolution on the Texas-Mexican Border, 1910–1916" (Ph.D. dissertation, Texas Tech University, 1981); Don M. Coerver and Linda B. Hall, *Texas and the Mexican Revolution: A Study in State and National Border Policy* (San Antonio: Trinity University Press, 1984); James A. Sandos, *Rebellion in the Borderlands: Anarchism and the Plan of San Diego, 1904–1923* (Norman: University of Oklahoma Press, 1992); Benjamin Heber Johnson, *Revolution in Texas: How A Forgotten Rebellion and Its Bloody Suppression Turned Mexicans Into Americans* (New Haven, CT: Yale University Press, 2003); and Charles R. Harris III and Louis R. Sadler, *The Texas Rangers and the Mexican Revolution: The Bloodiest Decade, 1910–1920* (Albuquerque, NM: University New Mexico Press, 2004).

35. Cumberland, "Border Raids in the Lower Rio Grande Valley, 1915," 291–305; Utley, *Lone Star Lawmen*. 26–47.
36. Walter Prescott Webb, *The Texas Rangers: A Century of Frontier Defense* (Boston: Houghton Mifflin, 1935), 478, reported that estimates of the number killed in South Texas during this time was between 500 and 5,000. Johnson, *Revolution in Texas*, 120, says that a "number in the low thousands is possible." Harris and Sadler, *Texas Rangers and the Mexican Revolution*, 296, believe that "about three hundred seems a reasonable estimate of Hispanic and Mexican deaths." This is the number given by Don E. Coerver, "Plan of San Diego," *Handbook of Texas*, 5: 228.
37. There are numerous accounts of the *Lusitania*. Among the most recent is Diane Preston, *Lusitania: An Epic Tragedy* (New York: Walker & Co., 2002). For Wilson's role in the crisis, see Arthur S. Link, *Wilson: The Struggle for Neutrality, 1914–1915* (Princeton, NJ: Princeton University Press, 1960), 368–455, and Ray Stannard Baker, *Woodrow Wilson, Life and Letters*. 8 vols. (New York: Doubleday & Co., 1937), 5: 245–260.
38. Quote, *Fort Worth Star-Telegram*, May 9, 1914, p. 4, in McCawley, "American Attitude Toward England and Germany," 82. Senate and House resolutions, *Journal of the Senate of Texas Being the First Called Session of the Thirty-Fourth Legislature* (Austin: A. C. Baldwin & Son, 1915), 37–36, 42; *Journal of the House of Representatives of the First Called Session of the Thirty-Fourth Legislature* (Austin: Von Boeckmann-Jones Co., 1915), 117.
39. Newspapers all quoted in McCawley, "American Attitude Toward England and Germany," 78–83.
40. Arthur S. Link, *Woodrow Wilson and the Progressive Era, 1913–1917* (New York: Harper & Row, 1954), 179–188; George C. Herring, Jr., "James Hay and the Preparedness Controversy, 1915–1916," *Journal of Southern History* 30 (November 1964): 388–391.
41. Thomas Lloyd Miller, "Oscar Callaway and Preparedness," *West Texas Historical Association Year Book* 43 (October 1967): 80–93.
42. *Congressional Record*, 64th Congress, First Session, Appendix, 367–368, 384, 386, 495, 635–636; James H. "Cyclone" Davis, *Memoir* (Sherman: Courier Press, 1935), 14–15; Anthony Gaughan, "Woodrow Wilson and the Rise of Militant Interventionism in the South," *Journal of Southern History* 65 (November 1999): 779, 782.
43. *Congressional Record*, 64th Congress, First Session, Appendix, 514–516; John Milton Cooper, *The Vanity of Power: American Isolationism and the First World War, 1914–1917* (Westport, CN: Greenwood Publishing, 1969), 94.
44. Quote, Grantham, "Texas Congressional Leaders," 39. For more on Dies, see Dennis K. McDaniel, "The First Congressman Martin Dies of Texas," *Southwestern Historical Quarterly* 102 (October 1998): 131–162; A. John Impson, "Martin Dies, John Henry Kirby, and Timber Politics," *East Texas Historical Journal* 35 (Fall 1997): 20–29.
45. *Congressional Record*, 64th Congress, First session, 4731, 6376, 12697–12700; Herring, "James Hay and the Preparedness Controversy, 1915–1916," 400–401.
46. Link, *Woodrow Wilson and the Progressive Era, 1910–1917*, 187–188.
47. Ibid., 180–190; Grantham, "Texas Congressional Leaders," 44. Oscar Callaway, a bitter opponent of the naval expansion bill, was in Texas campaigning for reelection.

48. Atkins Jefferson McLemore, a native of Tennessee, had a colorful career as cowboy, printer, newspaper reporter, gold prospector, state legislator, Austin alderman, poet, and magazine publisher. See John D. Thompson, "Atkins Jefferson McLemore," *New Handbook of Texas*, 4: 426–429; Robert L. Wagner, "The Congressional Career of Jeff McLemore as Seen in His Letters," *The Historian of the University of Texas* 1 (September 1962): 65–81. Thomas P. Gore, sponsor of the resolutions in the Senate, lived in Texas in the 1890s and married a native of Palestine. He moved to Oklahoma in 1901 and was elected to the U.S. Senate in 1907.
49. *Congressional Record*, 64th Congress, First Session, 3463–3469, 3519, 3598–3599, 3660–3662, 3689–3720, 3886–3898. For more, see Timothy C. McDonald, "The Gore-McLemore Resolutions: Democratic Revolt Against Wilson's Submarine Policy," *The Historian* 26 (November 1963): 52–74; and Thomas W. Ryley, *A Little Group of Willful Men: A Study of Congressional-Presidential Authority* (Port Washington, NY: Kennikat Press, 1975), 47–50.
50. Frank E. Vandiver, *Black Jack: The Life and Times and John J. Pershing*, 2 vols. (College Station: Texas A&M University Press, 1977), 2: 603–604; Cox, " 'An Enemy Closer to Us Than Any European Power,' " 66–73; Lonnie J. White, *Panthers to Arrowheads: The 36th (Texas-Oklahoma) Division in World War I* (Austin: Presidial Press, 1984), 2–4.
51. Herbert M. Mason Jr., *The Great Pursuit: General John J. Pershing's Punitive Expedition Across the Rio Grande to Destroy the Mexican Bandit Pancho Villa* (New York: Random House, 1970); Clarence C. Clendenen, *The United States and Pancho Villa* (Ithaca, NY: Cornell University Press, 1961); Clendenen, *Blood on the Border: The United States Army and the Mexican Irregulars* (London: Macmillan Company, 1969); and Joseph A. Stout Jr., *Border Conflict: Villistas, Carrancistas and the Punitive Expedition, 1915–1920* (Fort Worth: Texas Christian University Press, 1999).
52. Martin D. Kohout, "Glenn Springs Raid," *New Handbook of Texas*, 3: 189; David Montejano, *Anglos and Mexicans in the Making of Texas, 1836–1936* (Austin: University of Texas Press, 1987), 122–123; Frank C. Pierce, *A Brief History of the Lower Rio Grande Valley* (Menasha, WS: George Banta Publisher, 1917), 99–100.
53. Culberson, suffering from Bright's disease and alcoholism, resigned as Senate minority leader in 1910 but remained as chairman of the Judiciary Committee. Robert L. Wagner, "Charles Allen Culberson," *New Handbook of Texas*, 2: 435–436. The Texas Democratic Party required all candidates for public office to run in the primary contest (even though prior to the adoption of the 17th Amendment, state legislators chose U.S. senators). See Mike Kingston, Sam Attlesey, and Mary G. Crawford, *The Texas Almanac's Political History of Texas* (Austin: Eakin Press, 1992), 116.
54. Colquitt received 119,598 votes in the first primary; Culberson got 87,421. Seth S. McKay, *Texas Politics, 1906–1944: With Special Reference to the German Counties* (Lubbock: Texas Tech Press, 1952), 66; *Austin American*, July 23–24, 1916; *Houston Post*, July 23, 24, 1916; Gould, *Progressives and Prohibitionists*, 178–179; Hockaby, "Oscar Branch Colquitt," 424–437.
55. Culberson received 155,460 votes and Colquitt got 88,435 in the primary runoff election. McKay, *Texas Politics*, 68–71; Cox " 'An Enemy Closer to Us Than Any European Power,' " 55.

56. Presidential returns, Kingston, *Texas Almanac's Political History of Texas*, 80–83. Hughes carried only eight Texas counties: Comal, DeWitt, Gillespie, Guadalupe, Kendall, Lee, Maverick, and Washington. These "German" counties traditionally voted Republican in presidential elections. Wilson carried two "German" counties, Austin and Fayette. McKay, *Texas Politics*, 72. Historian Patrick L. Cox notes that although Wilson's "Kept Us Out of War" theme helped him in Texas, his tough policy with Mexico was another factor. Cox, " 'An Enemy Closer to Us Than Any European Power,' " 56–57.
57. Arthur S. Link, *Wilson: Campaigns for Progressivism and Peace, 1916–1917* (Princeton, NJ: Princeton University Press, 1965), 265–268. The address may be found in Link, ed., *Papers of Woodrow Wilson*, 40: 533–539.
58. Link, *Wilson: Campaigns for Progressivism and Peace, 1916–1917*, 271–293.
59. Robert H. Zieger, *America's Great War: World War I and the American Experience* (New York: Rowman & Littlefield, 2000), 49–50.
60. *Houston Chronicle*, Feb. 1, 1917; *Galveston Weekly News*, Feb. 2, 1917; *Fort Worth Star-Telegram*, Feb. 2, 1917; *Austin Statesman*, Feb. 2, 1917; *Dallas Morning News*, Feb. 3, 1917; *San Antonio Express*, Feb. 1, 1917, all quoted in McCawley, "American Attitude Toward England and Germany," 103–108.
61. Charles Seymour, ed., *The Intimate Papers of Colonel House*, 4 vols. (Boston: Houston Mifflin Co., 1926), 2: 438.
62. "An Address to a Joint Session of Congress," Link, ed., *Papers of Woodrow Wilson*, 41: 108–112.
63. *Houston Post*, February 4, 1917. Even Ellen Maury Slayden, wife of San Antonio congressman James L. Slayden, believed "the President never made a better impression" in his address to Congress. In her diary, Mrs. Slayden, who had known Wilson at the University of Virginia, was generally critical of the president. In this instance, she added "he was *almost* modest, not dogmatic and school masterish but like a normal man seeking advice and help of other men in a moment of awful responsibility." Terrell D. Webb, ed., *Washington Wife: Journal of Ellen Maury Slayden from 1897–1919* (New York: Harper & Row, 1963), 291.
64. Quote, Link, *Wilson: Campaigns for Progressivism and Peace, 1916–1917*, 304.
65. Link, ed., *Papers of Woodrow Wilson*, 286; David F. Houston, *Eight Years With Wilson's Cabinet, 1913 to 1920*, 2 vols. (Garden City, NY: Doubleday, Page, & Co., 1926),1: 229–231.
66. The thirteen congressmen who voted against the armed-ship bill were from New York, California, and the Midwest. Although the Senate did not vote on the bill, seventy-five members, including Morris Sheppard of Texas, signed a petition expressing support for it. Sen. Charles Culberson of Texas, who was ill and seldom present at this time, did not sign the petition. See Ryley, *A Little Group of Willful Men*, 98–118.
67. Details pertaining to the Zimmermann message may be found in "A Memorandum by Robert Lansing," March 4, 1917, in Link, ed., *Papers of Woodrow Wilson*, 41: 321–327, and Barbara Tuchman, *The Zimmermann Telegram* (new ed., New York: Houghton Mifflin, 1966).
68. Cox, " 'An Enemy Closer to Us Than Any European Power' " 74–77; *Houston Post*, April 4, 1917; *Fort Worth Star-Telegram*, April 4, 1917; *San Antonio Express*, April 6, 1917.

69. Ryley, *A Little Group of Willful Men*, 149–150; Link, *Campaigns for Progressivism and Peace, 1916–1917*, 371–376.
70. Link, *ibid.*, 394–400.
71. Houston, *Eight Years With Wilson's Cabinet*, 1: 242.
72. Gregory quoted in "A Memorandum by Robert Lansing," *Papers of Woodrow Wilson*, 41: 442.
73. Burleson quotation, "A Memorandum by Robert Lansing," *Papers of Woodrow Wilson*, 41: 442. According to his biographer, Adrian Anderson, Burleson was "neither a warhawk nor a pacifist [who] accepted the horror of war only when confronted with the humiliation of submission." Anderson, "Albert Sidney Burleson: A Southern Politician in the Progressive Era" (Ph.D. dissertation, Texas Technological College, 1967), 213.
74. Link, ed., *Papers of Woodrow Wilson*, 41: 446, 483–484, 496–498.
75. "An Address to a Joint Session of Congress," *ibid.*, 41: 519–527.
76. *Congressional Record*, 65th Congress, First Session, 201–261, 412; Cox, " 'An Enemy Closer to Us Than Any European Power,' " 78; Carl Wittke, *German-Americans and the World War* (Columbus, OH: Ohio State Archaeological and Historical Society, 1936), 128. Ryley, *A Little Group of Willful Men*, 154–167, provides a good account of congressional debates about the war resolution.
77. Ryley, *A Little Group of Willful Men*, 166; McDaniel, "The First Congressman Martin Dies," 154. In her diary, Ellen Slayden explains that her husband, a longtime opponent of war, believed that "the war was an accomplished fact, the President had plunged us into it long ago, and the only thing we could do now was to work to finish it as decently and promptly as possible." Webb, ed., *Washington Wife*, 301. Mrs. Slayden noted that her "antiwar sisters gave me some evil moments during the next few days."
78. Link, ed., *Papers of Woodrow Wilson*, 45: 224n; *Congressional Record*, 65th Congress, Second Session, 67–68, 99–100.

CHAPTER TWO

1. These are numbers *authorized* by Congress. John Keegan, *The First World War* (New York: Alfred A. Knopf, 1998), 372, points out that at the time the regular Army actually numbered 107,643 men and the National Guard 132,000 men. In addition, 15,500 were in the Marine Corps. For the bill, see John Whiteclay Chambers II, *To Raise an Army: The Draft Comes to Modern America* (New York: Free Press, 1987), 153. For Baker's role, see Daniel R. Beaver, *Newton D. Baker and the American War Effort, 1917–1919* (Lincoln, NB: University of Nebraska Press, 1966), 24–32.
2. These factors are discussed fully by Chambers, *To Raise an Army*, 125–151. Chambers argues that the key to Wilson's change was his old political rival, former President Theodore Roosevelt, who was requesting that he be placed in command of two divisions of volunteers that would be sent to France. Wilson was determined to avoid what he believed would be a military and political disaster.
3. For more on this controversy, see Seward W. Livermore, *Politics Is Adjourned: Woodrow Wilson and the War Congress, 1916–1918* (Middletown, CN: Wesleyan University Press, 1966), 15–31.

4. Steen, *Twentieth Century Texas*, 205; *Journal of the Senate, State of Texas, First Called Session of Thirty-Fifth Legislature* (Austin: A. C. Baldwin, 1917), 29–31; *Journal of the House of Representatives of the First Called Session of the Thirty-Fifth Legislature* (Austin: Von Boeckmann-Jones, 1917), 120–121.
5. Chambers, *To Raise an Army*, 154–177; Livermore, *Politics Is Adjourned*, 24–30. In the various votes on the Army bill, Texans in Congress overwhelmingly supported the administration. On a key vote to recommit an earlier version that made no provision for the Roosevelt volunteers, only Reps. Eugene Black of Clarksville, Thomas Blanton of Abilene, and Jeff McLemore of Houston voted to recommit and thus reconsider requiring the Roosevelt volunteers. *Congressional Record*, 65th Congress, First Session, 2197–2215, 2457.
6. *Second Report of the Provost Marshal General to the Secretary of War on the Operations of the Selective Service System to December 20, 1918* (Washington: Government Printing Office, 1919), 316.
7. *Order of Battle of the United States Land Forces in the World War*, 3 vols. (Org. pub., 1931–1949; Facsimile report, Washington: Center of Military History, United States Army, 1988), III, Pt. 1: 377: *Second Report of the Provost Marshal General*, 1–2, 396. These figures differ slightly from those provided to Ralph Steen by the adjutant general of Texas, March 12, 1940. These give total Texas registration as 989,571. Steen, *Twentieth Century Texas*, 285.
8. Chambers, *To Raise an Army*, 185. Although the bulk of those drafted went into the national Army, some would be used to fill out National Guard divisions. See White, *Panthers to Arrowheads*, 40–42.
9. *Second Report of the Provost Marshal General*, 6.
10. Ibid., 453; Chambers, *To Raise an Army*, 182.
11. Jeanette Keith, *Rich Man's War, Poor Man's Fight: Race, Class, and Power in the Rural South during the First World War* (Chapel Hill, NC: University of North Carolina Press, 2004), 61; David M. Kennedy, *Over Here: The First World War and American Society* (New York: Oxford University Press, 1980), 156–157; *Second Report of the Provost Marshal General*, 401.
12. Nationally, Selective Service drafted one-third of black registrants but only one-fourth of whites. *Second Report of the Provost Marshal General*, 458–459. For more on this subject, see Chambers, *To Raise an Army*, 222–226; Kennedy, *Over Here*, 161–162; Edward M. Coffman, *The War to End All Wars: The American Military Experience in World War I* (Madison, WS: University of Wisconsin Press, 1986), 70–71; and Keith, *Rich Man's War, Poor Man's Fight*, 126–133.
13. *Final Report of the Provost Marshal General to the Secretary of War on the Operation of the Selective Service System to July 15, 1919* (Washington: Government Printing Office, 1920), 19, 54; *Second Report of the Provost Marshal General*, 468; *Order of Battle*, III, Pt. 1: 404. Again, the total figures for Texans in service given by the provost marshal, 184,463, differ slightly from the 197,789 number provided by Ralph Steen, *Twentieth Century Texas*, 285. Not all Texans were eager to serve. In a recent work describing resistance to military service, *Rich Man's War, Poor Man's Fight*, 179, Jeanette Keith notes that 13.1 percent of Texans deserted—the same percentage as those from New York state. Desertion rates from other Southern states ranged from 7 percent in North Carolina to 20.4 percent in Florida.

14. Lonnie J. White, "The Call to Arms," *Military History of Texas and the Southwest* 17 (No. 2, 1982): 2–5; Bruce L. Brager, *The Texas 36th Division* (Austin: Eakin Press, 2002), 34–35.
15. White, *Panthers to Arrowheads*, 29–30.
16. White, "The Call to Arms," 8–11.
17. Descriptions of these posts are found in the *New Handbook of Texas*.
18. White, "The Call to Arms," 15; Zeiger, *America's Great War*, 86.
19. Lonnie J. White, *The 90th Division in World War I* (Manhattan, KS: Sunflower University Press, 1996), 2–3.
20. Ibid., 3–5; *Order of Battle*, III, Pt. 2: 931–932. For more on Camp Travis, see E. B. Johns, comp., *Camp Travis and Its Part in the World War* (New York: priv. publ., 1919).
21. *Order of Battle*, III, Pt.2: 900–902; White, "The Call to Arms," 17–19; Lonnie J. White, "The Formation of the 36th Division," *Military History of Texas and the Southwest* 17 (No. 2, 1982): 25–29; White, "Camp Bowie," *New Handbook of Texas*, 1: 929–930.
22. *Houston Chronicle*, June 11, 12, July 25, August 17, 1917; *Waco Times-Herald*, June 19, July 20–21, 1917.
23. Robert V. Haynes, *A Night of Violence: The Houston Riot of 1917* (Baton Rouge: Louisiana State University Press, 1976), 1–2; Garna L. Christian, *Black Soldiers in Jim Crow Texas, 1899–1917* (College Station: Texas A&M University Press, 1995), 132–133. For more on the 24th Infantry, see William G. Muller, *The Twenty-fourth Infantry: Past and Present* (Reprint: Fort Collins, Colorado, 1972).
24. Haynes, *A Night of Violence*, 51–54.
25. Robert V. Haynes, "The Houston Mutiny and Riot of 1917," *Southwestern Historical Quarterly* 76 (April 1973): 420–421.
26. Haynes, *A Night of Violence*, 63–65.
27. Five of the men received five years' imprisonment; the sixth, considered the leader of the group, was sentenced to ten years. The latter's sentence was later reduced to five years. Christian, *Black Soldiers in Jim Crow Texas*, 134–142.
28. Garna L. Christian, "The Ordeal and the Prize: The 24th Infantry and Camp MacArthur," *Military Affairs* 50 (April 1986): 65–70, credits the military leadership of the 1st Battalion for acting quickly to control the situation.
29. Haynes, "The Houston Mutiny and Riot of 1917," 424–431.
30. C. Calvin Smith, "The Houston Riot of 1917 Revisited," *Houston Review* 13 (No. 2, 1991): 96, argues that the claim that Henry led the men in a conspiracy is unsupported by reliable, documented evidence.
31. Haynes, *A Night of Violence*, 171–184; Christian, *Black Soldiers in Jim Crow Texas*, 154–155; *Houston Post*, August 24, 1917; *Houston Press*, August 24, 1917.
32. Haynes, *A Night of Violence*, 171–192; *Houston Chronicle*, August 26–27, 1917.
33. Ibid., 192–230; Christian, *Black Soldiers in Jim Crow Texas*, 153–160.
34. Haynes, *A Night of Violence*, 235–273.
35. Ibid., 285–296. An NAACP delegation appealed to President Wilson for clemency after the second trial. The president commuted the sentences of ten of the men condemned to death. For additional accounts of the Houston riot, see Edgar A. Scholar, "The Houston Race Riot, 1917," *Journal of Negro History* 29 (July 1944): 300–338; Phocion S. Park Jr., "The Twenty-fourth Infantry Regiment and the Houston Riot of 1917" (M.A. thesis, University of Houston, 1971); and Thomas Richard Adams, "The Houston Riot of 1917" (M.A. thesis, Texas A&M University, 1972).

36. *Order of Battle*, III, Pt. 2: 900–922.
37. *Ibid.*, III, Pt. 2: 918–919. In spite of local protests, Company C, 8th Illinois, an all-black National Guard unit, completed its training at Logan. Coffman, *War to End All Wars*, 73.
38. Quote, Garna L. Christian, "Newton Baker's War on El Paso Vice," *Red River Historical Review* 5 (Spring 1980): 67. For expenditures at various Texas posts, see *Order of Battle*, III, Pt. 1. For more on Baker's war on vice, see Coffman, *War to End All Wars*, 77–78.
39. Roger D. Launius, "A New Way of War: The Development of Military Aviation in the American West, 1908–1945," *Military History of the West* 25 (Fall 1995): 167–171; Roger E. Bilstein and Jay Miller, *Aviation in Texas* (Austin: Texas Monthly Press, 1985), 18–20; William C. Pool, "The Origin of Military Aviation in Texas, 1910–1913," *Southwestern Historical Quarterly* 58 (April 1955): 319–330; Pool, "Military Aviation in Texas, 1913–1917," *ibid.* 59 (April 1956): 429–454.
40. James J. Hudson, *Hostile Skies: A Combat History of the American Air Service in World War I* (Syracuse, NY: Syracuse University Press, 1968), 2–3.
41. Coffman, *War to End All Wars*, 196–198; Hudson, *Hostile Skies*, 27–29. The School of Military Aeronautics of the University of Texas opened on May 21, 1917. Barney M. Giles of Mineola, later deputy commander of the U.S. Air Forces in World War II, was among the first cadets at the University of Texas school. Giles describes his early training in "Early Military Aviation Activities in Texas," *Southwestern Historical Quarterly* 54 (October 1950): 149–158.
42. *Order of Battle*, III, Pt. 1: 164; Robert H. Hays, Jr., "Military Aviation in Texas, 1917–1919," *Texas Military History* 3 (Spring 1963): 5; Thomas E. Alexander, *The Wings of Change: The Army Air Force Experience in Texas During World War II* (Abilene, TX: McWhiney Foundation Press, 2003), 27. For more on Kelly Field, see Ann Hussey and Robert S. Browning III, *A History of Service: Seventy-five Years of Military Aviation at Kelly Air Force Base, 1916–1991* (San Antonio: Office of History, San Antonio Air Logistics Center, Kelly Air Force Base, 1991).
43. Edward B. Alcott, "Brooks Air Force Base," *New Handbook of Texas*, 1: 752; Hays, "Military Aviation in Texas, 1917–1919," 6.
44. David Minor, "Hicks, Texas," *New Handbook of Texas*, 3: 588; Art Leatherwood and Chris Cravens, "Hicks Field," *ibid.* 3: 588; Art Leatherwood, "Benbrook Field," *ibid.*, I: 486; Art Leatherwood, "Barron Field," *ibid.*, 1: 395; *Order of Battle*, III, Pt. 1: 163–164.
45. David Minor, "Call Field," *New Handbook of Texas*, 1: 903–904; *Order of Battle*, III, Pt. 2: 903–904.
46. Art Leatherwood, "Ellington Field," *New Handbook of Texas*, 2: 827–828; *Order of Battle*, III, Pt. 2: 909–910; Alexander, *Wings of Change*, 62.
47. *Order of Battle*, III, Pt. 2: 925.
48. *Ibid.*, III, Pt. 2: 921; Art Leatherwood, "Love Field," *New Handbook of Texas*, 4: 306.
49. *Order of Battle*, III, Pt. 2: 934–935; Hays, "Military Aviation in Texas, 1917–1919," 8; Hudson, *Hostile Skies*, 42–43.
50. *Order of Battle*, III, Pt. 2: 907, 908, 913, 933.
51. Zeiger, *America's Great War*, 64–65.
52. Robert H. Ferrell, *Woodrow Wilson and World War I, 1917–1920* (New York: Harper & Row, 1985), 103; Kennedy, *Over There*, 114–115.

53. Oran Elijah Turner, "History of the Texas State Council of Defense" (M.A. thesis, University of Texas, 1926), 20–21.
54. Steen, *Twentieth Century Texas*, 293–294; "Texas State Council of Defense," *New Handbook of Texas*, 6: 422.
55. Grosvenor B. Clarkson, *Industrial America in the World War: The Strategy Behind the Line, 1917–1918* (Boston: Houghton Mifflin Co., 1923), 36–37, 145, 301; Robert D. Cuff, *The War Industries Board: Business-Governmental Relations during World War I* (Baltimore: Johns Hopkins University Press, 1973), 1–2, 114–115, 119–120; S. G. Reed, "Robert Scott Lovett," *New Handbook of Texas*, 4: 308–309; Richard T. Fleming, "Edwin B. Parker," *ibid.*, 5: 59.
56. Beaver, *Newton D. Baker*, 73–75, 104–105; Zieger, *America's Great War*, 69–71; Kennedy, *Over There*, 126–137; Cuff, *The War Industries Board*, 212.
57. Ferrell, *Woodrow Wilson and World War I*, 98–99.
58. *Ibid.*, 99–100; Robert S. Maxwell and Robert D. Baker, *Sawdust Empire: The Texas Lumber Industry, 1830–1940* (College Station, Texas A&M University, 1983), 184–185.
59. Richard W. Bricker, *Wooden Ships from Texas: A World War I Saga* (College Station: Texas A&M University Press, 1998), 20–30.
60. *Ibid.*, 161–174; William Allen and Sue Hasting Taylor, *Aransas: The Life of a Texas Coastal County* (Austin: Eakin Press, 1997), 230–235.
61. Maxwell and Baker, *Sawdust Empire*, 187–190; Mary Lasswell, *John Henry Kirby: Prince of the Pines* (Austin: Encino Press, 1967), 160–161.
62. Maxwell and Baker, *Sawdust Empire*, 193–195; Bricker, *Wooden Ships from Texas*, 172–175. In his book, 20–65, Bricker describes the wooden sailing vessels built in Texas ports. See also Frank O. Karpii, "The Last Sailing Ships Built in Texas," *Texas Gulf Historical and Biographical Record* 16 (November 1980): 55–68; William J. Webb, "The United States Wooden Steamship Program During World War I," *American Neptune* 35 (1975): 275–288; James E. Johnson, "An Economic History of Orange County Prior to 1940" (M.A. thesis, Lamar State College of Technology, 1966), 107–114.
63. *Texas Almanac, 1941–42* (Dallas: A. H. Belo Co., 1941), 229; Forbes, *Flush Production: The Epic of Oil in the Gulf-Southwest*, 42–43, 45, 53; Olien and Olien, *Oil in Texas*, 77–94; Richard R. Moore, *West Texas After the Discovery of Oil: A Modern Frontier* (Austin: Jenkins Publishing Co., 1971), x–xi.
64. Bruce Andre Beauboeuf, "War and Change: Houston's Economic Ascendancy During World War I," *Houston Review* 14 (No. 2, 1992): 109; David McComb, *Houston: The Bayou City* (Austin: University of Texas Press, 1989), 116.
65. Diana J. Kleiner, "Sulphur Industry," *New Handbook of Texas*, 6: 141; James A. Creighton, *A Narrative History of Brazoria County* (Waco: Brazoria Historical Commission, 1975), 324, 329.
66. William Haynes, *Brimstone: The Stone That Burns* (Princeton, NJ: D. Van Nostrand Co., 1959), 99–100; Kleiner, "Sulphur Industry," 6: 141.
67. Kenneth B. Ragsdale, *Quicksilver: Terlingua and the Chisos Mining Company* (College Station: Texas A&M University, 1976) is the standard source. Bernard M. Baruch, *American Industry in the War* (New York: Prentice-Hill, Inc., 1941), 160–161, provides national data.
68. Ragsdale, *Quicksilver*, 102–105; Baruch, *American Industry in the War*, 160.

69. Herbert H. Lang, "Fort Worth's Role in the Origins of the Helium Industry," *West Texas Historical Association Year Book* 47 (1971): 127–129; Diana J. Kleiner, "Helium Production," *New Handbook of Texas*, 3: 545–546.
70. Lang, "Fort Worth's Role in the Origins of the Helium Industry," 129.
71. Ferrell, *Woodrow Wilson and World War I*, 91.
72. Kennedy, *Over Here*, 117–118; William C. Mullendore, *History of the United States Food Administration, 1917–1919* (Palo Alto, CA: Stanford University Press, 1941), 42–57.
73. Ferrell, *Woodrow Wilson and World War I*, 91; Cynthia Brandimarte, "Using Government Documents: The Food Administration Papers for Texas," *Southwestern Historical Quarterly* 104 (October 2000): 264–265.
74. Henry George Hendricks, "The Federal Food Administration for Texas, 1917–1919" (M.A. thesis, University of Texas, 1925), 32–42.
75. *Ibid.*, 42–50.
76. Zieger, *America's Great War*, 72–74.
77. Fourteenth Census of United States, *Agriculture*, Vol. 5: 736, 745, 751.
78. *Ibid.*, 839; *Texas Almanac*, 1941–42, 207; Truman McMahon, "The Fight Against the Pink Bollworm in Texas," *Southwestern Historical Quarterly* 94 (July 1990): 37–64; Walter L. Buenger, " 'This Wonder Age': The Economic Transformation of Northeast Texas, 1900–1930," *ibid.*, 98 (April 1995): 527, 533–540.
79. Baruch, *American Industry in the War*, 191–182, 244–246; Clarkson, *Industrial America in the World War*, 401–402, 446; Mary M. Standifier, "Cottonseed Industry," *New Handbook of Texas*, 2: 357.
80. Paul H. Carlson, *Texas Woolybacks: The Range Sheep and Goat Industry* (College Station: Texas A&M University Press, 1982), 193–194; Baruch, *American Industry in the World War*, 247–250.
81. Carlson, *Texas Woolybacks*, 195–200.
82. Colonel House Diary, in Link, ed., *Papers of Woodrow Wilson*, 46: 23; quoted in Meiron & Susie Harris, *The Last Days of Innocence: America At War, 1917–1918* (New York: Random House, 1997), 202–204. See also Kennedy, *Over Here*, 128–143. Ferrell, *Woodrow Wilson and World War I*, 96–97, is slightly less critical.

CHAPTER THREE

1. Rupert N. Richardson, *Colonel Edward M. House: The Texas Years, 1858–1912* (Abilene, TX: Hardin-Simmons University, 1964), 3–40; Charles E. Neu, "In Search of Colonel Edward M. House: The Texas Years, 1858–1912," *Southwestern Historical Quarterly* 93 (July 1989): 30–32.
2. Charles E. Neu, "Edward Mandell House," *New Handbook of Texas*, 3: 710–711. One biographer, Arthur D. Howden Smith, *Mr. House of Texas* (New York: Funk & Wagnalls Co., 1940), 1, states that House "detested the honorary title of Colonel." According to Smith, House "regarded it—and endured it good-humoredly as a political nickname." Richardson, *Colonel Edward House*, 223, says House "could have shaken it off, if he had been opposed to it."
3. Quote, Robert C. Hilderbrand, "Edward M. House," in Kenneth E. Hendrickson Jr. and Michael L. Collins, eds., *Profiles in Power: Twentieth-Century Texans in Washington* (Arlington Heights, Il: Harlan-Davidson, 1993), 3.

4. Charles Seymour, ed., *The Intimate Papers of Colonel House Arranged as a Narrative*, 4 vols. (Boston: Houghton Mifflin Co., 1926), 1: 46. For the early relationship between House and Wilson, see Godfrey Hodgson, *Woodrow Wilson's Right Hand: The Life of Colonel Edward M. House* (New Haven: Yale University Press, 2006), 54–68.
5. Hilderbrand, "Edward M. House," 8. For more on the Wilson-House relationship, see Alexander L. and Juliette L. George, *Woodrow Wilson and Colonel House: A Personality Study* (New York: The John Day Company, 1956); and George Sylvester Viereck, *The Strangest Friendship in History: Woodrow Wilson and Colonel House* (New York: Liveright, Inc., 1932).
6. Diary of Colonel House, Link, ed., *Papers of Woodrow Wilson*, 46: 24.
7. In his diary, reprinted in *Papers of Woodrow Wilson*, 41: 528, House stated that Wilson did not show members of the Cabinet his address prior to delivery. For more, see Lewis L. Gould, ed., "A Texan in London: A British Editor Lunches with Colonel Edward H. House, February 15, 1916," *Southwestern Historical Quarterly* 84 (April 1981): 426–434; and Robert W. Tucker, *Woodrow Wilson and the Great War: Reconsidering America's Neutrality, 1914–1917* (Charlottesville: University of Virginia Press, 2007), esp. 145–173.
8. House, who was constantly concerned about his health, was frequently in Massachusetts during the summer. In early September 1917, President Wilson and his wife journeyed to Gloucester to visit House. Seymour, ed., *Intimate Papers of Colonel House*, 3: 174–178, 205–206. For more on House's health, see Hodgson, *Woodrow Wilson's Right Hand*, 19–20.
9. Seymour, *Intimate Papers of Colonel House*, 3: 210–290. For more on the Supreme War Council, see David F. Trask, *The United States in the Supreme War Council: American War Aims and Inter-Allied Strategy, 1917–1918* (Middleton, CN: Wesleyan University Press, 1961).
10. Seymour, ed., *Intimate Papers of Colonel House*, 3: 316–318; Hilderbrand, "Edward M. House," 22; Hodgson, *Woodrow Wilson's Right Hand*, 161–167.
11. Biographical information drawn from Adrian Anderson, "Albert Sidney Burleson: A Southern Politician in the Progressive Era" (Ph.D. dissertation, Texas Technological College, 1967) and Anderson, "President Wilson's Politician: Albert Sidney Burleson of Texas," *Southwestern Historical Quarterly* 77 (January 1974): 338–354.
12. Anderson, "Albert Sidney Burleson," 100–123.
13. Gould, *Progressives and Prohibitionists*, 98–100; Anderson, "President Wilson's Politician," 342–344. Anderson points out that "Burleson and his wife believed Mrs. Wilson influenced the decision."
14. Anderson, "President Wilson's Politician," 347. Anderson discusses Burleson's prewar role in the Cabinet more fully in his dissertation, 167–195.
15. Quote, Anderson, "President Wilson's Politician," 345.
16. Quote, Anderson, "Albert Sidney Burleson," 214.
17. Anderson, "Albert Sidney Burleson," 226; Donald Johnson, "Wilson, Burleson, and Censorship in the First World War," *Journal of Southern History* 28 (February 1962): 47–48; Paul L. Murphy, *World War I and the Origin of Civil Liberties in the United States* (New York: W. W. Norton & Co., 1979), 97–98. For more on the Espionage Act of 1917, see Geoffrey R. Stone, *Perilous Times: Free Speech in Wartime* (New York: W. W. Norton & Co., 2004), 146–153.
18. Quote, Johnson, "Wilson, Burleson, and Censorship in the First World War," 49.

19. Woodrow Wilson to Burleson, July 13, 1917; Burleson to Wilson, July 16, 1917, in Link, ed., *Papers of Woodrow Wilson*, 43: 164, 187–188.
20. First quote, Kennedy, *Over Here*, 77; second quote, *Literary Digest* 55 (October 6, 1917), 12; Anderson, "Albert Sidney Burleson," 227. For more on Burleson's role in suppressing criticism of the administration, see two articles in the *Southwestern Social Science Quarterly* by Ora H. Hilton, "Public Opinion and Civil Liberties in Wartime, 1917–1919," 28 (December 1947): 201–224, and "Freedom of the Press in Wartime, 1917–1919," 28 (March 1948): 346–361.
21. Evan Anders, "Thomas Watt Gregory," *New Handbook of Texas*, 3: 331; Anders, "Thomas Watt Gregory and the Survival of His Progressive Faith," *Southwestern Historical Quarterly*, 93 (July 1989): 17; Gould, *Progressives and Prohibitionists*, 78, 102; Stone, *Perilous Times*, 184–185.
22. Kennedy, *Over Here*, 79–81; Murphy, *World War I and the Origins of Civil Liberties in the United States*, 79–80.
23. Kennedy, *Over Here*, 81–82; Murphy, *World War I and the Origins of Civil Liberties in the United States*, 89–90, 123–124; Harries and Harries, *Last Days of Innocence*, 203–205.
24. McAdoo to Gregory, June 2, 1917, and Wilson to Gregory," June 14, 1917, in Link, ed., *Papers of Woodrow Wilson*, 42: 441–446.
25. Jensen, *Price of Vigilance*, 210–215; Harold M. Hyman, *To Try Men's Souls: Loyalty Tests in American History* (Berkeley, CA: University of California Press, 1959), 272–291.
26. John W. Payne, Jr., "David Franklin Houston," *New Handbook of Texas*, 3: 715. For Houston's role at A&M, see Payne, "David F. Houston's Presidency of Texas A. & M.," *Southwestern Historical Quarterly* 58 (July 1954): 22–35. For more on Houston's early life, see Payne's dissertation, "David F. Houston: A Biography," (Ph.D. dissertation, University of Texas, 1953).
27. Houston, *Eight Years With Wilson's Cabinet, 1913 to 1920*, 1: 9–11, 21–22.
28. *Ibid.*, 1: 96–97; Payne, "David Franklin Houston," 3: 715.
29. Houston, *Eight Years With Wilson's Cabinet, 1913 to 1920*, 1: 256–266; "The Diary of Colonel House," in Link, ed., *Papers of Woodrow Wilson*, 46: 116–117.
30. James A. Tinsley, "Thomas Bell Love," *New Handbook of Texas*, 4: 306; Gould, *Progressives and Prohibitionists*, 61–67, 230. See also Sue E. Winston Moore, "Thomas B. Love, Texas Democrat" (M.A. thesis, University of Texas, 1971).
31. "Stockton Axson," *New Handbook of Texas*, 1: 321–322; Wilson James Battle, "Sidney Edward Mezes," *ibid.*, 4: 701–702; Walter Buenger, "Jesse Jones," in Hendrickson and Collins, eds., *Profiles in Power*, 67.
32. *Congressional Record*, 65th Congress, First Session, 2215, 2197–2215, 2457.
33. "James Luther Slayden," *New Handbook of Texas*, 5: 1084–1085. See also Sandra Wyatt Day, "The Political Career of James Luther Slayden" (M.A. thesis, University of Texas, 1962). In spite of his work for world peace, Slayden was a prime mover on the House Military Affairs Committee in the prewar years. Indeed, fellow congressmen on the committee recommended Slayden for the position of secretary of war in the Wilson Cabinet. Members of the Army general staff, however, considered Slayden was too much of a pacifist and opposed his nomination. See James W. Pohl, "Slayden's Defeat: A Texas Congressman Loses His Bid as Wilson's Secretary of War," *Military History of Texas and the Southwest* 10 (No. 1, 1972): 43–50.

34. Quote, Walter P. Webb, introduction, *Washington Wife*, xi. Mrs. Slayden, a member of a distinguished Virginia family, knew Wilson when she was a student at the University of Virginia. According to Webb, "she did not like him then, and she did not like him any better when he became President."
35. Robert L. Wagner, "Charles Allen Culberson," *New Handbook of Texas*, 2: 434–435; James William Madden, *Charles Allen Culberson: His Life, Character, and Public Service* (Austin: Gammel's Book Store, 1929), 153–154; Kennedy, *Over Here*, 25.
36. Richard Bailey, "Morris Sheppard," in Hendrickson and Collins, eds., *Profiles in Power*, 30–31; Gould, *Progressives and Prohibitionists*, 94–97. See also Richard Bailey, "Morris Sheppard of Texas, Southern Progressive and Prohibitionist" (Ph.D. dissertation, Texas Christian University, 1980); Escal F. Duke, "The Political Career of Morris Sheppard, 1875–1941" (Ph.D. dissertation, University of Texas, 1958); Karen J. Salas, "Senator Morris Sheppard and the Eighteenth Amendment" (M.A. thesis, University of Texas, 1970).
37. Lionel V. Patenaude, "John Nance Garner," in Hendrickson and Collins, eds., *Profiles in Power*, 43–45; Bascom N. Timmons, *Garner of Texas: A Personal History* (New York: Harper & Brothers, 1948), 82–84; Gould, *Progressives and Prohibitionists*, 110–111, 162, 183. See also Alwyn Barr, "John Nance Garner's First Campaign for Congress," *West Texas Historical Association Year Book* 48 (1972): 105–110; S. S. McKay, "John Nance Garner," *ibid.* 37 (1961): 10–20.
38. McDaniel, "The First Congressman Martin Dies of Texas," 140–154. See also A. John Impson, "Martin Dies, John Henry Kirby and Timber Politics, 1908–1918," *East Texas Historical Journal* 35 (Fall 1997): 20–29.
39. Thompson, "Atkins Jefferson McLemore," *New Handbook of Texas*, 4: 428–429. See also Wagner, "Congressional Career of Jeff McLemore as Seen in His Letters," 65–81.
40. The quote on Young is from Tom Connally, *My Name Is Tom Connally* (New York: Thomas Y. Crowell Co., 1954), 92.
41. Alexander Graham Shanks, "Sam Rayburn in the Wilson Administration, 1913–1920," *East Texas Historical Journal* 6 (March 1968): 63–76; Irvin M. May Jr., *Marvin Jones: The Public Life of an Agrarian Advocate* (College Station: Texas A&M University Press, 1980), 35–40; May, "Marvin Jones, Representative of and from the Panhandle," *West Texas Historical Association Year Book* 52 (1976): 91–104; Ron Law, "Congressman Hatton W. Sumners of Dallas, Texas: His Life and Congressional Career, 1875–1937" (Ph.D. dissertation, Texas Christian University, 1990); Connally, *My Name Is Tom Connally*, 94–95. In his autobiographical account, 90–92, Connally describes a number of his wartime colleagues. He describes Blanton, who was bitterly anti-labor, as the "most controversial"; Dies as "a brilliant debater who would have gone far if he had bothered to extend himself"; Buchanan, "who was noted chiefly for his foolhardiness in playing poker with John Garner"; Rayburn as "a hard worker"; Joe Mansfield, "who worried about waterways"; and Eugene Black as "a serious man given to no frivolity."
42. Richard L. Watson, "A Testing Time for Southern Congressional Leadership," *Journal of Southern History* 44 (February 1978): 16–19; Kennedy, *Over Here*, 17–18; May, *Marvin Jones*, 35–37; Livermore, *Politics Is Adjourned*, 57–61. Robert H. Zieger, *America's Great War*, 76–77, points out that the United States financed about 23 percent of its direct war expenses through taxation and the rest through borrowing.

The recently adopted income tax, which provided 16 percent of all federal revenues in 1916, provided 70 percent by 1918. Charles Gilbert, *American Financing of World War I* (Westport, CT: Greenwood Press, 1970), 76, 83–111.
43. Steen, *Twentieth Century Texas*, 207–231; K. Austin Kerr, "Prohibition," *New Handbook of Texas*, 5: 355.
44. Gould, *Progressives and Prohibitionists*, 46–57.
45. *Ibid.*, 226–227; Bailey, "John Morris Sheppard," *New Handbook of Texas*, 5: 1016.
46. *Congressional Record*, 65th Congress, First Session, 5549–5554; Watson, "A Testing Time for Southern Congressional Leadership," 27–28; Madden, *Charles Allen Culberson*, 156.
47. *Congressional Record*, 65th Congress, First Session, 5636–5666; Second Session, 469–470. Voting for passage were Black, Connally, Garrett, Gregg, Jones, Rayburn, Sumners, and Young. In opposition were Buchanan, Dies, Garner, Hardy, McLemore, Mansfield, Slayden, and Wilson. Tom Blanton and Joe Eagle did not vote.
48. Walter P. Webb, *The Great Plains* (Boston: Ginn & Co., 1931), 504; A. Elizabeth Taylor, "Woman Suffrage," *New Handbook of Texas*, 6: 1039–1041.
49. Grantham, "Texas Congressional Leaders and the New Freedom, 1913–1917," 46; Watson, "A Testing Time for Southern Congressional Leadership," 29–34.
50. Blanton, considered by Tom Connally as the most controversial member of the Texas delegation, was in his first term as congressman. His sister Annie Webb Blanton was the first woman to hold a state office in Texas, winning election as superintendent of public instruction in 1918. Thomas Lloyd Miller, "Thomas Lindsay Blanton," *New Handbook of Texas*, 1: 588; Connally, *My Name is Tom Connally*, 90–91; Watson "A Testing Time for Southern Congressional Leadership," 32fn.
51. *Congressional Record*, 65th Congress, Second Session, 810. Five of the six favoring the women's suffrage amendment had voted for prohibition. The sixth, Tom Blanton, failed to vote on the prohibition resolution. Three Texas congressmen (Black, Rayburn, and Young) voted for prohibition but against the suffrage resolution. Six Texas congressmen (Buchanan, Dies, Hardy, McLemore, Slayden, and Wilson) voted against both resolutions.
52. Quote, Richard L. Watson, "A Testing Time for Southern Congressional Leadership," 34; Livermore, *Politics Is Adjourned*, 182–184.
53. Ralph W. Steen, "James Edward Ferguson," *New Handbook of Texas*, 2: 979–981; Randolph B. Campbell, *Gone To Texas: A History of the Lone Star State* (New York: Oxford University Press, 2003), 350.
54. Lewis L. Gould, "The University Becomes Politicized: The War With Jim Ferguson, 1915–1918," *Southwestern Historical Quarterly* 86 (October 1982): 262–266; Gould, *Progressives and Prohibitionists*, 190–197; Ralph Steen, "Ferguson's War on the University of Texas," *Southwestern Social Science Quarterly* 35 (March 1955): 356–362.
55. *Dallas Morning News*, February 9–11. 1917; *Houston Post*, February 9, 1917.
56. Gould, *Progressives and Prohibitionists*, 205, points out Ferguson did provide for the issuance of deficiency warrants that would have allowed the school to operate under gubernatorial supervision and reduced circumstances.
57. Apparently Ferguson was convinced that the Legislature would meet with or without his action and wanted to be certain that his supporters were in attendance. Steen, "James Edward Ferguson," *New Handbook of Texas*, 2: 980; Robert E. Vinson, "The University Crosses the Bar," *Southwestern Historical Quarterly* 43

(January 1940): 287–288. Gould, *Progressives and Prohibitionists*, 209–211, points out that Fuller and Ferguson had been in a controversy over the location of a proposed West Texas A&M College.
58. *Journal of the House of Representatives, Second Called Session, Thirty-fifth Legislature* (Austin: Von Boeckmann-Jones, 1917), 78–103. The loan had come from members of the brewing industry who had a promise from the governor that he would not reveal their names. Ferguson kept the promise, although as Lewis Gould points out, "his reticence gave enemies ample opportunity for innuendo." Gould, *Progressives and Prohibitionists*, 214.
59. *Journal of the Senate, State of Texas, Third Called Session, Thirty-Fifth Legislature* (Austin: A. C. Baldwin & Sons, 1917), 940–943. Votes on the ten charges ranged from 21–17 in favor and 4–10 in opposition. Four senators voted against every article of impeachment.
60. Gould, *Progressives and Prohibitionists*, 217–218; *Journal of the Senate, Third Called Session, Thirty-Fifth Legislature*, 951–996; *Houston Post*, September 22–23, 1917.
61. Hobby served as acting governor during Ferguson's trial in the Senate. Under the Texas Constitution, the action of the House in voting impeachment articles automatically suspended Ferguson from office. Hobby, the lieutenant governor, served as acting chief executive pending the outcome of the trial in the Senate. James A. Clark, with Weldon Hart, *The Tactful Texan: A Biography of Governor Will Hobby* (New York: Random House, 1958), 71.

CHAPTER FOUR

1. See the chronology table in the appendix.
2. Clark, *Tactful Texan*, 45–56.
3. Gilbert, *American Financing of World War I*, 124–128; Clark, *Tactful Texan*, 76–78.
4. Clark, *Tactful Texan*, 77–79; John F. Griffiths and Greg Ainsworth, *One Hundred Years of Texas Weather, 1880–1979* (College Station: Office of the State Climatologist, 1981), 60–62; Glenn Smith, "Drought in Runnels County, 1915–1918," *West Texas Historical Association Year Book* 40 (October 1964): 52–70. The drought continued through most of 1918. Rains in late autumn and winter, 1918–1919, ended the drought. The year 1919 was one of the wettest years on record.
5. Gould, *Progressives and Prohibitionists*, 227–232; Clark, *Tactful Texan*, 79–80.
6. *Journal of the House of Representatives of the Fourth Called Session of the Thirty-Fifth Legislature* (Austin: Von Boeckmann-Jones, 1918), 2–3, 5–8, 53–55.
7. Ibid., 42, 90–91; *Journal of the Senate Fourth Called Session of the Thirty-Fifth Legislature* (Austin: A. C. Baldwin & Sons, 1918), 60–61, 133; Steen, *Twentieth Century Texas*, 229–230; *San Antonio Express*, March 5, 1918; *Houston Post*, March 2, 5, 7, 1918.
8. *Journal of the House of the Fourth Called Session of the Thirty-Fifth Legislature*, 142–143; *Journal of the Senate Fourth Called Session of the Thirty-Fifth Legislature*, 262–263; Gould, *Progressives and Prohibitionists*, 233; Clark, *Tactful Texan*, 81–82.
9. Clark, *Tactful Texan*, 82; Steen, *Twentieth Century Texas*, 230. For local efforts to eliminate alcohol near training camps, see James B. Seymour Jr., "Evils More Deadly than the Carnage of the Battlefield: The Fight for Prohibition in McLennan County in 1917," *East Texas Historical Journal* 40 (Spring 2002): 58–69; Christian, "Newton Baker's War on El Paso Vice," 55–67.

10. Gould, *Progressives and Prohibitionists*, 233–235; *Houston Post*, March 13, 1918.
11. A. Elizabeth Taylor, "The Woman Suffrage Movement in Texas," *Journal of Southern History* 17 (May 1951): 207; Taylor, "Woman Suffrage," *New Handbook of Texas*, 6: 1039–1041; Judith N. McArthur, *Creating the New Woman: The Rise of the Southern Women's Progressive Culture in Texas,1893–1918* (Urbana, Il.: University of Illinois Press, 1998), 136–137.
12. Quote, Judith N. McArthur, *Creating the New Woman*, 137. See also Judith N. McArthur and Harold L. Smith, *Minnie Fisher Cunningham: A Suffragist's Life in Politics* (New York: Oxford University Press, 2003) 61–62; John Carroll Eudy, "The Vote and Lone Star Women: Minnie Fisher Cunningham and the Texas Equal Suffrage Association," *East Texas Historical Journal* 14 (Fall 1976): 52–59.
13. *Journal of the House, Fourth Called Session*, 325; *Journal of the Senate, Fourth Called Session*, 355; Taylor, "Woman Suffrage," *New Handbook of Texas*, 6: 1040; Debbie Mauldin Cottrell, "Texas Association Opposed to Woman Suffrage," *New Handbook of Texas*, 6: 291–292. McArthur and Smith, *Minnie Fisher Cunningham*, 61, point out that Metcalf, a West Texas rancher, told Cunningham to stay out of the limelight during the legislative process.
14. Clark, *Tactful Texan*, 84; *Houston Post*, March 24, 1918.
15. McKay, *Texas Politics, 1906–1944*, 77; Clark, *Tactful Texan*, 85.
16. Ferguson quotes, *Dallas Morning News*, July 19, 25, 1918, printed in McKay, *Texas Politics, 1906–1944*, 79–80. See also Clark, *Tactful Texan*, 85; Gould, *Progressives and Prohibitionists*, 236; S. S. McKay and Odie B. Faulk, *Texas After Spindletop* (Austin: Steck-Vaughn Co., 1965), 66–67; *Ferguson Forum*, April 11, 1918.
17. McKay, *Texas Politics, 1906–1944*, 77–78; McArthur and Smith, *Minnie Fisher Cunningham*, 64.
18. Clark, *Tactful Texan*, 87–88; McKay and Faulk, *Texas After Spindletop*, 68–69.
19. First quote, Gould, *Progressives and Prohibitionists*, 240; second quote, Clark, *Tactful Texan*, 87; third quote, Clark, *Tactful Texan*, 89.
20. McKay, *Texas Politics, 1906–1944*, 76–79; Gould, *Progressives and Prohibitionists*, 241–242; *Dallas Morning News*, June 23, July 4, 1918; *Houston Post*, August 11, 1918.
21. Gould, *Progressives and Prohibitionists*, 245; Clark, *Tactful Texan*, 94–95. Ferguson acknowledged that women voted 10–1 in favor of Hobby.
22. Gould, *Progressives and Prohibitionists*, 245–246; V. O. Key Jr., *Southern Politics in State and Nation* (New York: Alfred A. Knopf, 1949), 265–266. McKay, *Texas Politics, 1906–1944*, 82–83, notes that while Hobby received almost 70 percent of the total state vote, the German counties gave him only a little more than 40 percent of their vote. McKay points out that 250,000 more Texans voted in the 1918 primary than in 1916, largely because of the women's vote.
23. Debbie Mauldin Cottrell, "Annie Webb Blanton," *New Handbook of Texas*, 1: 587–588; A. Elizabeth Taylor, "The Woman Suffrage Movement in Texas," in Ruthe Winegarten and Judith N. McArthur, eds., *Citizens At Last: The Woman Suffrage Movement in Texas* (Austin: Ellen C. Temple, 1987), 38.
24. McDaniel, "The First Congressman Martin Dies of Texas," 157. McDaniel notes that aspects of Dies' last years, his final illness, and death remain obscure. He suggests that Dies may not have "defeated his alcohol problem and was still erratic and unstable." *Ibid.*, 158.
25. Quote, James Slayden, in Webb, ed., *Washington Wife*, 334.

26. *New Handbook of Texas*, 1: 734; 3: 98; 4: 428–29; Gould, *Progressives and Prohibitionists*, 242–243; Gaughan, "Woodrow Wilson and the Rise of Militant Interventionism in the South," 799–800.
27. Leonard P. Ayres, *The War With Germany: A Statistical Summary* (Washington: Government Printing Office, 1919), 33; Laurence Stallings, *The Doughboys: The Story of the AEF, 1917–1918* (New York: Harper & Row, 1963), 375.
28. Dorman H. Winfrey, "The 90th Infantry Division," in *Soldiers of Texas* (Waco: Texian Press, 1973), 121–125; White, *The 90th Division in World War I*, 75–76; White, *Panthers to Arrowheads*, 89–98.
29. Gilbert, *American Financing of World War I*, 119–139; Zieger, *America's Great War*, 75–76.
30. Gilbert, *American Financing of World War I*, 163–165.
31. Ibid., 75–76.
32. Ibid., 26–27, 77, 96–99.
33. Kennedy, *Over Here*, 118–119; Mullendore, *History of the United States Food Administration, 1917–1919*, 221, 263.
34. Hendricks, "Federal Food Administration in Texas," 54–56; Brandimarte, "Using Government Documents: The Food Administration in Texas," 274–276.
35. Hendricks, "Federal Food Administration in Texas," 65; Steen, *Twentieth Century Texas*, 296–297.
36. Hendricks, "Federal Food Administration in Texas," 165–166; Steen, *Twentieth Century Texas*, 297; McArthur, *Creating the New Woman*, 121–122.
37. Hendricks, "Federal Food Administration in Texas," 152–162.
38. Ibid., 132–145; Steen, *Twentieth Century Texas*, 297–298.
39. William R. Hunt, "Thomas Aloysius Hickey," *New Handbook of Texas*, 3: 585; James R. Green, *Grass-Roots Socialism: Radical Movements in the Southwest, 1895–1943* (Baton Rouge: Louisiana State University Press, 1978), 45–46, 96; Green, "Tenant Farmer Discontent and Socialist Protest in Texas, 1901–1917," *Southwestern Historical Quarterly* 81 (October 1977): 137–139; Steven Boyd and Daniel Smith, "Thomas Hickey, the Rebel, and Civil Liberties in Wartime Texas," *East Texas Historical Journal* 45 (No. 1, 2007), 45–47.
40. Green, *Grass-Roots Socialism*, 355–356; Boyd and Smith, "Thomas Hickey," 45–47. For more on the Farmers' and Laborers' Protective Association, see Jennette Keith, *Rich Man's War, Poor Man's Fight*, 90–98; Robert Wilson, "The Farmers' and Laborers' Protective Association of America, 1915–1916" (M.A. thesis, Baylor University, 1978).
41. Quote, Tom Hickey, in Green, *Grass-Roots Socialism*, 356. Neal Foley, *The White Scourge: Mexicans, Blacks, and Poor Whites in Texas Cotton Culture* (Berkeley, CA: University of California Press, 1997), 115, says that Burleson despised Hickey for making him front-page news when he replaced the tenant farmers on his plantation in Bosque County with convict labor.
42. H. C. Peterson and Gilbert C. Fite, *Opponents of War, 1917–1918* (Madison, WS: University of Wisconsin Press, 1957), 38–39; Keith, *Rich Man's War, Poor Man's Fight*, 96.
43. Peterson and Fite, *Opponents of War, 1917–1918*, 90.
44. Ibid., 187.
45. First quote, Peterson and Fite, *Opponents of War, 1917–1918*, 141; second quote, McKay and Faulk, *Texas After Spindletop*, 73.

46. W. T. Burns, in *Congressional Record*, 65th Congress, First Session, October 6, 1917, p. 7878, quoted in Peterson and Fite, *Opponents of War, 1917–1918*, 152.
47. "Texas State Council of Defense," *New Handbook of Texas*, 6: 422; Kennedy, *Over Here*, 61–62.
48. William E. Nicholas, "World War I and Academic Dissent in Texas," *Arizona and the West* 14 (Autumn 1972): 218–219; William C. Pool, *Eugene C. Barker: Historian* (Austin: Texas State Historical Association, 1971), 88.
49. Walter F. Pilcher, "Lindley Miller Keasbey," *New Handbook of Texas*, 3: 1043. Joe B. Frantz, a longtime professor of history at the University of Texas, later wrote that he had heard at least a dozen University of Texas professors say that Keasbey "was the most profound influence in their lives." Frantz, *The Forty-Acre Follies* (Austin: Texas Monthly Press, 1983), 35. For Webb's views, see "History as High Adventure" in *An Honest Preface and Other Essays*, ed. Joe B. Frantz (Boston: Houghton Mifflin Co., 1959), 198.
50. Quote, William Nicholas, "World War I and Academic Dissent in Texas," 222. Keasbey never returned to teaching. He moved to Arizona for health reasons, began raising dogs, and converted to Catholicism. He later wrote a philosophical study entitled *Three Worlds in One*. He died in Whittier, California, in September 1946. For Keasbey's influence on Webb, see Mazie E. Mathews, "On the Hither Edge of Free Land: Lindley Miller Keasbey and Evolution of the Frontier Thesis" (M.A. thesis, Southwest Texas State University, 1973).
51. Nicholas, "World War I and Academic Dissent in Texas," 222–223. The same year (1919), Hobby vetoed the appropriation for the German Department, but the Legislature overrode the veto.
52. Ibid., 225–229.
53. Oliver Knight, *Fort Worth: Outpost on the Trinity* (Norman, OK: University of Oklahoma Press, 1953), 192–193.
54. Ibid., 193.
55. Ibid., 193–194.
56. Frederick C. Luebke, *Bonds of Loyalty: German-Americans and World War I* (DeKalb, IL: Northern Illinois University Press, 1974), 280.
57. Lola Bracht Woellert, quoted in Allen and Taylor, *Aransas: The Life of a Texas Coastal County*, 229.
58. Glen E. Lich, *The German Texans* (San Antonio: Institute of Texan Cultures, 1981), 110,138; McKay and Faulk, *Texas After Spindletop*, 74; Bera Flach, *A Yankee in German-America Texas Hill Country* (San Antonio: Naylor Co., 1973), 72; Christopher Long, "King William Historic District," *New Handbook of Texas*, 3: 1116; Carl Wittke, *German-Americans and the World War* (Columbus,OH: Ohio State Archaeological and Historical Society, 1936), 179–180; Clara Trenckmann Studer, "William Andreas Trenckmann," *New Handbook of Texas*, 6: 560–561; Joan Druesedow Grigg, "Old Glory Texas," *ibid.*, 4: 1134. Joseph Wilson, "Texas German and Other Immigrant Languages: Problems and Prospects," *Eagle in the New World: German Immigration to Texas and America* (College Station: Texas A&M University Press, 1986), 231–240. Benjamin Paul Hegi, " 'Old Time Good Germans': German-Americans in Cooke County, Texas, during World War I," *Southwestern Historical Quarterly* 109 (October 2005): 235–257, points out that although some tension existed between residents of the county's two German settlements, Muenster and Lindsay, and the rest of the county, no violence or rash actions occurred.

59. McArthur, *Creating the New Woman*, 120.
60. *Ibid.*, 120–121.
61. Maurine Weiner Greenwald, *Women, War, and Work: The Impact of World War I on Women Workers in the United States* (Westport, CN: Greenwood Press, 1980), 5, 13, 15, 21, 93. See also Carrie Brown, *Rosie's Mom: Forgotten Women Workers of the First World War* (Boston: Northeastern University Press, 2002).
62. Christine A. Keffeler, "Katherine Stinson," *New Handbook of Texas*, 6: 105. See also Mary Beth Rogers, et al., *We Can Fly: Stories of Katherine Stinson and Other Gutsy Texas Women* (Austin: Texas Foundation for Woman's Resources, 1983).
63. Lettie Gavin, *American Women in World War I: They Also Served* (Niwot, CO: University Press of Colorado, 1997), x, 77–94, 101–119. See also Susan Zeiger, *In Uncle Sam's Service: Women Workers With the American Expeditionary Force, 1917–1918* (Ithaca, NY: Cornell University Press, 1999) and Dorothy Schneider and Carl J. Schneider, *Into the Breach: American Women Overseas in World War I* (New York: Viking Press, 1991).
64. *Ibid.*, 2–15. Also Eunice Dessez, *The First Enlisted Women, 1917–1918* (Philadelphia: Dorrance & Co., 1955); and Jean Ebbert and Marie-Beth Hall, *The First, The Few, The Forgotten: Navy and Marine Corps Women in World War I* (Annapolis: Naval Institute Press, 2002).
65. Gavin, *American Women in World War I*, 25–36. Theresa Lake is identified in this work as a "Texas statistician" whose sweetheart was killed overseas. I have found no additional information on her. Another female Marine, Lela Leibrand (later McMath), settled in Texas. Her daughter later became movie star Ginger Rogers. *Ibid.*, 36.
66. These are identified as Kate Dodson (Casa Blanca), Alma Furr (Austin), Elina W. Hill (San Antonio), Mamie Jones (Pontotoc), Ebba C. Lindel (Georgetown), Jessie McDowell (Port Arthur), and Anna K. Shirley (San Antonio) in Gavin, *American Women in World War I*, 253–256.
67. Debbie Mauldin Cottrell, "May Agness Hopkins," *New Handbook of Texas*, 3: 692–693; Elizabeth York Enstam, *Women and the Creation of Urban Life: Dallas, Texas, 1843–1920* (College Station: Texas A&M University Press, 1998), 164. For more on the struggle by female physicians to serve in the war, see Ellen S. More, " 'A Certain Restless Ambition': Women Physicians and World War I," *American Quarterly* 41 (December 1989): 636–660.
68. Wilda M. Smith and Eleanor A. Bogart, "Henrietta Eleanor Goodnought Duell," *New Handbook of Texas*, 2: 608–609. For her complete story, see Smith and Bogart, *The Wars of Peggy Hull: The Life and Times of a War Correspondent* (El Paso: Texas Western Press, 1991) .
69. Steven A. Reich, "Soldiers of Democracy: Black Texans and the Fight for Citizenship, 1917–1921," *Journal of American History* 82 (March 1996): 1478–1504, is an excellent account of these hopes and frustrations.
70. Margaret B. Baker, "The Texas Negro and the World War" (M.A. thesis, University of Texas, 1938), 44–45, 53–54; Barr, *Black Texans*, 114.
71. Hendricks, "Federal Food Administration for Texas," 87–93; Baker, "Texas Negro and the World War," 48–51; Forest G. Hill, "The Negro in the Texas Labor Supply" (M.A. thesis, University of Texas, 1946), 105; Barr, *Black Texans*, 114; Diana J. Kleiner, "William Leonard Davis," *New Handbook of Texas*, 2: 535; McArthur, *Creating the New Woman*, 123.

72. Bruce Alden Glasrud, "Black Texans, 1900–1930: A History" (Ph.D. dissertation, Texas Technological College, 1969), 314; Emmett J. Scott, *Negro Migration During the War* (org. pub. 1920; New York: Arno Press, 1969), 13–25, 31, 86–94; Robert T. Higgs, "The Boll Weevil, The Cotton Economy, and Black Migration, 1910–1930," *Agricultural History* 50 (April 1976): 335–350; Neil Fligstein, *Going North: Migration of Blacks and Whites from the South, 1900–1950* (New York: Academic Press, 1981), 13, 15, 76; Jack Temple Kirby, "The Southern Exodus, 1910–1960: A Primer for Historians," *Journal of Southern History* 49 (November 1983): 585–600.
73. Quoted in Carter Woodson, ed., "Letters of Negro Migrants of 1916–1918," *Journal of Negro History* 4 (July 1919): 298. The Texas State Council of Defense hired thirty African-American lecturers to discourage Texas blacks from leaving, but this apparently had little effect. Foley, *The White Scourge*, 52.
74. Baker, "The Texas Negro in the World War," 43–44; Emmett J. Scott, *Scott's Official History of the American Negro in the World War* (New York: Arno Press and New York Times, 1969), 32, 67–69; W. Allison Sweeney, *History of the American Negro in the Great War* (New York: Negro Universities Press, 1969), 106–109. There were 5,328 African-Americans in the Navy in June 1918; the number increased to slightly more than 6,000 by November 1918. Many black Texans served in the Army's 365th Regiment of the 92nd Division.
75. Scott, *Scott's Official History*, 471–481; Baker, "The Texas Negro and the World War," 23.
76. Sweeney, *History of the American Negro in the Great War*, 78; Barbara L. Green, "Emmett Jay Scott," *New Handbook of Texas*, 5: 935; David A. Williams, "Emmett Scott, Advocate for World War I African American Servicemen," paper delivered at Texas State Historical Association annual meeting, Austin, Texas, March 6, 2004.
77. Baker, "The Texas Negro and the World War," 28–29; Scott, *Scott's Official History*, 178, 181; Sweeney, *History of the American Negro in the Great War*, 159.
78. First quote, E. B. Hogan, *The Last Buffalo: Walter Potts and the 92nd "Buffalo" Division in World War I* (Austin: Eakin Press, 2000), 30; second quote, Steven A. Reich, "Soldiers of Democracy," 484. For more on the treatment of blacks in France, see Coffman, *War to End All Wars*, 231–233.
79. Glasrud, "Black Texans," 70–71.
80. James M. SoRelle, "The 'Waco Horror': The Lynching of Jesse Washington," *Southwestern Historical Quarterly* 86 (April 1983): 517–536; Glasrud, "Black Texans," 160–161; NAACP, *Thirty Years of Lynching in the United States, 1869–1918* (New York: Arno Press, 1969), 35; Fray Shay, *Judge Lynch: His First Hundred Years* (Montclair, NJ: Patterson Smith, 1969), 117. For more on the Washington lynching, see Patricia Bernstein, *The First Waco Horror: The Lynching of Jesse Washington and the Rise of the NAACP* (College Station: Texas A&M University Press, 2005).
81. David Montejano, *Anglos and Mexicans in the Making of Texas, 1836–1986* (Austin: University of Texas Press, 1987), 117; NAACP, *Thirty Years of Lynching*, 98–99; Buenger, *Path to a Modern South*, 171–172.
82. Quote, Carole Christian, "Joining the American Mainstream: Texas' Mexican Americans During World War I," *Southwestern Historical Quarterly* 92 (April 1989): 559.
83. Otey M. Scruggs, "The First Mexican Farm Labor Program," *Arizona and the West* 2 (Winter 1960): 319–326; Lawrence A. Cardoso, "Labor Emigration to the

Southwest, 1916–1920: Mexican Attitudes and Policy," *Southwestern Historical Quarterly* 79 (April 1976): 400–406; Emilio Zamora, *The World of the Mexican Worker in Texas* (College Station: Texas A&M University Press, 1993), 38–39; Mario T. Garcia, *Desert Immigrants: The Mexicans of El Paso, 1880–1920* (New Haven, CN: Yale University Press, 1981), 44–46.

84. Christian, "Joining the American Mainstream," 572–577, 592–594.
85. Christian, *ibid.*, 587, quotes a Defense Department publication, *Hispanics in America's Defense*, 36, that states the exact number of Texas Hispanics who served in the military cannot be ascertained at present.
86. Adjutant General of the Army, comp., *Congressional Medal of Honor, the Distinguished Service Cross, and the Distinguished Service Medal Issued by the War Department Since April 6, 1917* (Washington: Government Printing Office, 1920), 30, 701, 708, 715; Christian, "Joining America's Mainstream," 578, 583.
87. Quote, Carole Christian, "Joining the American Mainstream," 595.
88. Joseph A. McCartin, *Labor's Great War: The Struggle for Industrial Democracy and the Origins of Modern American Labor Relations, 1912–1921* (Chapel Hill: University of North Carolina Press, 1997), 40–42.
89. Patricia E. Hill, *Dallas: The Making of a Modern City* (Austin: University of Texas Press, 1996), 76; J. Eddie Johnson, "The Economic Development of Orange County, Texas, 1900–1920," *Texas Gulf Historical and Biographical Record* 13 (November 1977): 26–27. Ruth Allen, a noted Texas labor historian, observed "while there were many strikes in Texas during the war, detailed information about them is lacking." Allen, *East Texas Lumber Workers: An Economic and Social Picture, 1870–1950* (Austin: University of Texas Press, 1961), 183.
90. James C. Maroney, "The Texas-Louisiana Oil Field Strike of 1917," in Gary M. Fink and Merl E. Reed, eds., *Essays in Southern Labor History* (Westport, CT: Greenwood Press, 1976), 161–163. See also William Lee Greer, "The Texas Gulf Coast Oil Strike of 1917" (M.A. thesis, University of Houston, 1974).
91. Maroney, "Texas-Louisiana Oil Field Strike of 1917," 163–165.
92. *Ibid.*, 164–165.
93. *Ibid.*, 167.
94. *Ibid.*, 167–168.
95. Frederick Eby, *The Development of Education in Texas* (New York: Macmillan Co., 1925), 227.
96. Eby, *Development of Education in Texas*, 233; C. E. Evans, *The Story of Texas Schools* (Austin: Steck Co., 1955), 120–122; *Journal of the Senate, Third Called Session, Thirty-Fifth Legislature*, 993, 1130.
97. *Journal of the Senate, Third Called Session, Thirty-Fifth Legislature*, 998; *Journal of the House, Third Called Session, Thirty-Fifth Legislature*, 223, 264, 281–281; Evans, *Story of Texas Schools*, 124–125; V. R. Cordozier, "Higher Education," *New Handbook of Texas*, 3: 597.
98. Chambers, *To Raise An Army*, 233; *Order of Battle*, III, Pt. 2: 933; John Q. Adams Jr., *We Are the Aggies: The Texas A&M University Association of Former Students* (College Station: Texas A&M University Press, 1979), 101.
99. Adams, *We Are the Aggies*, 103, 105; Henry C. Dethloff, *A Centennial History of Texas A&M University*, 2 vols. (College Station: Texas A&M University Press, 1975), 1: 282–283.

100. John A. L. Scarborough, "The University of Texas and the Great War" (M.A. thesis, University of Texas, 1927), 114, 428.
101. Fredericka Meiners, *A History of Rice University: The Institute Years, 1907–1963* (Houston: Rice University Studies, 1982), 70–71; Johnston, *Houston: The Unknown City*, 196–197.
102. Bill O'Neal, *The Texas League, 1888–1987: A Century of Baseball* (Austin: Eakin Press, 1987), 46–50. The government gave major leagues until Labor Day to finish the season, with an additional two weeks for the World Series. In the series, played in September rather than October, the Boston Red Sox, behind the pitching and hitting of George Herman "Babe" Ruth, defeated the Chicago Cubs, four games to two. Richard M. Cohen, David S. Neff, and Roland Johnson, *The World Series* (New York: Dial Press, 1976), 71–75.
103. Kern Tips, *Football–Texas Style: An Illustrated History of the Southwest Conference* (Garden City, NY: Doubleday & Co., 1964), 21; Deane H. Freeman, *Hook 'Em Horns: A Story of Texas Football* (Huntsville, AL: Strode Publishers, 1974), 211; Harold Classen, comp., *Ronald's Encyclopedia of Football* (third ed., New York: Ronald Press, 1963), 254, 262.
104. Harold V. Ratliff, *Autumn's Mightiest Legions: History of Texas Schoolboy Football* (Waco: Texian Press, 1963), 2–3, 8–10, 16–18; Ty Cashion, *Pigskin Pulpit: A Social History of Texas High School Coaches* (Austin: Texas State Historical Association, 1998), 52–54.
105. Steen, *Twentieth Century Texas*, 261–262, 270.
106. Lota M. Spell, *Music in Texas* (reprint; New York: AMS, 1973), 89, 99.
107. Quote, Richard Schroeder, *Lone Star Picture Shows* (College Station: Texas A&M University Press, 2001), 47.
108. Larry Wayne Ward, *The Motion Picture Goes to War: The U.S. Film Effort During World War I* (Ann Arbor, MI: UMI Research Press, 1985), 52–54; Daniel Blum, *A Pictorial History of the Silent Screen* (New York: G. P. Putnam's, 1953), 153.
109. Edwin S. Gaustad, *A Religious History of America* (New York: Harper & Row, 1966), 325; Winthrop S. Hudson, *Religion in America: An Historical Account of the Development of American Religious Life* (second ed., New York: Charles Scribner's Sons, 1973), 324; Robert T. Handy, *A History of the Churches of the United States and Canada* (New York: Oxford University Press, 1977), 307–308, 329; Ray H. Abrams, *Preachers Present Arms: The Role of American Churches and Clergy in World War I and II* (rev. ed., Scottsdale, PA: Herald Press, 1969), 86–87, 171–176.
110. Keith, *Rich Man's War, Poor Man's Fight*, 77–79. There were 71,592 members and 1,240 congregations of the Churches of Christ in Texas in 1916. Bureau of Census, *Religious Bodies, 1916*, 224–225.
111. Lee Canipe, "Preaching the Gospel in a World Made Safe for Democracy: George W. Truett, Religious Liberty, and the American Expeditionary Force." Paper presented at Texas State Historical Association annual meeting, Austin, Texas, March 4, 2004.
112. Canipe, "Preaching the Gospel in a World Made Safe for Democracy;" Joan Jenkins Perez, "George Washington Truett," *New Handbook of Texas*, 6: 578; Powhatan W. James, *George W Truett: A Biography* (Nashville, TN: Broadman Press, 1939), 131–149.
113. Quote, Walter Buenger, *Path To A Modern South*, 129.

CHAPTER FIVE

1. Each of these individuals will be discussed in the narrative that follows. Lonnie J. White, *Panthers to Arrowheads: The 36th (Texas-Oklahoma) Division in World War I*, and White, *The 90th Division in World War I: The Texas-Oklahoma Draft Division in the Great War*, are the principal accounts of these two Texas-Oklahoma divisions in the First World War.
2. Coffman, *The War To End All Wars*, 43. The official letter of appointment and instructions to Pershing was signed by Secretary of War Newton D. Baker on May 26, 1917. John J. Pershing, *My Experiences in the World War*, 2 vols. (New York: Frederick A. Stokes Co., 1931), I: 38–39.
3. For more detail concerning Pershing's appointment, see Frank E. Vandiver, *Black Jack: The Life and Times of John J. Pershing*, 2 vols. (College Station: Texas A&M University Press, 1977), I: 671–695, and John S. D. Eisenhower, *Yanks: The Epic Story of the American Army in World War I* (New York: Simon & Schuster, 2000), 26–34.
4. *Order of Battle*, I: 82–85; Gary Mead, *The Doughboys: America and the First World War* (New York: The Overlook Press, 2000), 11; Eisenhower, *Yanks*, 41–42.
5. Stallings, *The Doughboys*, 375–377; *Order of Battle*, II: 275; Ayers, *War with Germany: Statistical Summary*, 33.
6. Robert Wooster, "Military History," *New Handbook of Texas*, 4: 729; Warren R. Jackson, *His Time in Hell: A Texas Marine in France* (Novato, CA: Presidio Press, 2000), xvi. Later, in August 1918, several hundred troops, largely Texans and Oklahomans from the 36th and 90th Divisions, were transferred to the 42nd Division. White, *Panthers to Arrowheads*, 109.
7. Beaumont Bonaparte Buck, *Memoirs of Peace and War* (San Antonio: Naylor Co., 1935), 148–155; George W. Cullum, *Biographical Register of the Officers and Graduates of the U. S. Military Academy . . .*, 3 vols. (Boston: Houghton, Mifflin, and Co., 1891), III: 390; Anne Cipriano Venzon, ed., *The United States in the First World War: An Encyclopedia* (New York: Garland Publishing Co., 1995), 108. Buck's division commander, Robert L. Bullard, was a classmate at West Point. Bullard's biographer, Allen R. Millett, describes Buck as "a short, dogmatic, inflexible, and not very bright officer." *The General: Robert L. Bullard and Officership in the United States Army, 1881–1925* (Westport, CT: Greenwood Press, 1975), 310.
8. Herbert M. Mason Jr., *The Lafayette Escadrille* (New York: Random House, 1964), 73–75; Robert Sidney Bowen, *They Flew to Glory: The Story of the Lafayette Flying Corps* (New York: Lothrop, Lee & Shepard, Inc., 1965), 62–63.
9. Bowen, *They Flew to Glory*, 63–65. For more detailed accounts of Balsley's injury, see Arch Whitehouse, *Legion of the Lafayette* (Garden City, NY: Doubleday & Co., 1962), 77–87; Edwin C. Parsons, *I Flew With the Lafayette Escadrille* (New York: Arno Press, 1972), 115–127.
10. Mason, *Lafayette Escadrille*, 83n.
11. Bowen, *They Flew to Glory*, 65.
12. Mason, *Lafayette Escadrille*, 10, 18, 45, 161–162, 295.
13. John H. Morrow Jr., *The Great War in the Air: Military Aviation from 1909 to 1921* (Washington: Smithsonian Institution Press, 1993), 203, 336; Bert Frandsen, *Hat in the Ring: The Birth of American Air Power in the Great War* (Washington: Smithsonian Books, 2003), 16.

14. James J. Hudson, *Hostile Skies: A Combat History of the American Air Service in World War I* (Syracuse, NY: Syracuse University Press, 1968), 308–310. Frandsen, *Hat in the Ring*, 265, lists the number of victories for the 94th Squadron as sixty-seven.
15. Frandsen, *Hat in the Ring*, 74, 217; Hudson, *Hostile Skies*, 124. Tobin survived the war, returned to San Antonio, and started the Tobin Aerial Surveys firm. He established a world reputation in mapping operations for oil companies. During World War II, he served as special civilian adviser to General Henry H. Arnold, chief of the U.S. Air Forces. Tobin died on January 10, 1954, in a plane crash near Shreveport that took the lives of eleven other prominent businessmen, including Thomas Elmer Braniff. *New Handbook of Texas*, 6: 511.
16. Hudson, *Hostile Skies*, 196, 212, 223–224.
17. *Ibid.*, 38, 308; Adjutant General of the Army, *Congressional Medal of Honor, the Distinguished Service Cross*, 702. Geoffrey Perret, *A Country Made By War* (New York: Random House, 1989), 338, points out that Pershing was reluctant to award medals, particularly to general and staff officers. Before 1918, the only Army awards were the Medal of Honor (commonly referred to as the "Congressional Medal of Honor") and the Certificate of Merit. Congress created the Distinguished Service Cross for acts of heroism not meriting the Medal of Honor, and the Distinguished Service Medal, mainly for staff officers. In 1920, the Silver Star was created for the 5,000 men recommended for the Distinguished Service Cross who had not received it.
18. Jane Leslie Newberry, "The World War I Diary of William S. Leslie, Private, 169th Aero Squadron, American Expeditionary Force," *East Texas Historical Journal* 32 (Spring 1964): 55–64.
19. *The Second Report of the Provost Marshal General*, 468, lists 16,889 Texans in the Navy. Another 2,073 Texans were in the Marines. For more on Richardson and Nimitz, see Christopher Long, "James Otto Richardson," *New Handbook of Texas*, 5: 568; Robert Weddle, "Chester William Nimitz," *ibid.*, 4: 1015–1017; *On the Treadmill to Pearl Harbor: The Memoirs of Admiral James O. Richardson, USN (Retired) as told to Vice Admiral George C. Dyer* (Washington: United States Naval Department, 1973); Skipper Steeley, *Pearl Harbor Countdown: Admiral James O. Richardson* (Gretna: Pelican Publishing Company. 2008), 57–61; and E. B. Potter, *Nimitz* (Annapolis: Naval Institute Press, 1976), 129–131.
20. Thomas G. Frothingham, *The Naval History of the World War: The United States in the War* (Freeport, NY: Books for Libraries Press, 1971), 173, 285; *Dictionary of American Naval Fighting Ships*, 8 vols. (Washington: Navy Department, Office of the Chief of Naval Operations, 1959–1981), VIII: 115. For the battleship *Texas*, see John C. Ferguson, *Historic Battleship Texas* (Abilene, TX: McWhiney Foundation Press, 2004).
21. Marc Wortham, *The Millionaires Unit: The Aristocratic Flyboys Who Fought the Great War and Invented American Air Power* (New York: Public Affairs, 2006), esp. 8–9, 117, 200–213; Walter Isaacson and Evan Thomas, *The Wise Men: Six Friends and the World They Made* (New York: Simon and Schuster, 1988), 60–63, 90–93.
22. Bureau of Navigation, *Officers and Enlisted Men of the United States Navy Who Lost Their Lives During the World War, From April 6, 1917 to November 11, 1918* (Washington: Government Printing Office, 1920) names 216 Texas naval enlisted men and five officers who died during the war.

23. Quote, *Dictionary of American Naval Fighting Ships*, II: 226. Names of Texans lost on the *Cyclops* are given in *Officers and Enlisted Men of the United States Navy Who Lost Their Lives*.
24. *Dictionary of American Naval Fighting Ships*, III: 181–182; Frothingham, *Naval History of the World War*, 265.
25. *Order of Battle*, II: 179, 195; Ayres, *War with Germany: A Statistical Summary*, 26.
26. White, *The 90th Division in World War I*, 13–14, 75; Dorman Winfrey, "The 90th Infantry Division," 119–120. White, 162, points out that the designation "Tough 'Ombres," was not commonly used during the First World War. For more on Henry T. Allen, see Heath Twitchell Jr., *Allen: The Biography of an Army Officer, 1859–1930* (New Brunswick, NJ: Rutgers University Press, 1974).
27. White, *The 90th Division in World War I*, 75–83; Winfrey, "The 90th Infantry Division," 123–124; George Wythe, *A History of the 90th Division* (New York: 90th Division Association, 1920), 13–18. Pershing was highly critical of British and French military doctrine, which he believed was too passive and wedded to trench warfare. See Pershing, *My Experiences in the World War*, I: 151–153.
28. Greble remained in command of Camp Bowie until his retirement for physical disability the following September. He returned home to Philadelphia, later lived in Washington, D.C., and died in New Jersey in September 1931. White, *Panthers to Arrowheads*, 69–70, 89–95; White, "Major General Edwin St. John Greble," *Military History of Texas and the Southwest* 14 (No. l, 1978): 7–20; White, "Chief of the Arrowheads: Major General William R. Smith and the 36th Division in France," *ibid.*, 16 (No. 3, n. d.): 149–176.
29. Brager, *The Texas 36th Division*, 44–46.
30. White, *Panthers to Arrowheads*, 91–109; Brager, *The Texas 36th Division*, 45–48.
31. Stallings, *The Doughboys*, 25–36; *United States Army in the World War, 1917–1919*, 17 vols. (Org. pub. 1948; reprint, Washington: Center of Military History, United States Army, 1989), IV: 1–65.
32. Martin Donell Kohout, "Louis John Jordan," *New Handbook of Texas*, 3: 1002, states that Jordan was the first Texas officer killed in World War I. Jordan's body was reinterred in Fredericksburg in 1921. The American Legion post in Fredericksburg was named in his honor. In 1957, his name was inscribed in the University of Texas Longhorn Hall of Honor.
33. Buck, *Memoirs of Peace and War*, 171–182; Eisenhower, *Yanks*, 121–134.
34. Art Leatherwood, "Daniel R. Edwards," *New Handbook of Texas*, 2: 797.
35. General Orders No. 14, War Department, 1923, in *Texas Medal of Honor Recipients*, compiled by the Texas Veterans Commission Headquarters (Austin, 1993), 18; Debe Weldon Casad, *Texans of Valor: Military Heroes in the 20th Century* (Austin: Eakin Press, 1998), 16–17. Edwards became a celebrity after the war. His life was chronicled by Lowell Thomas, *This Side of Hell: Dan Edwards, Adventurer* (New York: P. F. Collier & Son, 1932). Art Leatherwood, writing in the *New Handbook of Texas*, 2: 797, cautions that Edwards' "exploits as he reported them approached the unbelievable, however, and doubts have been raised about some of them."
36. George B. Clark, *Devil Dogs: Fighting Marines of World War I* (Novato, CA: Presidio Press, 2000), 62–86.
37. First quote, C. A. Brannen, *Over There: A Marine in the Great War*, annotated by Rolfe L. Hillman Jr. and Peter F. Owen (College Station: Texas A&M University

Press, 1995), 19; second quote, Brannen, 21. Clark, *Devil Dogs*, 101, notes that June 6 "would be the most catastrophic day in Marine Corps history." More Marines were killed or wounded on that day than in all the previous history of the Corps.

38. Quote, Warren R. Jackson, *His Time in Hell*, 104.
39. Quote, Jackson, *His Time in Hell*, 105.
40. *Congressional Medal of Honor, Distinguished Service Cross*, 707; Clark, *Devil Dogs*, 122.
41. John W. Thomason Jr., *Fix Bayonets!* (New York: Charles Scribner's Sons, 1928), 1–66; Martha Anne Turner, *The World of Colonel John W. Thomason, USMC* (Austin: Eakin Press, 1984), 79–81; Casad, *Texans of Valor*, 2–8.
42. Mead, *The Doughboys*, 247–255; Eisenhower, *Yanks*, 149–162.
43. The most complete account of the battle is Douglas V. Johnson II and Rolfe L. Hillman, Jr., *Soissons, 1918* (College Station: Texas A&M University Press, 1999).
44. Thomason, *Fix Bayonets!*, 98.
45. Brannen, *Over There*, 31.
46. Jackson, *His Time in Hell*, 145.
47. Johnson and Hillman, *Soissons, 1918*, 144. These authors point out that casualty statistics for the campaign are a source of controversy. *Ibid.*, 189 fn.
48. *Congressional Medal of Honor, Distinguished Service Cross*, 703, 713, 718, 720; Johnson and Hillman, *Soissons, 1918*, 68, 100–101; Thomas, *This Side of Hell*, 275–291.
49. Johnson and Hillman, *Soissons, 1918*, 117, are quite critical of Buck, whom they say "rode off into the blue." For Buck's account, see his *Memoirs of Peace and War*, 187–209.
50. Quote, Johnson and Hillman, *Soissons, 1918*, 133. Johnson and Hillman, 139, believe that Buck's absence in the early fighting "counts for more than his tardy, final presence."
51. Buck, *Memoirs of Peace and War*, 216. Robert H. Ferrell, *America's Deadliest Battle: Meuse-Argonne, 1918* (Lawrence: University Press of Kansas, 2007), 79, 113, points out that Buck was later relieved of command of his division in the Meuse-Argonne campaign.
52. Pershing, *My Experiences in the World War*, 2: 243–255.
53. White, *The 90th Division in World War I*, 107.
54. Pershing, *My Experiences in the World War*, 2: 259–265; Coffman, *War to End All Wars*, 275. The 82nd Division had been organized and originally commanded by Major General Eben Swift, born at Fort Chadbourne, Texas. Camp Swift, a World War II training facility at Bastrop, was named in his honor.
55. Quote, Coffman, *War to End All Wars*, 275; White, *The 90th Division in World War I*, 100–101; Winfrey, "The 90th Infantry Division," 120.
56. Quote, Chris Emmett, *Give 'Way To The Right: Serving With the A.E.F. in France, during the World War* (San Antonio: Naylor Co., 1934), 172.
57. Wythe, *History of the 90th Division*, 38–48. These are figures given by White, *The 90th Division in World War I*, 107. Winfrey, "The 90th Infantry Division," 127, lists 1,972 casualties.
58. Maury Maverick, *A Maverick American* (New York: Corici, Friade, 1937), 123.
59. Coffman, *War to End All Wars*, 280; *Medal of Honor, Distinguished Service Cross*, 701.
60. Quote, *Texas Medal of Honor Recipients*, 34.
61. *Medal of Honor, Distinguished Service Cross*, 701, 703.
62. Eisenhower, *Yanks*, 198–207; Stallings, *The Doughboys*, 223–227.

63. Mead, *The Doughboys*, 300–310; James G. Harbord, *The American Army in France, 1917–1919* (Boston: Little, Brown, and Co., 1936), 446–447.
64. Clark, *Devil Dogs*, 288–334; Brannen, *Over There*, 44–51; Jackson, *His Time in Hell*, 181–194.
65. White, *Panthers to Arrowheads*, 126; Brager, *The Texas 36th Division*, 56–57.
66. Hutchings had received low efficiency ratings from the inspector general before leaving for overseas duty but was saved from transfer at the time by Greble. White, *Panthers to Arrowheads*, 68–69, 107–108.
67. Ibid., 133–141; White, "The 71st Brigade at St. Etienne," *Military History of Texas and the Southwest* 17 (No. 4, 1982): 123–145; Brager, *The Texas 36th Division*, 58–66; Jay A. Matthews Jr., "Taps for the Bugler: Major Edwin Hutchings and the First Combat Action of the 36th Division," *Military History of Texas and the Southwest* 11 (No. 2, 1973): 71–75. Another Texan, Albert E. "Jack" Chatham of the 132nd Machine Gun Battalion, a twenty-eight-year-old teacher from Callahan County, was wounded in his left foot in the first day of the St. Etienne campaign. See Russell Chatham, "World War I: The Letters of a County School Teacher to His Girl," *West Texas Historical Association Year Book* 72 (1996): 162.
68. White, *Panthers to Arrowheads*, 147–155; Jimmy M. Skaggs, "Lieutenant General John A. Hulen: Portrait of a Citizen-Soldier," *Texas Military History* 8 (No. 3, 1970): 135–143; Henry L. Krench, "John Augustus Hulen: Service in the Philippine Insurrection, 1899–1901," *Military History of Texas and the Southwest* 9 (No. 1, 1971): 34–48.
69. G.O. No. 59, War Department, 1919, in *Texas Medal of Honor Recipients*, 68. See also Casad, *Texans of Valor*, 9–15.
70. *Medal of Honor, Distinguished Service Cross*, 702, 706, 708, 717.
71. Ibid., 711–715, 721. Dreben, known as the "Fighting Jew," had a colorful career as a soldier in the Spanish-American War, the Philippine insurrection, the Boxer Rebellion, the Mexican Revolution, and the Pershing expedition. He received not only the Distinguished Service Cross but also the Croix de Guerre with palms and the Medaille Militaire. Dreben served as an honor guard at the funeral of the Unknown Soldier. See Jane Burges Perrenot, "Samuel Dreben," *New Handbook of Texas*, 2: 697.
72. Brager, *The Texas 36th Division*, 72–73.
73. Ibid., 74–75; White, *Panthers to Arrowheads*, 164; White, "Indian Soldiers of the 36th Division," *Military History of Texas and the Southwest* 15 (No. 1, n. d.): 17–18.
74. Quote, White, *Panthers to Arrowheads*, 167.
75. Ibid., 170–172; Brager, *The Texas 36th Division*, 77.
76. White, *Panthers to Arrowheads*, 169. These figures differ slightly from Ayers, *War with Germany: A Statistical Summary*, 117, which lists 600 battle deaths and a total of 2,528 casualties for the division.
77. Twitchell, *Allen: The Biography of an Army Officer*, 207; Wythe, *History of the 90th Division*, 199; White, *The 90th Division in World War I*, 114–115.
78. White, *The 90th Division in World War I*, 119–123.
79. Winfrey, "The 90th Infantry Division," 130–131.
80. White, *The 90th Division in World War I*, 126.
81. Ibid., 130–131; Winfrey, "The 90th Infantry Division," 131; Edward G. Lengel, *To Conquer Hell: The Meuse-Argonne, 1918* (New York: Henry Holt and Co., 2008), 369–370.

82. Wythe, *History of the 90th Division*, 202; *Medal of Honor, Distinguished Service Cross*, 706.
83. Quote, Strickland, *Adventures of the A.E.F. Soldier*, 142–143.
84. *Medal of Honor, Distinguished Service Cross*, 704.
85. White, *The 90th Division in World War I*, 133–134.
86. *Ibid.*, 137–147; Winfrey, "The 90th Infantry Division," 131; Stallings, *The Doughboys*, 350–351. Joseph E. Persico, *Eleventh Month, Eleventh Day, Eleventh Hour* (New York: Random House, 2004), 234–235, states that division commander Major General William H. Smith ordered one of his brigade commanders to "push patrols as far as possible into Stenay before 11 o'clock."
87. Ayres, *War with Germany: A Statistical Summary*, 117. White, *The 90th Division in World War I*, 152, points out the difficulties in arriving at exact casualty numbers. He notes that Major George Wythe, whose *History of the 90th Division* was compiled immediately after demobilization, reported 9,710 casualties, of which 1,096 were battle deaths. Leonard P. Ayers, who compiled statistics for the Army general staff in 1919, listed 7,277 total casualties for the division, 1,392 of whom were killed. The American Battle Monuments Commission in its *American Armies and Battlefields in Europe* (Washington: Government Printing Office, 1938) reported total casualties for the division as 7,739, with 1,498 battle deaths.
88. Ayres, *War with Germany: A Statistical Summary*, 33, 115; Twitchell, *Allen: Biography of An Army Officer*, 214.
89. *Medal of Honor, Distinguished Service Cross*, 715, 717.
90. James M. Myers, "David Bennes Barkley," *New Handbook of Texas*, 1: 383. Family records indicate that he did not want to be known as of Mexican descent because he feared it would keep him from front-line action. He is listed as Barkeley in *Medal of Honor, Distinguished Service Cross*, 30, and Casad, *Texans of Valor*, 16. Camp Barkeley, near Abilene, a World War II training facility, was named in his honor. According to the *New Handbook of Texas*, I: 923, a clerical error caused the discrepancy in spelling of his name.
91. Ezwoh Barton Snead, "Robert Lee Howze," *New Handbook of Texas*, 3: 753; *Medal of Honor, Distinguished Service Medal*, 912.
92. Skaggs, "Lieutenant General John A. Hulen," 139.
93. *Medal of Honor, Distinguished Service Cross*, 906, 911, 945–947.

CHAPTER SIX

1. Quote, Warren R. Jackson, *His Time in Hell*, 211.
2. Kennedy, *Over Here*, 201–202; *Houston Post*, November 11, 1918; *Dallas Morning News*, November 11, 1918; Johnston, *Houston: The Unknown City*, 209.
3. Quote, C. A. Brannen, *Over There*, 56. Joe Persico, *Eleventh Month, Eleventh Day, Eleventh Hour*, notes that there were heavy casualties on the last day of the war as Allied commanders pushed to occupy as much territory as possible. Many of these casualties came after the 11 o'clock hour that day. Persico, *ibid.*, 178, states there were nearly 11,000 casualties, many in the six hours after the armistice was effective. This is more than the total number of casualties at D-Day in World War II. For general reactions, see Mead, *The Doughboys*, 397–398; Coffman, *War to End All Wars*, 355–357.

4. Laurence N. Martin, *Peace Without Victory: Woodrow Wilson and the British Liberals* (New Haven, CT: Yale University Press, 1958), 184–185; Arthur Walworth, *Woodrow Wilson*, two books in one (org. pub. 1958; new edition, Boston: Houghton Mifflin, 1965), 2: 9–12; Bullitt Lowry, *Armistice, 1918* (Kent, OH: Kent State University Press, 1996), 31–44.
5. Harry R. Rudin, *Armistice, 1918* (New Haven, CN: Yale University Press, 194), 274–275; Hodgson, *Woodrow Wilson's Right Hand*, 183–194. House also met with Pershing to discuss a letter that the general sent to the Supreme War Council advocating unconditional surrender instead of an armistice. This letter had outraged Secretary of War Baker, normally a Pershing supporter. In the meeting with House, Pershing apologized for acting without prior consultation with civilian authorities. House then recommended to President Wilson that the matter be dropped. According to David F. Trask, *The AEF and Coalition Warmaking, 1917–1918* (Lawrence, KS: University Press of Kansas, 1993), 157, "this tactful advice" was accepted, and Pershing escaped censure. Trask does note that although Pershing apologized, he never changed his personal opposition to an armistice. See also Vandiver, *Black Jack*, 2: 982–983, 985, 1075.
6. The literature upon the American intervention, especially in Siberia, is extensive. The classic account of the American decision to send American troops is George F. Kennan, *The Decision to Intervene* (Princeton, NJ: Princeton University Press, 1958). See also Daniel S. Foglesong, *America's Secret War Against Bolshevism* (Chapel Hill, NC: University of North Carolina Press, 1995); Richard Goldhurst, *The Midnight War: The American Intervention in Russia, 1918–1920* (New York: McGraw Hill Book Co., 1978); Betty Miller Unterberger, *America's Siberian Expedition: A Study in National Policy* (Durham, NC: Duke University Press, 1956); John Albert White, *The Siberian Intervention* (Princeton, NJ: Princeton University Press, 1950); Ernest M. Halliday, *The Ignorant Armies: The Anglo-American Archangel Expedition, 1918–1919* (New York: Harper & Brothers, 1958).
7. *Order of Battle*, I: 381–382; Harries and Harries, *Last Days of Innocence*, 198–199; Halliday, *Ignorant Armies*, 30–48.
8. Cullum, *Biographical Register of the Officers and Graduates of the U. S. Military Academy*, III: 381; *Order of Battle*, I: 383; Brian Hart, "Wilds Preston Richardson," *New Handbook of Texas*, 5: 571.
9. *Order of Battle*, I: 384; Hart, "Wilds Preston Richardson," 5: 571. Halliday, *Ignorant Armies*, 194–195, is less charitable to Richardson, whom Halliday criticizes for excessive emphasis upon military courtesy and close-order drill.
10. *Order of Battle*, I: 386–387; Margaret Royalty Edwards, "William Sidney Graves," *New Handbook of Texas*, 3: 291; Goldhurst, *Midnight War*, 73.
11. William S. Graves, *America's Siberian Adventure, 1918–1920* (New York: Jonathan Cape & Harrison Smith, 1931), 1–3; Goldhurst, *Midnight War*, 73–74; Robert J. Maddox, *The Unknown War With Russia: Wilson's Siberian Intervention* (San Rafael, CA: Presidio Press, 1977), 56. For more on Graves, see Donald John Curtis, "Hard Times Come Again No More: General William S. Groves and the American Intervention in Siberia, 1918–1920" (Ph.D. dissertation, Texas A&M University, 2000).
12. Quote, William S. Graves, *America's Siberian Adventure*, 3.
13. Graves reprints the aide-mémoire in his *America's Siberian Adventure*, 5–10.
14. Quote, Newton D. Baker, in Graves, *America's Siberian Adventure*, 4.

15. Kennan, *Decision to Intervene*, 414.
16. Maddox, *Unknown War With Russia*, 98–99; Unterberger, *America's Siberian Expedition*, 123–125. Kennan, *Decision to Intervene*, 414–416, describes "the wonderland to which he [Graves] had now been admitted."
17. Unterberger, *America's Siberian Expedition*, 123–125; Maddox, *Unknown War With Russia*, 98–99; Major Jeff Stamp, "Lost in the Snow: The US Intervention in Siberia During the Russian Civil War," *Armed Diplomacy: Two Centuries of American Campaigning* (Fort Leavenworth: KS; Combat Institute Press, 2003): 98–100.
18. *Order of Battle*, I: 389; Graves, *America's Siberian Adventure*, 302–306; Stamp, "Lost in the Snow," 101–102. In his biography of Wilson, H. W. Brands says the Russian intervention "accomplished nothing good and left a legacy of distrust among the Russians who never forgot—or allowed the West to forget—that the capitalists had tried to smother the socialist revolution in its cradle." Brands, *Woodrow Wilson* (New York: Henry Holt & Co., 2003), 93.
19. David S. Minor, "Kearie Lee Berry," *New Handbook of Texas*, 1: 503–504; Josephine Hejl Legg, "Josef H. Kopecky," *ibid.*, 3: 1156; Smith and Bogart, *The Wars of Peggy Hull*, 135–155.
20. John M. Barry, *The Great Influenza: The Epic Story of the Deadliest Plague in History* (New York: Viking, 2004), 95–96.
21. *Ibid.*, 169–171; Gina Kolata, *Flu: The Story of the Great Influenza Pandemic of 1918 and the Search for the Virus That Caused It* (New York: Simon & Schuster, 1999), 10–11.
22. Barry, *The Great Influenza*, 172–174.
23. *Ibid.*, 198–252; A. A. Hoehling, *The Great Epidemic* (Boston: Little, Brown, and Co., 1961), 36–37, 64, 151–188; Alfred W. Crosby Jr., *Epidemic and Peace, 1918* (Westport, CT: Greenwood Press, 1976), 39–140.
24. Bradford Luckingham, *Epidemic in the Southwest, 1918–1919* (El Paso: Texas Western Press, 1984), 5–17; June E. Osborn, ed., *Influenza in America, 1918–1976* (New York: Wilson Academic Publications, 1977), 8–9; Bureau of Census, *Mortality Statistics, 1918* (Washington: Government Printing Office, 1920), 232.
25. Michelle Baxley, "The Year That Changed America and Texas: The Great Influenza Epidemic of 1918," *Touchstone* 21 (2002): 40; Johns, *Camp Travis and Its Part in the World War*, 37–38; *Mortality Statistics, 1918*, 232.
26. *Mortality Statistics, 1918*; Johnston, *Houston: The Unknown City*, 208; Judith Walker Linsley and Ellen Walker Rienstra, *Beaumont: A Chronicle of Promise* (Woodland Hills, CA: Windsor Publications, 1982), 88; James G. Partin, et al., *Nacogdoches* (Lufkin: Best of Texas Publishers, 1995), 140; Baxley, "The Year That Changed America and Texas," 40.
27. Ruben E. Ochoa, "Macie, Texas," *New Handbook of Texas*, 4: 411.
28. Hoehling, *The Great Epidemic*, 159; Bureau of Navigation, *Officers and Enlisted Men of the United States Navy Who Lost Their Lives During the World War*; Alfred W. Crosby, *America's Forgotten Pandemic: The Influenza of 1918* (Cambridge, England: Cambridge University Press, 2003), 57, 205.
29. Crosby, *America's Forgotten Pandemic*, 140, 159. Efforts of Army medical personnel to combat the influenza virus are covered fully by Carol R. Byerly, *Fever of War: The Influenza Epidemic in the U. S. Army during World War I* (New York: New York University Press, 2005).

30. *Ibid.*, 206–207; Richard Collier, *The Plague of the Spanish Lady: The Influenza Pandemic of 1918–1919* (New York: Atheneum, 1974), 305; Bureau of Census, *Mortality Statistics, 1919* (Washington: Government Printing Office, 1921), 220–221. Texas was one of the twenty-three states that did not report total deaths in 1918 or 1919. Only statistics from Beaumont, Cleburne, Dallas, El Paso, Galveston, Houston, and San Antonio are included in the Census Bureau's mortality figures.
31. Crosby, *America's Forgotten Pandemic*, 317–318; Joan Givner, "Katherine Ann Porter," *New Handbook of Texas*, 5: 274–275.
32. Quote, Crosby, *America's Forgotten Pandemic*, 318. For more on Porter, see Joan Givner, *Katherine Ann Porter: A Life* (New York: Simon & Schuster, 1982); Clinton Machann and William Bedford Clark, eds., *Katherine Ann Porter and Texas: An Uneasy Relationship* (College Station: Texas A&M University Press, 1990).
33. McKay, *Texas Politics, 1906–1944*, 82–83. Charles A. Boynton, Republican candidate for governor, received 26,713 votes. W. D. Simpson, Socialist candidate, polled only 1,660. Hobby received 148,982 votes. In the Democratic primary, Hobby and Ferguson together totaled 670,000 votes. Joseph E. and Jessamine S. Kallenbach, *American State Governors*, 3 vols. (Dobbs Ferry, NY: Oceano Publishers, 1977), 1: 576.
34. Thomas A. Fleming, *The Illusion of Victory: America in World War I* (New York: Basic Books, 2003), 206–207; Kennedy, *Over Here*, 240–245; Selig Adler, "The Congressional Election of 1918," *South Atlantic Quarterly* 36 (October 1937): 447–465.
35. Hilberbrand, "Edward M. House," 24; Hodgson, *Woodrow Wilson's Right Hand*, 206–207; Crosby, *America's Forgotten Pandemic*, 180; Margaret MacMillan, *Paris 1919: Six Months That Changed the World* (New York: Random House, 2001), 17–19, 53–59; Inga Floto, *Colonel House in Paris: A Study of American Policy at the Paris Peace Conference* (Princeton, NJ: Princeton University Press, 1973), 99.
36. Crosby, *America's Forgotten Pandemic*, 189–190; MacMillan, *Paris 1919*, 200–201; Floto, *Colonel House in Paris*, ix.
37. Hilderbrand, "Edward M. House," 26–27; Hodgson, *Woodrow Wilson's Right Hand*, 215–231; Admiral Cary T. Grayson, "The Colonel's Folly and the President's Distress," *American Heritage* 15 (October 1964): 99–100; Floto, *Colonel House in Paris*, 11–13; John Milton Cooper, *Breaking the Heart of the World: Woodrow Wilson and the Fight for the League of Nations* (Cambridge, England: Cambridge University Press, 2001), 89.
38. Grayson, "The Colonel's Folly," 101; Cooper, *Breaking the Heart of the World*, 100; George and George, *Woodrow Wilson and Colonel House*, 266–267. The Georges emphasize that the second Mrs. Wilson, Edith Bolling Galt, never cared for House and may have played a role in the rupture. See pp.185–188, 246–247. Kendrick A. Clements, *Woodrow Wilson: World Statesman* (Rev. ed., Chicago: Ivan R. Dee, 1999), 198, makes a similar point.
39. Quote, Robert C. Hilderbrand, "Edward M. House," 27. Charles Seymour, who was House's official biographer, points out that on three later occasions Wilson sent notes to House and that there was never a quarrel between the two but admits that "the friendship had lapsed." Seymour, *Intimate Papers of Colonel House*, 4: 516–517. For House's views on the treaty-making, see Edward Mandell House and Charles Seymour, eds., *What Really Happened at Paris: The Story of the Peace Conference, 1918–1919* (London: Hodden & Staughton, 1920), 425–444.

40. White, *Panthers to Arrowheads*, 208–222; White, *The 90th Division in World War I*, 200–203.
41. White, *Panthers to Arrowheads*, 173–174.
42. *Ibid.*, 181–203.
43. *Ibid.*, 208–222.
44. As noted earlier, White, *The 90th Division in World War I*, 162, points out that the designation "Tough 'Ombres," widely used in the Second World War, was seldom used in the First World War.
45. *Ibid.*, 165–172; Winfrey, "The 90th Infantry Division," 133.
46. White, *The 90th Division in World War I*, 176–186; Wythe, *History of 90th Division*, 147–148; Strickland, *Adventures of the A.E.F. Soldier*, 267–309.
47. White, *The 90th Division in World War I*, 200–203.
48. Quote, White, *ibid.*, 212. Wythe, *History of the 90th Division*, 201–203, provides the names and addresses of all division recipients of the Distinguished Service Cross. Paul F. Braim, *The Test of Battle: The American Expeditionary Forces in the Meuse-Argonne Campaign* (Newark, DL: University of Delaware Press, 1987) ranked the 90th Division as fourteenth among twenty-nine combat divisions on the basis of performance. White believes that the 90th, and possibly the 36th, was equal to or ahead of at least six divisions ranked higher by Braim.
49. Steen's figures in *Twentieth Century Texas*, 288, differ slightly from those he gave in the *New Handbook of Texas*, 6: 1076. In the *Handbook* article, 4,748 Army deaths are given; in *Twentieth Century Texas*, Army deaths total 4,742. In his book, Steen lists 292 Texas Navy and 133 Marine Corps deaths.
50. *The Literary Digest* (April 5, 1919), reported that eighty-eight of the 117 daily newspapers in Texas-Oklahoma-Louisiana supported the League of Nations; twenty-one gave conditional support, and only eight opposed. See Thomas A. Bailey, *Woodrow Wilson and the Great Betrayal* (New York: Macmillan Co., 1945), 47.
51. Cooper, *Breaking the Heart of the World*, 191; Arthur S. Link, *Wilson the Diplomatist: A Look at His Major Foreign Policies* (Baltimore, MD: Johns Hopkins Press, 1957), 141–150.
52. Link, *Wilson the Diplomatist*, 150; Bailey, *Woodrow Wilson and the Great Betrayal*, 113–114; Fleming, *Illusion of Victory*, 416–420.
53. Quote, Bailey, *Woodrow Wilson and the Great Betrayal*, 175. Bailey points out that House sent Colonel Stephen Bonsal to meet with Lodge. Bonsal secured a conciliatory note from Lodge, which House forwarded to Wilson. According to Bailey, "the Colonel packed his bags, sick though he was, expecting a summons to come to Washington and work out a compromise with Lodge. The summons never came; the letter was never acknowledged; no action was apparently ever taken as a result of it."
54. Dewey Grantham Jr., "The Southern Senators and the League of Nations, 1918–1920," *North Carolina Historical Review* 26 (April 1949): 193–195, notes that a total of twenty-eight Southern votes were cast for the fourteen Lodge reservations. Culberson and Sheppard voted against all of the reservations in the November balloting. For more on the factions involved in the November Senate voting (and later) see Bailey, *Woodrow Wilson and the Great Betrayal*, 180–197, and Cooper, *Breaking the Heart of the World*, 234–270.

55. Colonel House to President Wilson," November 24, 1919 and November 27, 1919, in Seymour, ed., *Intimate Papers of Colonel House*, 4: 509–511.
56. Grantham, "Southern Senators and the League of Nations, 1919–1920," 196–197.
57. Ibid., 194, 197–198. Cooper, *Breaking the Heart of the World*, 360–361, provides percentages for Southern voting on the March reservations. Culberson voted against reservations 94 percent of the time on seventy-one roll call votes. Only eight senators, all Democrats, had a higher percentage of support for the president. The other Texas senator, Morris Sheppard, supported the president on 88 percent of the roll calls. Nineteen senators, all Democrats, gave a higher percentage of support than Sheppard.
58. Culberson's vote is described in various sources, including Bailey, *The Great Betrayal*, 266–267; Fleming, *Illusion of Victory*, 446–447; and Cooper, *Breaking the Heart of the World*, 366–367. For the Senate vote, see *Congressional Record*, 66th Congress, Second Session, (March 19, 1920), 4598–4599.
59. Fleming, *Illusion of Victory*, 449–470.
60. *Texas Almanac's Political History of Texas*, 83; *Galveston Daily News*, March 7, 1920; Gould, *Progressives and Prohibitionists*, 263–265. In this election, former Gov. Jim Ferguson ran a one-state campaign for president, receiving 47,684 votes in Texas. Gould, ibid., 278.
61. Gould, ibid., 260–276; *Fort Worth Star Telegram*, August 19, 1920; *Austin Statesman*, August 30, 1920. Kenneth Durham, "The Longview Race Riot of 1919," *East Texas Historical Journal* 18 (Fall, 1980): 13–24; McKay and Faulk, *Texas After Spindletop*, 77–82; Norman Brown, *Hood, Bonnet, and Little Brown Jug: Texas Politics, 1921–1928* (College Station: Texas A&M University Press, 1984), 15–17.
62. Total population in Texas increased from slightly more than 3 million in 1900 to more than 4.5 million in 1920.
63. Norman D. Brown, "Texas In The 1920s," *New Handbook of Texas*, 6: 375.
64. Ibid., 375.
65. Gould, *Progressives and Prohibitionists*, 253.
66. Christian, "Joining the American Mainstream," 559.
67. Buenger, *Path To A Modern South*, 129.

APPENDIX I
CHRONOLOGY

1914

June 28	Assassination of Francis Ferdinand in Sarajevo, Bosnia
July 25	James E. Ferguson wins Democratic nomination for governor of Texas
July 28	Austria-Hungary declares war on Serbia
July 30	Russia mobilizes troops
Aug 1	Germany declares war on Russia
Aug 3	Germany declares war on France
Aug 4	German troops invade Belgium; England declares war on Germany
Aug 6	Death of Ellen Axson Wilson, wife of Woodrow Wilson
Aug 19	President Wilson's neutrality message to Congress
Sept 5–14	First battle of the Marne
Oct 22	Congress passes Emergency Revenue Act

1915

Jan 6	Signing of "Plan of San Diego"
Jan 15	Colonel Edward House sails for Europe on *Lusitania*
Jan 19	Ferguson inaugurated governor of Texas
Feb 4	German submarine warning
Feb 10	Wilson protests German policy
May 7	Sinking of *Lusitania*
Jun 13	Colonel House returns from Europe
Jul–Oct	Disturbances in South Texas
Aug 15	Sinking of *Arabic*
Sept 1	Germany pledges to limit submarine warfare
Dec 18	Marriage of Woodrow Wilson and Edith Bolling Galt
Dec 25	Colonel House sails for England

1916

Jan 5	House lands in England
Feb 6	Germans open battle for Verdun
Mar 3	U.S. Senate tables Gore-McLemore resolutions
Mar 6	House returns from Europe
Mar 7	U.S. House tables Gore-McLemore resolutions
Mar 8–9	Francisco Villa attacks Columbus, New Mexico
Mar 11	John J. Pershing ordered to lead expedition into Mexico
Mar 24	Sinking of *Sussex*
Apr 18	Lansing warns German regarding submarine policy
May 4	German *Sussex* pledge restricting submarine warfare
May 20	Passage of national defense bill by Congress
May 31–Jun 1	Naval Battle of Jutland
July 1	British open Somme offensive
Aug 19	Passage of naval expansion bill by Congress
Sept 8	Passage of Revenue Act of 1916 by Congress
Nov 8	Wilson re-elected president; Ferguson re-elected governor
Dec 18	Wilson asks European belligerents to state war aims

1917

Jan 16	Ferguson inaugurated governor second time
Jan 22	Wilson's "Peace Without Victory" speech to Congress
Jan 27	Beginning of withdrawal of Pershing expedition from Mexico
Jan 31	Germany announces resumption of unrestricted submarine warfare policy
Feb 3	United States breaks relations with Germany
Feb 26	Wilson asks Congress for power to arm ships
Mar 1	Zimmermann note published in newspapers; U.S. House passes armed-ship bill

Mar 3	Congress passes Revenue Act of 1917 to be used for military preparedness
Mar 4	Wilson takes oath of office second time (Sunday; inauguration next day)
Mar 5	Wilson inaugurated president; Senate blocks armed ship bill
Mar 15	Czar Nicholas II of Russia forced to abdicate
Mar 16–18	German submarines sink three U.S. merchant vessels
Apr 2	Wilson asks Congress for declaration of war
Apr 6	Congress declares war on Germany
May 18	Passage of Selective Service Act
May 18	Pershing appointed commander of American Expeditionary Force
June 5	First registration for Selective Service
June 7	Ferguson vetoes University of Texas appropriation
June 13	Pershing arrives in Paris
June 15	Passage of Espionage Act
June 26	First American troops arrive in France
July 20	Secretary of War Newton Baker draws first number in draft lottery
Aug 1	Senate passes prohibition resolution
Aug 5	Texas-Oklahoma National Guard federalized as 36th Division
Aug 11	Kelly Field opens for training
Aug 23	Riot and mutiny involving African-American troops at Camp Logan
Aug 24	Camp Bowie officially open
Aug 25	90th Division activated
Sept 4	First trainees arrive at Camp Travis
Sept 25	Texas Senate convicts Ferguson on ten counts; W. P. Hobby becomes governor
Oct 3	Passage of War Revenue Act of 1917

Oct 24	Opening of German-Austrian offensive at Caporetto
Oct 29	American mission headed by Colonel House sails for Europe
Nov 1	Beginning of Texas-Louisiana oil field strike
Nov 7	Bolsheviks seize power in Russia; Allies create Supreme War Council
Nov 27	First aircraft fly from Ellington Field
Dec 11	United States declares war on Austria-Hungary
Dec 17	American mission returns to Washington; U.S. House passes prohibition resolution

1918

Jan 8	Wilson's "Fourteen Points" speech to Congress
Mar 3	Treaty of Brest-Litovsk between Russia and Germany
Mar 4	Texas Legislature ratifies 18th Amendment
Mar 7	Legislature prohibits alcohol within ten-mile zone of military camps
Mar 11	Report of influenza outbreak, Fort Riley, Kansas
Mar 15	Legislature passes bill permitting women to vote in state primary elections
Apr 6	Ferguson opens campaign for re-election as governor
May 26	Opening of Ludendorff offensive against Allied left flank
May 28	U.S. 1st Infantry Division in battle at Cantigny
June 6	U.S. troops in action at Belleau Wood
June 22	First units of 90th Infantry Division arrive in France
July 15	Opening of last phase of Ludendorff offensive (Second Battle of the Marne)
July 18	Allied counterattack at Soissons
July 26	Hobby defeats Ferguson in Democratic primary
July 30	First units of 36th Infantry Division arrive in France
Aug 1	American expedition ordered to Murmansk, Russia

Aug 8	German army suffers defeats; "black day of German army"
Aug 10	U.S. 1st Army activated
Aug 23	90th Division relieves 1st Division in the line
Sept 3	Gen. William Graves sets up headquarters at Vladivostok, Siberia
Sept 10	St. Mihiel offensive begins
Sept 26	Opening of Meuse-Argonne offensive
Sept–Nov	Major influenza outbreak in United States and Europe
Oct 8	First combat action of 36th Division (St. Etienne)
Oct 25	Wilson asks voters to elect Democratic Congress
Oct 26	Col. House arrives in Paris
Nov 5	U.S. elections; Republicans gain control of Congress
Nov 9	Kaiser Wilhelm II abdicates
Nov 11	Armistice
Nov 17	90th Division moves to Germany for occupation duty
Dec 4	Wilson sails for France
Dec 13	Wilson arrives in Paris

1919

Jan 18	Opening of Paris Peace Conference
Jan 29	18th Amendment to U.S. Constitution ratified
Feb 15	Wilson leaves Paris
Feb 24	Wilson back in United States
Mar 5	Wilson leaves United States heading back to Europe
Mar 14	Wilson back in Paris
Apr 9	General Wilds P. Richardson assumes command of AEF, north Russia
May 17	First units of 90th Division leave Germany for home
May 24	Texas voters approve prohibition amendment to state constitution; reject women's suffrage
June 11	First units of 36th Division arrive at Camp Bowie for demobilization

June 28	Legislature ratifies 19th Amendment (women's suffrage)
June 28	Signing of Treaty of Versailles; Wilson leaves Paris
July 8	Wilson arrives back in Washington
July 11	Longview race riot
July 31	Senate hearings on Treaty of Versailles begin
Aug 5	Withdrawal of AEF, north Russia
Sept 4	Wilson begins Western speaking tour
Sept 25	Wilson becomes ill after speech in Pueblo, Colorado
Oct 2	Wilson suffers massive stroke
Nov 6	Senate Foreign Relations Committee proposes Lodge resolutions
Nov 19	Senate rejects Lodge resolutions and Treaty of Versailles
Dec 31	War Department orders withdrawal of U.S. troops from Siberia

1920

Jan 20	18th Amendment becomes effective
Mar 19	Senate again rejects Treaty of Versailles
Apr 1	Last U.S. troops leave Siberia
Aug 26	19th Amendment Constitution ratified
Aug 28	Pat Neff defeats Joe Bailey in Democratic gubernatorial primary
Nov 2	Warren G. Harding elected president; Neff elected governor

1921

July 2	Joint congressional resolution declares war with Germany and Austria-Hungary ended
Oct 10	Senate ratifies treaties with Germany and Austria

1924

Feb. 13	Woodrow Wilson dies in Washington, D.C.

APPENDIX II
AFTER THE WAR

Below are brief sketches of the postwar careers and activities of many of the individuals mentioned in the text.

Allen, Henry T., major general, commander of the 90th Division. Became commander of the VIII Corps. From 1918 until retirement in 1923, commander American forces in Germany. Wrote *My Rhineland Journal* and *The Rhineland Occupation*. Died August 30, 1930, in Buena Vista Springs, Pa.

Axson, Stockton, national secretary of the Red Cross. Returned to Rice Institute and continued to teach there until his death February 12, 1935.

Bailey, Joseph W., U.S. senator, Texas. Unsuccessful candidate for governor in 1920. Resumed law practice in Dallas. Died April 13, 1929, during trial in Sherman.

Ball, Thomas H., unsuccessful candidate for Texas governor, 1914. Resumed law practice in Houston; served as general counsel to Houston Port Commission. Died May 7, 1944, in Houston. Town of Tomball named in his honor.

Battle, William J., acting president, University of Texas, 1915–16. Taught at University of Cincinnati, 1917–20. Returned to University of Texas as professor of classical languages in 1920. Received many honors. Retired in 1948. Moved to Rocky Mount, North Carolina in 1955. Died there October 9, 1955.

Beall, Jack Andrew, Texas congressman, 1904–15. Resumed law practice. President, Texas Electric Railway, Dallas Union Transit Company. Died February 11, 1929, in Dallas.

Bee, Carlos, Texas congressman, 1919–21. Resumed law practice after one term in Congress. Died April 20, 1932, in San Antonio.

Bible, Dana X., head football coach, Texas A&M. Resumed coaching, Texas A&M. Left in 1929 to coach University of Nebraska. Returned to Texas to coach University of Texas, 1936. Retired in 1946; served as athletic director, 1946–56. Charter member, National Football Hall of Fame. President, American Football Coaches Association. Died January 19, 1980, in Austin.

Black, Eugene, Texas congressman, 1915–29. Defeated in 1928 by Wright Patman. Appointed judge, U.S. tax court, 1928–66. Died May 22, 1975, in Washington, D.C.

Blanton, Annie Webb, state superintendent of public instruction. Served as superintendent of public instruction through 1922. Unsuccessful candidate for Congress. Returned to University of Texas, earned master's degree, taught in education department until 1926. Earned Ph.D., Cornell. Returned to University of Texas, professor of education until death October 2, 1945, in Austin. Dormitory at University of Texas named for her.

Blanton, Thomas L., Texas congressman, 1917–29, 1930–37. Defeated in race for U.S. Senate, 1928; upon death of successor Robert Q. Lee in 1930 was again elected to Congress. Remained in House until defeated in 1936. Resumed law practice. In 1954, withdrew from race for Congress. Died August 11, 1957, in Albany, Texas.

Bliss, Tasker Howard, Army major general, U.S. representative to Supreme War Council. Retired after the war. Governor of Soldier's Home in Washington, 1920–27. Helped organize the Council of Foreign Relations. Served on editorial board of *Foreign Affairs*. Died in November 1930 in Washington.

Bruce, Andrew D., commander, 4th Machine Gun Battalion, 2nd Division. Remained in Army; attended various staff schools. Organized Tank Destroyer Center at Fort Hood in early 1930s. Commanded 77th Infantry Division in Pacific campaigns in World War II. Commanded 7th Division in Korean War. Retired from Army in 1953. Became president and later chancellor, University of Houston. Died July 28, 1969.

Buchanan, James Paul, Texas congressman, 1903–37. Serving as chairman of House Committee on Appropriations at time of death on February 12, 1937. Seat taken by Lyndon B. Johnson. Buchanan Dam named for him.

Buck, Beaumont Bonaparte, commander, 2nd Brigade, 1st Infantry Division, and later 3rd Infantry Division. Relieved of command by Pershing on Oct. 18, 1918. Retired from Army in June 1925; made home in San Antonio. Headed San Antonio Bicentennial Commission. Wrote *Memories of Peace and War*. Died February 10, 1950, in San Antonio.

Burgess, George F., Texas congressman, 1901–17. Unsuccessful candidate for U.S. Senate, 1916. Resumed law practice in Gonzales. Died December 31, 1919, in Gonzales.

Burleson, Albert Sidney, U.S. postmaster general, 1913–21. Retired from public life in 1921. Returned to Austin to devote time to agricultural interests. Supported Alfred E. Smith and Franklin D. Roosevelt. Died November 24, 1937, in Austin.

Callaway, Francis Oscar, Texas congressman, 1911–17. Defeated for renomination in 1916. Returned to Comanche, resumed law practice, and engaged in farming and stock raising. Died January 31, 1917.

Colquitt, Oscar B., Texas governor, 1911–15, unsuccessful candidate for U.S. Senate, 1916. Resumed business activities; president, Dallas oil firm. Headed Hoover Democrats in Texas in 1928. Member, U.S. Board of Mediation, 1919–33. Field representative of Reconstruction Finance Corporation, 1935 until death on March 8, 1940.

Connally, Thomas T., Texas congressman, 1917–29. Elected to U.S. Senate in 1928. Chairman, Foreign Relations Committee, 1941–47, 1949–53. Helped write charter of the United Nations. Retired in 1953. Died October 28, 1963.

Crowder, Enoch, Army provost marshal, charged with administration of selective service. After war, appointed to represent United States in Cuba; worked to get Cubans to cut budget and eliminate corruption. Left Army in 1923; became ambassador to Cuba. Later practiced law in Chicago. Died May 7, 1932, in Washington, D.C.

Culberson, Charles A., former Texas governor, U.S. senator, 1899–1923. In ill health, defeated for re-election in 1922. Died of pneumonia March 19, 1925, in Washington.

Cunningham, Minnie Fisher, suffragist leader. After adoption of suffrage for women, helped organize the National League of Women Voters; served as executive secretary. Unsuccessful candidate for U.S. Senate in 1928. Editor, Texas A&M Extension Service, 1930–39. Information specialist, Woman's Division of Agricultural Adjustment Administration, 1939–43. Unsuccessful candidate for governor in 1944. Continued to work for progressive causes. Died December 9, 1964.

Davis, James H. "Cyclone," Texas congressman, 1915–17. Lost bid for re-election in 1916. Engaged in lecturing and working for progressive causes. Unsuccessful candidate for Congress in 1932. Died January 31, 1940.

Deuell, Henrietta Goodnough (pseudonym Peggy Hull), war correspondent. Worked on newspapers in Shanghai. In 1933, married *New York Daily News* editor Harvey Deuell. In World War II, served as correspondent in Pacific campaigns for North American Newspaper Alliance. Awarded Navy Commendation. Spent last years in Carmel Valley, California. Died July 19, 1967.

Dies, Martin Sr., Texas congressman, 1909–19. Chose not to run for re-election in 1918. Died July 13, 1922, in Kerrville. Son Martin Dies Jr. later represented his old district in Congress.

Eagle, Joe Henry, Texas congressman, 1913–21. Resumed law practice in Houston; returned to Congress, 1933–37. Championed Social Security reform. Unsuccessful candidate for U.S. Senate in 1936. Returned to law practice. Died January 10, 1963.

Edwards, Daniel R., Medal of Honor recipient. Celebrity after war; served as press aide to Warren G. Harding in 1920. Held job aiding veterans. Later worked as fishing guide in Arkansas. Lowell Thomas wrote his story, *This Side of Hell: Dan Edwards, Adventurer.* Died October 21, 1967.

Emmett, Chris, 359th Infantry, 90th Division. Lawyer, Southern Pacific Railroad for more than thirty years. Prolific author; works included *Texas Camel Tales* (1932), *Give 'Way to the Right* (1934), and *Shanghai Pierce* (1953). After retirement from Southern Pacific, lived in Santa Fe. Died October 20, 1971.

Ferguson, James E. "Pa," Texas governor, 1915–17. Unsuccessful candidate for president, 1920 and U.S. Senate, 1922. Ran wife's campaign for governor in 1924, 1930, and 1932. Died September 21, 1944.

Foulois, Benjamin D., commander, Air Service, American Expeditionary Force. After war, reverted to rank of major. Air attaché, Berlin, 1920–24; assistant chief of Air Corps, 1927; brigadier general, 1931, chief of Air Corps with rank of major general. Retired 1935. Died April 25, 1967, at Andrews Air Force Base.

Garner, John Nance, Texas congressman, 1903–33. Vice president of United States, 1933–41. Opposed Franklin Roosevelt's third term; retired to Uvalde. Lived in virtual seclusion. Died November 7, 1967.

Garrett, Daniel E., Texas congressman, 1913–15, 1917–18. Re-elected to Congress in 1920; served until death December 13, 1932, in Washington.

Graves, William S., Siberian expedition commander. After return from Siberia, commanded 1st Brigade, 1st Division, 1920–25. Promoted to major general; commanded 1st Division, 1925. Commander of Panama Canal Division, 1926–27. Retired 1928. Wrote *America's Siberian Adventure* (1931). Died February 27, 1940, at New Jersey home.

Greble, Edwin St. John, commander of 36th Division prior to overseas movement. After 36th Division departed for France, he remained in command of Camp Bowie. Retired for physical disability, September 1918. Returned home to Philadelphia; died in September 1931 in New Jersey.

Gregg, Alexander W., Texas congressman, 1903–19. Died April 30, 1919, in Palestine, Texas, shortly after last term in Congress ended.

Gregory, Thomas Watt. Resigned as U.S. attorney general on March 4, 1919. Brief role at Paris Peace Conference. Served on Wilson's second Industrial Commission, 1919–20. Resumed law practice, first in Washington, then Houston. Died February 26, 1933.

Hardy, Rufus, Texas congressman, 1907–23. Not a candidate for re-election in 1922. Resumed law practice in Corsicana, where he died March 13, 1943.

Hayden, David E., Medal of Honor recipient. Died March 18, 1974, in Fresno, California.

Henry, Robert L., Texas congressman, 1897–1917. Unsuccessful candidate for U.S. Senate in 1916, 1922, and 1928. Resumed law practice; moved to Houston in 1923. Died July 9, 1931 in Houston.

Hickey, Thomas, editor, *The Rebel*. In October 1919, he and other socialists organized National Workers Drilling and Production Company. Also advertising manger of Desdemona *Oil News* and correspondent for fourteen other newspapers. Withdrew from drilling company in 1920 and lived on farm. Was publishing *Tom Hickey's Magazine* in Fort Worth shortly before his death on May 7, 1928.

Hobby, William P., Texas governor, 1917–21. After completing second term as governor, returned to publish *Beaumont Enterprise*; later purchased *Beaumont Journal*. In 1924, became president of *Houston Post-Dispatch*; later acquired ownership. In February 1931, married Oveta Culp of Killeen; she was later head of Women's Army Corps in World War II and first secretary of health, education, and welfare. Hobby died June 7, 1964, in Houston, where Hobby Airport is named for him.

Hoover, Herbert, U.S. food administrator. Secretary of commerce, 1921–28. U.S. president, 1929–33; defeated for re-election. Remained active in national affairs. Appointed head of Commission on Organization of Executive Branch of Government (better known as Hoover Commission) by President Harry S. Truman. Died October 20, 1964, in New York City.

Hopkins, May Agnes, Texas physician, served overseas. Returned to Dallas after end of war. Resumed practice of medicine. Taught at Baylor University College of Medicine; active in medical societies. Died May 30, 1972, in Dallas.

House, Edward M., adviser to President Wilson. Ceased to exercise influence in public affairs but maintained contact with national and international figures. Not invited to Wilson's funeral. Died March 28, 1939, in New York City.

Houston, David F., secretary of agriculture, Wilson administration. Served as secretary of treasury during last years of Wilson administration. Business career, president of Mutual Life Insurance Company of New York, 1930; held position for ten years. Director of several corporations. Overseer of Harvard University and member of Cornell board of trustees. Died September 2, 1940, in New York City.

Howze, Robert L., major general; commander, 38th Division. After occupation duty with 3rd Army, assigned command of military district of El Paso. Organized and trained 1st Cavalry Division. Later commanded 5th Army Corps Area at Columbus, Ohio, where he died September 19, 1926.

Hulen, John A., commander, 72nd Brigade, 36th Division. Railroad executive; president of Houston Terminal Railway, 1919–20; traffic manager (1920–30) and president (1930–41) of Fort Worth and Denver Railway. In 1920, promoted to major general, Texas National Guard. In 1922, became commander of 36th Division, a position he held until retirement in 1935. Retired from railway in 1941. Died September 14, 1957, in Palacios. Camp Hulen named for him.

Hutchings, Henry, commander, 71st Brigade, 36th Division. Texas secretary of state under Gov. Pat Neff. Adjutant general of Texas, 1922–35. Executive officer in charge of narcotics division of Texas Department of Public Safety. Died July 27, 1939, in Austin.

Jackson, Warren, corporal, 6th Marines. Little known of postwar activity. Probably attended Sam Houston Normal and University of Texas. Wrote manuscript describing war experiences; gave copy to University of Texas. Manuscript recently discovered and published by Marine Corps historian George R. Clark.

Jester, Beauford, captain; commander, D Company, 1st Battalion, 357th Infantry, 90th Division. Entered University of Texas law school; received law degree, 1920. Moved back to Corsicana to practice law. Member University of Texas board of regents,

1929–35. Texas Railroad Commission, 1942–47. Elected governor 1946 and 1948. Died July 11, 1949, on train en route to Houston.

Jones, Jesse H., director general of American Relief for American Red Cross during World War I. Returned to Houston and resumed business career. Became owner of *Houston Chronicle* in 1926. Instrumental in bringing Democratic National Convention to Houston in 1928. Chairman, Reconstruction Finance Corporation, 1933–39. Secretary of commerce, 1940–45. Broke with Democratic Party. Died June 1, 1956. Jones Hall for Performing Arts named for him.

Jones, Marvin, Texas congressman, 1917–40. After long tenure as chairman of House Agriculture Committee, became justice of U.S. court of claims. War food administrator, 1943–45. Returned to court of claims after war; became chief judge in 1947. Served until 1964, then became senior judge. Died March 4, 1976, in Amarillo.

Keasbey, Lindley B., professor of institutional history, University of Texas. After dismissal from University of Texas, had difficulty finding new position. Moved to Arizona in 1925, began raising dogs; gained national recognition in so doing. Later moved to California, where he died September 17, 1946.

Kirby, John Henry, lumber company president, lumber administrator, U.S. Shipping Board. Continued to be active in lumber industry; served two terms as president of National Lumber Manufacturers Association, 1917–21. Opposed Franklin D. Roosevelt; co-founder of Southern Committee to Uphold the Constitution. Contributed to various anti-New Deal groups. Died November 9, 1940.

La Follette, Robert M., U.S. senator from Wisconsin, 1906–25. In 1924, ran for president on Progressive ticket; carried only one state (Wisconsin). Died June 18, 1925; succeeded in Senate by son Robert La Follette Jr.

Lodge, Henry Cabot, chairman, Senate Foreign Relations Committee. Majority leader in Senate, 1918–24. U.S. representative in Conference on Limitations of Armament in 1921. Died November 9, 1924, in Cambridge, Massachusetts.

Love, Thomas B., assistant secretary of treasury. Elected national Democratic committeeman for Texas in 1920; served until 1924. Opposed nomination of Alfred E. Smith; helped organize Hoover Democrat clubs. State Senate, 1927–31. Died September 17, 1948, in Dallas.

Lovett, Robert Abercrombie, commander, Naval Night Bombing Squadron. Joined Brown Brothers Harriman banking firm on Wall Street. Assistant secretary of war for air in Second World War; secretary of defense, 1951. One of the "wise men," a group of influential advisers to American presidents in Cold War. Died March 7, 1986, at age 90.

Lovett, Robert Scott, member of War Industries Board. Continued to serve as president and chairman of board of Union Pacific Railroad. Retired from active supervision in 1923. Died June 19, 1932.

Mansfield, Joseph J., Texas congressman, 1916–47. After war, continued congressional service. Longtime chairman, House Rivers and Harbors Committee. Became paralyzed in 1920 and thereafter used wheelchair. Died July 5, 1947. Mansfield Dam on Lake Travis named for him.

Maverick, Maury, lieutenant, 28th Infantry, 1st Division. Law practice, tax collector, Bexar County, 1930–34. Congress, 1935–38; mayor of San Antonio, 1939–41. Chairman of Smaller War Plants Corporation, 1941–46. Died June 7, 1954, in San Antonio.

Mayfield, Earle, Texas Railroad Commission, 1913–23. Elected to U.S. Senate in 1922. Defeated in 1928 by Thomas T. Connally. Unsuccessful candidate for governor in 1930. Practiced law and served as president of Mayfield Wholesale Grocery Company until retirement in 1952. Died June 23, 1964.

McAdoo, William G., secretary of treasury, Wilson administration. Unsuccessful candidate for Democratic presidential nomination, 1920 and 1924. Elected to U.S. Senate from California in 1932; defeated for re-election in 1938. Practiced law in California. Died February 1, 1941, in Washington, D. C.

McDonald, William M., political activist. Remained active in politics, supported Gen. Leonard D. Wood for president in 1920. Became distrustful of Republicans; supported La Follette, Al Smith, FDR. In 1940, returned to Republican Party; supported Thomas E. Dewey. Died July 5, 1950, in Fort Worth.

McLemore, Atkins Jefferson, Texas congressman, 1915–19. Defeated for re-election in 1918. Returned to newspaper work in Hebbronville. Unsuccessful candidate for U.S. Senate, 1928. Died March 4, 1929, in Laredo.

Mezes, Sidney E., chairman, "The Inquiry." After service at Paris Peace Conference and Central Territorial Commission, resumed presidency of CCNY; continued until retirement in 1927. Made president emeritus of University of Texas in 1929. Spent rest of life in Arizona, California, and Europe. Died September 10, 1931, in Altadena, California. Mezes Hall, University of Texas, named for him.

Mouzon, E. D., Methodist bishop. Continued work as bishop. Member, Southern Methodist University board of trustees. First dean of School of Theology. President of Board of Christian Education of the Methodist Episcopal Church, South. Died February 10, 1937, in Charlotte, North Carolina.

Nimitz, Chester W., naval officer U.S. Fleet. Served in various capacities during inter-war period, rising to rank of rear admiral. In 1939, appointed chief of Bureau of Navigation. After attack on Pearl Harbor, placed in command of Pacific Fleet and Pacific Ocean Area. Promoted to rank of Admiral of the Fleet. Became commander of U.S. Fleet in 1945. Died February 20, 1966, in San Francisco.

Parker, Edwin B., member, War Industries Board. Chairman, U.S. Liquidation Commission. Commissioner, Tripartite Claims Commission for United States, Austria, and Hungary. Board of trustees for Carnegie Endowment and board of George Washington University. Received U.S. Distinguished Service Medal and various foreign awards. Died October 30, 1929, in Washington, D.C.

Peden, Edward A., Texas food administrator. Continued business and civic work in Houston, where he died July 10, 1934.

Pershing, John J., commander, American Expeditionary Force. Promoted to General of the Armies. Army chief of staff, 1921–24. Wrote memoirs, *My Experiences in the World War* (1931); received Pulitzer Prize, 1932. Continued to have considerable influence in military affairs. Suffered from heart trouble; died July 15, 1948, at Walter Reed Hospital.

Porter, Katherine Anne, reporter. After recovery from influenza, lived in New York City. Traveled to Mexico and Europe. Wrote short stories and novels. Taught at various universities. Novel *Ship of Fools* (1962) brought her fame and fortune. Moved to Maryland. Died September 18, 1980.

Rayburn, Sam, Texas congressman, 1913–61. Majority leader of U.S. House, 1937–40. House speaker, 1940–47, 1949–53, 1955–61. Died of cancer on November 16, 1961. Sam Rayburn Library in Bonham named for him.

Richardson, James Otto, naval officer, Atlantic Fleet. After war, gradually rose in rank. In 1940, named commander, Pacific Fleet. Opposed move to Pearl Harbor ordered by President Roosevelt. Relieved of command January 5, 1941. Returned to permanent rank of rear admiral. Executive vice president, Navy Relief Society, 1942–45. Released from active duty in January 1947. Died May 2, 1974, in Washington, D.C.

Richardson, Wilds P., commander, American Expeditionary Force, north Russia. Retired from Army on October 31, 1920. Lived in Army and Navy Club in Washington. Wrote article "Alaska" for 1928 *Atlantic Monthly* calling for development of Alaska that would not destroy natural resources. Died May 10, 1929, in Washington, D.C.

Sampler, Samuel, corporal, 142nd Infantry, 36th Division, Medal of Honor. Honored by several presidents. Worked at Naval Supply Depot in Philadelphia. Died November 19, 1979, in Fort Myers, Florida.

Scott, Emmett Jay, special assistant for Negro affairs, War Department. Secretary-treasurer, Howard University, 1919–34. Personnel director, Sun Shipbuilding Company, Chester, Pennsylvania, during World War II. Author of *Scott's Official History of the American Negro in World War I* (1919) and *Negro Migration During World War* (1920). Died December 11, 1957, in Washington, D.C.

Sheppard, John Morris, U.S. senator from Texas, 1913–41. Longtime supporter of prohibition. Supported most New Deal legislation. Chairman, Senate Military Affairs Committee. Died April 9, 1941.

Slayden, Ellen Maury, wife of U.S. Rep. James L. Slayden. Died April 20, 1926, in San Antonio. Left her notebooks describing social and political life in Washington to nephew Maury Maverick. Maverick's widow, Terrell Webb, with her second husband, Walter P. Webb, had journal published in 1962 as *Washington Wife*.

Slayden, James L., Texas congressman, 1897–1919. Dropped out of race for re-election in 1918. After retirement from Congress, devoted attention to orchard in Virginia, ranch in Texas, and mine in Mexico. Died February 18, 1924, in San Antonio.

Smith, William R., major general; commander, 36th Division in France. Postwar assignments in Philippines, Fort Sam Houston, Fort Monroe, and Hawaii. Superintendent, West Point, 1928 until retirement from Army in 1932. Served as superintendent, Sewanee Military Academy in Tennessee until death on July 15, 1941.

Smith, William R., Texas congressman, 1903–17. Defeated in re-election campaign, 1917. Appointed U.S. judge for Western District of Texas by President Wilson. Died August 16, 1924, in El Paso.

Stephens, John H., Texas congressman, 1897–1917. Defeated for re-election, 1916. Moved to Monrovia, California, where he died November 18, 1924.

Sterling, Ross, president, Humble Oil & Refining Company. In 1925, sold Humble interest; started developing real estate. Purchased Houston *Dispatch* and Houston *Post*; combined them as *Houston Post*. Chairman, Texas Highway Commission. Elected governor in 1930; defeated in re-election campaign in 1932. Returned to Houston; president of Sterling Oil Company, 1933–46. President of American Maid Flour Mills; chairman, Houston National Bank. Died March 25, 1949, in Fort Worth.

Stinson, Katherine, pilot in Texas, ambulance driver in France. Ill when returned from France; moved to Santa Fe for health. Became architectural designer. Died July 18, 1977, in Santa Fe.

Sumners, Hatton W., Texas congressman, 1913–47. Chairman, House Judiciary Committee, 1932–46. Opposed FDR court reorganization bill. Retired from Congress, 1947. Served as director of research in law and government, Southwestern Legal Foundation. Died April 19, 1962.

Thomason, John W. Jr., lieutenant, 5th Marines. Remained in Marines after war. Served in Cuba, Nicaragua, and China. Received Silver Star, Navy Cross, and Air Medal. Prolific writer and illustrator; published more than sixty articles and eleven books, five of which were about Marines. Died March 11, 1934, in San Diego. Navy destroyer and Graphic Arts Building, Sam Houston State University, named for him.

Thompson, Ernest O., lieutenant colonel, 36th Infantry. Practiced law; bought and managed Amarillo Hotel. Mayor of Amarillo in 1928. Appointed to Texas Railroad Commission in 1932. Became dominant figure on commission. Unsuccessful candidate for governor in 1938 and 1940. Resigned from Railroad Commission in January 1965. Died June 28, 1966.

Truett, George W., pastor, First Baptist Church of Dallas, and overseas minister. President, Southern Baptist Convention, 1927–29. President, Baptist World Alliance, 1934–39. Published ten volumes of sermons, two volumes of addresses, and two volumes of Christmas messages. Pastor of First Baptist Church of Dallas, until death on July 7, 1944.

Villa, Francisco "Pancho," Mexican revolutionary leader. Continued to commit acts of banditry in Chihuahua. Mexican federalists bought his retirement in 1920 by giving him an estate in Durango. Assassinated in 1923.

Vinson, Robert E., president, University of Texas, 1917–23. Resigned from university presidency in 1923 to become president of Case Western Reserve, where he remained until retirement in December 1933. Served fourteen years as trustee of Carnegie Foundation of Teaching. Died September 2, 1945, in Cleveland, Ohio.

Wilson, James C., Texas congressman, 1917–19. Resigned from Congress to take appointment as federal judge. Served as judge until retirement in 1947.

Wilson, Woodrow, U.S. president, 1913–21. Became ill on Western speaking tour; suffered massive stroke on October 2, 1919; finished term as virtual recluse. Died February 13, 1924, in Washington, D.C.

BIBLIOGRAPHY

Government Documents

Adjutant General of the Army. *Congressional Medal of Honor the Distinguished Service Cross, and the Distinguished Service Medal Issued by the War Department Since April 6, 1917*. Washington: Government Printing Office, 1920.

American Battle Monuments Commission. *American Armies and Battlefields in Europe*. Washington: Government Printing Office, 1938.

Ayres, Leonard. *The War With Germany: A Statistical Summary*. Washington: Government Printing Office, 1919.

Bureau of Navigation. *Officers and Enlisted Men of the United States Navy Who Lost Their Lives During the World War, From April 6, 1917 to November 11, 1918*. Washington: Government Printing Office, 1920.

Bureau of the Census. *Thirteenth Census of the United States. Vol. Agriculture, 1909 and 1910*. Washington: Government Printing Office, 1913.

Bureau of the Census. *Thirteenth Census of the United States: 1910. Vol. Manufactures*. Washington: Government Printing Office, 1913.

Bureau of the Census. *Thirteenth Census of the United States: 1910. Vol. Mines and Quarries*. Washington: Government Printing Office, 1913.

Bureau of the Census. *Thirteenth Census of the United States: 1910. Vol. Population*. Washington: Government Printing Office, 1913.

Bureau of the Census. *Fourteenth Census of the United States Taken in the Year 1920. Vol. Population*. Washington: Government Printing Office, 1922.

Bureau of the Census. *Mortality Statistics, 1918*. Washington: Government Printing Office, Washington: Government Printing Office, 1920.

Bureau of the Census. *Religious Bodies, 1916*. Washington: Government Printing Office, 1919.

Texas Legislature. *Journal of the House of Representatives of the First Called Session of the Thirty-Fourth Legislature*. Austin: Von Boeckmann-Jones Co., 1915.

Texas Legislature. *Journal of the House of Representatives of the First Called Session of the Thirty-Fifth Legislature*. Austin: Von Boeckmann-Jones Co., 1917.

Texas Legislature. *Journal of the House of Representatives, Second Called Session, Thirty-Fifth Legislature*. Austin: Von Boeckmann-Jones, 1917.

Texas Legislature. *Journal of the House of Representatives, Third Called Session, Thirty-Fifth Legislature*. Austin: Von Boeckmann-Jones, 1917.

Texas Legislature. *Journal of the House of Representatives of the Fourth Called Session of the Thirty-Fifth Legislature*. Austin: Von Boeckmann-Jones, 1918.

Texas Legislature. *Journal of the Senate of Texas, Being the First Called Session of the Thirty-Fourth Legislature*. Austin: A. C. Baldwin & Sons, 1915.

Texas Legislature. *Journal of the Senate, State of Texas, First Called Session of Thirty-Fifth Legislature*. Austin: A. C. Baldwin & Sons, 1917.

Texas Legislature. *Journal of the Senate of Texas, Third Called Session of the Thirty-Fifth Legislature*. Austin: A. C. Baldwin & Sons, 1917.

Texas Legislature. *Journal of the Senate of Texas, the Fourth Called Session of the Thirty-Fifth Legislature*. Austin: A. C. Baldwin & Sons, 1918.

Texas Veterans Commission. *Texas Medal of Honor Recipients*. Austin: Texas Veterans Commission Headquarters, 1993.

United States Army. *Order of Battle of the United States Land Forces in the World War*. 3 vols. Reprint. Washington: Center of Military History, United States Army, 1938.

United States Army. *United States Army in the World War, 1917–1919*. 17 vols. Reprint. Washington: Center of Military History, United States Army, 1989.

United States Army Provost Marshal. *Final Report of the Provost Marshal General to the Secretary of War on the Operations of the Selective Service System to July 15, 1919*. Washington: Government Printing Office, 1920.

United States Army Provost Marshal. *Second Report of the Provost Marshal to the Secretary of War on the Operations of the Selective Service System to December 20, 1918*.

Washington: Government Printing Office, 1919. United States Congress. *Congressional Record, 64th Congress*. Washington: Government Printing Office, 1915–1917.

United States Congress. *Congressional Record, 65th Congress*. Washington: Government Printing Office, 1917–1919.

United States Navy. *Dictionary of American Fighting Ships*. 8 vols. Washington: Navy Department, Office of Chief of Naval Operations, 1959–1981.

Memoirs and Personal Accounts

Baruch, Bernard M. *American Industry in the War*. New York: Prentice-Hall, Inc., 1940.

Brannen, C. A. *Over There: A Marine in the Great War*. College Station: Texas A&M University Press, 1996.

Buck, Beaumont Bonaparte. *Memoirs of Peace and War*. San Antonio: Naylor Co., 1935.

Connally, Tom. *My Name is Tom Connally*. New York: Thomas Y. Crowell Co., 1954.

Davis, James H. "Cyclone." *Memoirs*. Sherman, TX: Courier Press, 1935.

Emmett, Chris. *Give 'Way To The Right: Serving with the A.E.F. in France, during the World War*. San Antonio: Naylor Co., 1934.

Flach, Bera. *A Yankee in German-America Texas Hill Country*. San Antonio: Naylor Co., 1973.

Graves, William S. *America's Siberian Adventure, 1918–1920*. New York: Jonathan Cape & Harrison Smith, 1931.

Harbord, James G. *The American Army in France, 1917–1919*. Boston: Little, Brown and Co., 1936.

House, Edward Mandell and Charles Seymour, eds. *What Really Happened at Paris: The Story of the Peace Conference, 1918–1919*. London: Hodden & Staughton, 1921.

Houston, David F. *Eight Years with Wilson's Cabinet, 1913 to 1920*. 2 vols. Garden City, N. Y.: Doubleday, Page, & Co., 1926.

Jackson, Warren R. *His Time in Hell: A Texas Marine in France*. Novoto, CA: Presidio Press, 2001.

Link, Arthur S., ed. *The Papers of Woodrow Wilson*. 69 vols. Princeton, NJ: Princeton University Press, 1966–1994.

Maverick, Maury. *A Maverick American*. New York: Corici, Friade. 1937.

Parsons, Edwin C. *I Flew With the Lafayette Escadrille*. New York: Arno Press, 1972.

Pershing, John J. *My Experiences in the World War*. 2 vols. New York: Frederick A. Stokes Co., 1931.

Richardson, James A. *On the Treadmill to Pearl Harbor: The Memoirs of Admiral James O. Richardson, USN (Retired) as told to Vice Admiral George C. Dyer*. Washington: U. S. Naval Department, 1973.

Seymour, Charles, ed. *The Intimate Papers of Colonel House*. 4 vols. Boston: Houghton Mifflin Co., 1926.

Strickland, Riley. *Adventures of the A.E.F. Soldier*. Austin: Von Boeckmann-Jones Co., 1920.
Thomason, John W. *Fix Bayonets!* New York: Charles Scribner's Sons, 1928.
Webb, Terrell, ed. *Washington Wife: Journal of Ellen Maury Slayden from 1897 to 1919*. New York: Harper & Row, 1963.
Whiteman, Harold B. Jr., ed. *Letters from the Paris Peace Conference*. New Haven, CT.: Yale University Press, 1965.
Wilson, Edith Bolling. *My Memoir*. Indianapolis: Bobbs-Merrill Co., 1938.

Books

Abrams, Roy H. *Preachers Present Arms: The Role of American Churches and Clergy in World Wars I and II* . . . Rev. ed., Scottsdale, PA: Harold Press, 1969.
Adams, John Q. Jr. *We Are the Aggies: The Texas A&M University Association of Former Students*. College Station: Texas A&M University Press, 1979.
Alexander, Thomas E. *The Wings of Change: The Army Air Force Experience in Texas During World War II*. Abilene: McWhiney Foundation Press, 2003.
Allen, Ruth. *East Texas Lumber Workers: An Economic and Social Picture, 1870–1950*. Austin: University of Texas Press, 1961.
Bailey, Thomas A. *Woodrow Wilson and the Great Betrayal*. New York: Macmillan Co., 1945.
Baker, Ray Stannard. *Woodrow Wilson: Life and Letters*. 8 vols. Garden City, NY: Doubleday, Page & Co., 1927–1939.
Barbeau, Arthur E., and Florette Henri, *The Unknown Soldiers: African-American Troops in World War I*. Reprint, New York: DeCapo Press, 1996.
Barr, Alwyn. *Black Texans: A History of African Americans in Texas, 1528–1995*. 2nd ed. Norman: University of Oklahoma Press, 1996.
Barry, John M. *The Great Influenza: The Epic Story of the Deadliest Plague in History*. New York: Viking, 2004.
Beaver, Daniel R. *Newton D. Baker and the American War Effort, 1917–1919*. Lincoln, NB: University of Nebraska Press, 1966.
Bernstein, Patricia. *The First Waco Horror: The Lynching of Jesse Washington and the Rise of the NAACP*. College Station: Texas A&M University Press, 2005.

Bilstein, Roger E. and Jay Miller. *Aviation in Texas*. Austin: Texas Monthly Press, 1985.

Blum, Daniel. *A Pictorial History of the Silent Screen*. New York: G. P. Putnam's, 1953.

Bowen, Robert Sidney. *They Flew to Glory: The Story of the Lafayette Flying Corps*. New York: Lothrop, Lee & Shepard, Inc., 1964.

Brager, Bruce L. *The Texas 36th Division*. Austin: Eakin Press, 2002.

Braim, Paul F. *The Test of Battle: The American Expeditionary Forces in the Meuse-Argonne Campaign*. Newark, DL: University of Delaware Press, 1987.

Bricker, Richard H. *Wooden Ships from Texas: A World War I Saga*. College Station: Texas A&M University Press, 1998.

Brown, Carrie. *Rosie's Mom: Forgotten Women Workers of the First World War*. Boston: Northeastern University Press, 2002.

Brown, Norman. *Hood, Bonnet, and Little Brown Jug: Texas Politics, 1921–1928*. College Station: Texas A&M University Press, 1984.

Buenger, Walter L. *The Path To A Modern South: Northeast Texas between Reconstruction and the Great Depression*. Austin: University of Texas Press, 2001.

Byerly, Carol R. *Fever of War: The Influenza Epidemic in the U.S. Army during World War I*. New York: New York University Press, 2005.

Campbell, Randolph B. *Gone to Texas: A History of the Lone Star State*. New York: Oxford University Press, 2003.

Carlson, Paul H. *Texas Woolybacks: The Range Sheep and Goat Industry*. College Station: Texas A&M University Press, 1982.

Carrigan, William D. *The Making of a Lynching Culture: Violence and Vigilantism in Central Texas, 1836–1916*. Urbana: University of Illinois Press, 2004.

Casad, Debe Weldon. *Texans of Valor: Military Heroes in the 20th Century*. Austin: Eakin Press, 1998.

Cashion, Ty. *Pigskin Pulpit: A Social History of Texas High School Coaches*. Austin: Texas State Historical Association, 1998.

Chambers, John Whiteclay II. *To Raise an Army: The Draft Comes to Modern America*. New York: Free Press, 1987.

Chastine, Ben H. *Story of the 36th: The Experiences of the 36th Division in the World War*. Oklahoma City: Harlow Publishing Co., 1920.

Christian, Garna L. *Black Soldiers in Jim Crow Texas, 1899–1917*. College Station: Texas A&M University Press, 1995.

Clark, Jim, with Weldon Hart. *The Tactful Texan: A Biography of Governor Will Hobby*. New York: Random House, 1958.

Clark, George. *Devil Dogs: Fighting Marines of World War I*. Novato, CA: Presidio Press, 2000.
Clarkson, Grosvenor B. *Industrial America in the World War: The Strategy Behind the Line, 1917–1918*. Boston: Houghton Mifflin Co., 1923.
Clements, Kenrick A. *Woodrow Wilson: World Statesman*. Rev. ed., Chicago: Ivan R. Dee, 1999.
Clendenen, Clarence C. *Blood on the Border: The United States Army and the Mexican Irregulars*. London: Macmillan Co., 1969.
Clendenen, Clarence C. *The United States and Pancho Villa: A Study in Unconventional Diplomacy*: Ithaca, NY: Cornell University Press, 1961.
Coerver, Don M. and Linda B. Hall. *Texas and the Mexican Revolution: A Study in State and National Border Policy, 1910–1920*. San Antonio: Trinity University, 1984.
Coffman, Edward. *The War to End All Wars: The American Military Experience in World War I*. Madison, WI: University of Wisconsin Press, 1986.
Collier, Richard. *The Plague of the Spanish Lady: The Influenza Pandemic of 1918–1919*. New York: Atheneum, 1974.
Cooper, John Milton. *Breaking the Heart of the World: Woodrow Wilson and the Fight for the League of Nations*. Cambridge, England: Cambridge University Press, 2001.
Cooper, John Milton. *The Vanity of Power: American Isolationism and the First World War, 1914–1917*. Westport, CN: Greenwood Press, 1969.
Creighton, James A. *A Narrative History of Brazoria County*. Waco: Brazoria Historical Commission, 1975.
Crosby, Alfred W. *America's Forgotten Pandemic: The Influenza of 1918*. Cambridge, England: Cambridge University Press, 2003.
Crosby, Alfred W. *Epidemic and Peace, 1918*. Westport, CN: Greenwood Press, 1976.
Cuff, Robert D. *The War Industries Board: Business-Governmental Relations during World War I*. Baltimore: Johns Hopkins University Press, 1973.
Cullum, George W. *Biographical Register of the Officers and Graduates of the U.S. Military Academy* . . . 3 vols. Boston: Houghton Mifflin Co., 1891.
Dessez, Eunice. *The First Enlisted Women, 1917–1918*. Philadelphia: Dorrance & Co., 1955.
Dethloff, Henry C. *A Centennial History of Texas A.&M. University*. 2 vols. College Station: Texas A&M University Press, 1975.

Ebbert, Jean. *Crossed Currents: Navy Women from World War II to Tailhook.* Washington: Brassey's, 1993.

Ebbert, Jean and Marie-Beth Hall. *The First, The Few, The Forgotten: Navy and Marine Corps Women in World War I.* Annapolis: Naval Institute Press, 2002.

Eby, Frederick. *The Development of Education in Texas.* New York: Macmillan Co., 1925.

Eisenhower, John S. D. *Yanks: The Epic Story of the American Army in World War I.* New York: Simon & Schuster, 2001.

Enstam, Elizabeth York. *Women and the Creation of Urban Life; Dallas, Texas, 1843–1920.* College Station: Texas A&M University Press, 1998.

Evans, C. E. *The Story of Texas Schools.* Austin: Steck Co., 1955.

Ferguson, Niall. *The Pity of War.* New York: Basic Books, 1995.

Ferrell, Robert H. *America's Deadliest Battle: Meuse-Argonne, 1918.* Lawrence: University Press of Kansas, 2007.

Ferrell, Robert H. *Woodrow Wilson and World War I, 1917–1920.* New York: Harper & Row, 1985.

Fleming, Thomas. *The Illusion of Victory: America in World War I.* New York: Basic Books, 2003.

Fligstein, Neil. *Going North: Migration of Blacks and Whites from the South, 1900–1950.* New York: Academic Press, 1981.

Floto, Inga. *Colonel House in Paris: A Study of American Policy in the Paris Peace Conference.* Princeton: Princeton University Press, 1973.

Foglesung, Daniel S. *America's Secret War Against Bolshevism.* Chapel Hill, NC: University of North Carolina Press, 1995.

Foley, Neil. *The White Scourge: Mexicans, Blacks, and Poor Whites in Texas Cotton Culture.* Berkeley, CA: University of California Press, 1997.

Forbes, Gerald. *Flush Production: The Epic of Oil in the Gulf-Southwest.* Norman: University of Oklahoma Press, 1942.

Frandsen, Bert. *Hat in the Ring: The Birth of American Air Power in the Great War.* Washington, D.C.: Smithsonian Books, 2003.

Frantz, Joe B. *The Forty Acre Follies.* Austin: Texas Monthly Press, 1983.

Fromkin, David. *Europe's Last Summer.* New York: Alfred A. Knopf, 2004.

Frothingham, Thomas G. *The Naval History of the World War: The United States in the War.* Freeport, NY: Books for Libraries Press, 1971.

Garcia, Mario T. *Desert Immigrants: The Mexicans of El Paso, 1880–1980*. New Haven, CT: Yale University Press, 1981.
Gaustad. Edwin S. *A Religious History of America*. New York: Harper & Row, 1966.
Gavin, Lettie. *American Women in World War I: They Also Served*. Niwot, CO: University Press of Colorado, 1997.
George, Alexander L. and Juliette L. *Woodrow Wilson and Colonel House: A Personality Study*. New York: John Day Co., 1956.
Gilbert, Charles. *American Financing of World War I*. Westport, CN: Greenwood Press, 1970.
Givner, Joan. *Katherine Ann Porter: A Life*. New York: Simon & Schuster, 1982.
Goldhurst, Richard. *The Midnight War: The American Intervention in Russia, 1918–1920*. New York: McGraw Hill Book Co., 1978.
Gould, Lewis L. *Progressives and Prohibitionists: Texas Democrats in the Wilson Era*. Org. pub., 1973. Austin: Texas State Historical Association, 1992.
Green, James R. *Grass-Roots Socialism: Radical Movements in the Southwest, 1895–1943*. Baton Rouge: Louisiana State University Press, 1978.
Greenwald, Maurine Weiner. *Women, War, and Work: The Impact of World War I on Women Workers in the United States*. Westport, CN: Greenwood Press, 1980.
Griffiths, John F. And Greg Ainsworth. *One Hundred Years of Texas Weather, 1880–1979*. College Station: Texas A&M University Press, 1981.
Hagedorn, Ann. *Savage Peace: Hope and Fears in America, 1919*. New York: Simon & Schuster, 2007.
Harries, Merion and Susie. *The Last Days of Innocence: America At War, 1917–1918*. New York: Random House, 1997.
Halliday, Ernest M. *The Ignorant Armies: The Anglo-American Archangel Expedition, 1918–1919*. New York: Harper & Brothers, 1958.
Harris, Charles III and Louis P. Sadler. *The Texas Rangers and the Mexican Revolution: The Bloodiest Decade, 1910–1920*. Albuquerque, NM: University of New Mexico Press, 2004.
Haynes, Robert V. *A Night of Violence: The Houston Riot of 1917*. Baton Rouge: Louisiana State University Press, 1976.
Haynes, William. *Brimstone: The Stone That Burns*. Princeton: D. Van Nostrand Co., 1959.
Hendrick, George. *Katherine Ann Porter*. New York: Twayne, 1965.

Hendrickson, Kenneth E. Jr. and Michael L. Collins, eds. *Profiles in Power: Twentieth Century Texans in Washington*. Arlington Heights, IL: Harlan Davidson, 1993.

Hill, Patricia E. *Dallas: The Making of a Modern City*. Austin: University of Texas Press, 1996.

Hodgson, Godfrey, *Woodrow Wilson's Right Hand: The Life of Colonel Edward M. House*. New Haven: Yale University Press, 2006.

Hoehling, A. A. *The Great Epidemic*. Boston: Little, Brown, and Co., 1961.

Hogan, E. B. *The Last Buffalo: Walter Potts and the 92nd "Buffalo" Division in World War I*. Austin: Eakin Press, 2000.

Hough, Emerson. *The Web*. Orig. pub. 1919. New York: Arno Press, 1969.

Hudson, James J. *Hostile Skies: A Combat History of the American Air Service in World War I*. Syracuse, NY: Syracuse University Press, 1968.

Hudson, Winthrop S. *Religion in America: An Historical Account of the Development of American Religious Life*. Second ed. New York: Charles Scribner's Sons, 1973.

Hussey, Ann and Robert S. Browning III. *A History of Service: Seventy-five Years of Military Aviation at Kelly Air Force Base, 1916–1990*. San Antonio: Office of History San Antonio Air Logistics Center, Kelly Air Force Base, 1991.

Hyman, Harold M. *To Try Men's Souls: Loyalty Tests in American History*. Berkeley, CA: University of California Press, 1959.

James, Powhatan W. *George W. Truett: A Biography*. Nashville, TN: Broadman Press, 1939.

Jensen, Joan M. *The Price of Vigilance*. Chicago: Rand McNally, 1969.

Johns, E. B. *Camp Travis and Its Part in the World War*. New York: priv. pub., 1919.

Johnson, Benjamin H. *Revolution in Texas: How A Forgotten Rebellion and Its Bloody Suppression Turned Mexicans Into Americans*. New Haven, CN: Yale University Press, 2003.

Johnson, Douglas V. and Rolfe L. Hillman Jr. *Sossions*. College Station: Texas A&M University Press, 1999.

Kallenbach, Joseph E. and Jessamine S. *America's State Governors*. 3 vols. Dobbs Ferry, NY: Oceano Publishers, 1977.

Keegan, John. *The First World War*. New York: Alfred A. Knopf, 1999.

Keith, Jeannette. *Rich Man's War, Poor Man's Fight: Race, Class, and Power in the Rural South during the First World War*. Chapel Hill: University of North Carolina Press, 2001.

Kennan, George F. *The Decision to Intervene*. Princeton, NJ: Princeton University Press, 1958.
Kennedy, David M. *Over Here: The First World War and American Society*. New York: Oxford University Press, 1980.
Key, V. O. Jr. *Southern Politics in State and Nation*. New York: Alfred A. Knopf, 1949.
Kingston, Mike, Sam Attlesey, and Mary G. Crawford, comps. *The Texas Almanac's Political History of Texas*. Austin: Eakin Press, 1992.
Knight, Oliver. *Fort Worth: Outpost on the Trinity*. Norman: University of Oklahoma Press, 1953.
Kolata, Gina. *Flu: The Story of the Great Influenza Pandemic of 1918 and the Search for the Virus That Caused It*. New York: Simon & Schuster, 1999.
Krousser, J. Morgan. *The Shaping of Southern Politics, Suffrage Restrictions, and the Establishment of the One-Party South, 1880–1910*. New Haven, CN: Yale University Press, 1974.
Lasswell, Mary. *John Henry Kirby: Prince of the Pines*. Austin: Encino Press, 1967.
Lengel, Edward G. *To Conquer Hell: The Meuse-Argonne, 1918*. New York: Henry Holt, 2008.
Lich, Glen E. *The German Texans*. San Antonio: Institute of Texas Cultures, 1981.
Lich, Glen E. and Dana B. Reeves, eds. *German Culture in Texas: A Free Earth; Essays from the 1978 Southwest Symposium*. Boston: Twayne Publishers, 1980.
Link, Arthur S. *The Higher Realism of Woodrow Wilson and Other Essays*. Nashville: Vanderbilt University Press, 1971.
Link, Arthur S. *Wilson the Diplomatist: A Look at His Major Foreign Policies*. Baltimore: Johns Hopkins Press, 1957.
Link, Arthur S. *Wilson: The Struggle for Neutrality, 1914–1915*. Princeton, NJ: Princeton University Press, 1960.
Link, Arthur S. *Woodrow Wilson and the Progressive Era, 1910–1917*. New York: Harper & Row, 1954.
Linsley, Judith Walker and Ellen Walker Rienstra. *Beaumont: A Chronicle of Promise*. Woodland Hills, CA: Windsor Publications, 1982.
Livermore, Seward. *Politics Is Adjourned: Woodrow Wilson and the War Congress, 1916–1918*. Middlebury, CN: Wesleyan University Press, 1966.
Lowry, Bullitt. *Armistice, 1918*. Kent, OH: Kent State University Press, 1996.

Luckingham, Bradford. *Epidemic in the Southwest, 1918–1919*. El Paso: Texas Western Press, 1984.

Luebke, Frederick C. *Bonds of Loyalty: German-Americans and World War I*. Dekalb, IL: Northern Illinois University, 1974.

McArthur, Judith N. *Creating the New Woman: The Rise of Southern Women's Progressive Culture in Texas, 1893–1918*. Urbana, IL: University of Illinois Press, 1998.

McArthur, Judith N. and Harold L. Smith. *Minnie Fisher Cunningham: A Suffragist's Life in Politics*. New York: Oxford University Press, 2003.

McCartin, Joseph. *Labor's Great War: The Struggle for Industrial Democracy and the Origins of Modern American Labor Relations, 1912–1921*. Chapel Hill, NC: University of North Carolina Press, 1997.

McComb, David. *Galveston: A History*. Austin: University of Texas Press, 1986.

McComb, David. *Houston: The Bayou City*. Austin: University of Texas Press, 1989.

McKay, Seth S. *Texas Politics, 1906–1944: With Special Reference to German Counties*. Lubbock: Texas Tech Press, 1952.

McKay, Seth S. and Odie B. Faulk. *Texas After Spindletop*. Austin: Steck-Vaughn Co., 1965.

Machann, Clinton and William Bedford Clark, eds. *Katherine Ann Porter and Texas: An Uneasy Relationship*. College Station: Texas A&M University Press, 1990.

Macmillan, Margaret. *Paris 1919: Six Months That Changed the World*. New York: Random House, 2001.

Madden, James W. *Charles Allen Culberson: His Life, Character and Public Service*. Austin: Gammel's Book Store, 1929.

Maddox, Robert J. *The Unknown War With Russia: Wilson's Siberian Intervention*. San Rafael, CA: Presidio Press, 1977.

Malin, James C. *The United States After the World War*. Freeport, NY: Books for Libraries Press, 1972.

Martin, Laurence N. *Peace Without Victory: Woodrow Wilson and the British Liberals*.

New Haven, CN: Yale University Press, 1958. Mason, Herbert M. Jr. *The Great Pursuit: General John J. Pershing's Punitive Expedition Across the Rio Grande to Destroy the Mexican Bandit Pancho Villa*. New York: Random House, 1970.

Mason, Herbert M. Jr. *The Lafayette Escadrille*. New York: Random House, 1964.

Maxwell, Robert S. and Robert D. Baker. *Sawdust Empire: The Texas Lumber Industry, 1830–1940*. College Station: Texas A&M University Press, 1983.
May, Irvin M. Jr. *Marvin Jones: The Public Life of an Agrarian Advocate*. College Station: Texas A&M University Press, 1980.
Mead, Gary. *The Doughboys: America and the First World War*. New York: Overlook Press, 2000.
Meiners, Fredericka. *A History of Rice University: The Institute Years, 1907–1963*. Houston: Rice University Studies, 1982.
Millett, Allan R. *The General: Robert L. Bullard and Officership in the United States Army, 1881–1925*. Westport, CN: Greenwood Press, 1975.
Montejano, David. *Anglos and Mexicans in the Making of Texas, 1836–1987*. Austin: University of Texas Press, 1987.
Moore, Richard R. *West Texas After the Discovery of Oil: A Modern Frontier*. Austin: Jenkins Publishing Co., 1971.
Morrow, John H. Jr. *The Great War in the Air: Military Aviation from 1909 to 1921*. Washington: Smithsonian Institute Press, 1993.
Mullendore, William C. *History of the United States Food Administration, 1917–1919*. Stanford, CA: Stanford University Press, 1941.
Murphy, Paul. *World War I and the Origin of Civil Liberties in the United States*. New York: W. W. Norton & Co., 1979.
National Association for the Advancement of Colored People. *Thirty Years of Lynching in the United States, 1888–1919*. Org. pub. 1919. New York: Arno Press, 1969.
Olien, Dianna and Roger M. *Oil in Texas: The Gusher Age, 1895–1945*. Austin: University of Texas Press, 2002.
O'Neal, Bill. *The Texas League, 1888–1987: A Century of Baseball*. Austin: Eakin Press, 1987.
Osborne, June E., ed. *Influenza in America, 1918–1978*. New York: Neale Western Academic Publications, 1977.
Perret, Geoffrey. *A Country Made By War*. New York: Random House, 1989.
Persico, Joseph. *Eleventh Month, Eleventh Day, Eleventh Hour: Armistice Day, 1918, World War and Its Violent Climax*. New York: Random House, 2004.
Peterson, H. C. and Gilbert C. Fite. *Opponents of War, 1917–1918*. Madison, WS: University of Wisconsin Press, 1957.
Pierce, Frank C. *A Brief History of the Lower Rio Grande Valley*. Menasha, WS: George Banta Publishing, 1917.

Pitre, Merline. *The Struggle Against Jim Crow: Lula B. White and the NAACP, 1900–1957*. College Station: Texas A&M University Press, 1999.

Pool, William C. *Eugene C. Barker: Historian*. Austin: Texas State Historical Association, 1971.

Potter, E. B. *Nimitz*. Annapolis: Naval Institute Press, 1976.

Preston, Diane. *Lusitania: An Epic Tragedy*. New York: Walker & Co., 2002.

Ragsdale, Kenneth B. *Quicksilver: Terlingua and the Chisos Mining Company*. College Station: Texas A&M University Press, 1976.

Ransleben, Guido E. *A Hundred Years of Comfort in Texas: A Centennial History*. Rev. ed. San Antonio: Naylor Co., 1974.

Ratliff, Harold V. *Autumn's Mightiest Legions: A History of Texas Schoolboy Football*. Waco: Texian Press, 1963.

Richardson, Rupert N. *Colonel Edward M. House: The Texas Years, 1858–1912*. Abilene: Hardin-Simmons University, 1964.

Robinson, Charles M. III. *The Men Who Wore the Star*. New York: Random House, 2002.

Rogers, Mary Beth, et al. *We Can Fly: Stories of Katherine Stinson and Other Gutsy Texas Women*. Austin: Texas Foundation for Women's Resources, 1983.

Rudin, Harry R. *Armistice, 1918*. New Haven, CT: Yale University Press, 1944.

Ryley, Thomas W. *A Little Group of Willful Men: A Study of Congressional-Presidential Authority*. Port Washington, NY: Kennikat Press, 1975.

Sandos, James A. *Rebellion in the Borderland: Anarchism and the Plan of San Diego, 1904–1923*. Norman: University of Oklahoma Press, 1992.

Schneider, Dorothy and Carl J. Schneider, *Into the Breach: American Women Overseas in World War I*. New York: Viking Press, 1991.

Schroeder, Richard. *Lone Star Picture Shows*. College Station: Texas A&M University Press, 2001.

Scott, Emmett J. *Negro Migration During the War*. Org. pub. 1920. New York: Arno Press, 1969.

Scott, Emmett J. *Scott's Official History of the American Negro in the World War*. New York: Arno Press and New York Times, 1969.

Shay, Fray. *Judge Lynch: His First Hundred Years*. Montclair, NJ: Patterson Smith, 1969.

Smith, Arthur D. A. *Mr. House of Texas*. New York: Funk & Wagnalls Co., 1940.

Smith, Wilda M. and Eleanor A. Bogart. *The Wars of Peggy Hull: The Life and Times of a War Correspondent*. El Paso: Texas Western Press, 1991.
Spell, Lota M. *Music in Texas*. Austin, 1936; reprint New York: AMS, 1973.
Stallings, Laurence. *The Doughboys: The Story of the AEF, 1917–1918*. New York: Harper & Row, 1963.
Steen, Ralph W. *Twentieth Century Texas: An Economic and Social History*. Austin: Steck Company, 1942.
Stokesbury, James L. *A Short History of World War I*. New York: William Morrow and Co., 1981.
Stone, Geoffrey R. *Perilous Times: Free Speech in Wartime*. New York: W. W. Norton & Co., 2004.
Stout, Joseph A. Jr. *Border Conflict: Villistas, Carrrancistas, and the Punitive Expedition, 1915–1920*. Fort Worth: Texas Christian University Press, 1999.
Strachan, Hew. *The First World War*. New York: Viking, 2003.
Sweeney, W. Allison. *History of the American Negro in the Great War*. New York: Negro Universities Press, 1969.
Taylor, William Allen and Sue Hastings. *Aransas: The Life of A Texas Coastal County*. Austin: Eakin Press, 1987. *Texas Almanac and Industrial Guide, 1941–1942*. Dallas: A. H. Belo Co., 1941.
Thomas, Lowell. *This Side of Hell: Dan Edwards, Adventurer*. New York: P. F. Collier & Son, 1932.
Timmons, Bascom N. *Garner of Texas: A Personal History*. New York: Harper & Brothers, 1948.
Tindall, George B. *The Emergence of the New South, 1913–1945*. Baton Rouge: Louisiana State University Press, 1967.
Trask, David F. *The AEF and Coalition Warmaking, 1917–1918*. Lawrence, KS: University Press of Kansas, 1993.
Trask, David, F. *The United States in the Supreme War Council: American War Aims and Inter-Allied Strategy, 1917–1918*. Middleton, CN: Wesleyan University Press, 1961.
Tuchman, Barbara W. *The Guns of August*. New York: Macmillan Co., 1962.
Tuchman, Barbara W. *The Zimmermann Telegram*. New York: Houghton Mifflin, 1966.
Tucker, Robert W. *Woodrow Wilson and the Great War: Reconsidering America's Neutrality, 1914–1917*. Charlottesville, VA: University of Virginia Press, 2007.

Turner, Martha Anne. *The World of Col. John W. Thomason, USMC*. Austin: Eakin Press, 1984.

Twitchell, Heath Jr. *Allen: The Biography of an Army Officer, 1859–1930*. New Brunswick, NJ: Rutgers University Press, 1974.

Tyler, Ron, et al. *The New Handbook of Texas*. 6 vols. Austin: Texas State Historical Association, 1996.

Unterberger, Betty Miller. *America's Siberian Expedition: A Study in National Policy*. Durham, NC: Duke University Press, 1956.

Utley, Robert M., *Lone Star Lawmen: The Second Century of the Texas Rangers*. New York: Oxford University Press, 2007.

Vandiver, Frank E. *Black Jack: The Life and Times of John J. Pershing*. 2 vols. College Station: Texas A&M University Press, 1977.

Venzon, Anne Cipriano, ed. *The United States in the First World War: An Encyclopedia*. New York: Garland Publishing Co., 1995.

Viereck, George Sylvester. *The Strangest Friendship in History*. New York: Liveright, Inc., 1932.

Walworth, Arthur. *Woodrow Wilson*. Org. pub. 1958. Boston: Houghton Mifflin, 1965.

Ward, Larry Wayne. *The Motion Picture Goes to War: The U.S. Film Effort during World War I*. Ann Arbor, MI: UMI Research Press, 1985.

Webb, Walter P. *An Honest Preface and Other Essays*. Boston: Houghton Mifflin Co., 1959.

Webb, Walter P. *The Texas Rangers: A Century of Frontier Defense*. Boston: Houghton Mifflin Co., 1935.

White, John Albert. *The Siberian Intervention*. Princeton, NJ: Princeton University Press, 1950.

White, Lonnie J. *Panthers to Arrowheads: The 36th (Texas, Oklahoma) Division in World War I*. Austin: Presidial Press, 1984.

White, Lonnie J. *The 90th Division in World War I*. Manhattan, KS: Sunflower University Press, 1996.

Whitehouse, Arch. *Legion of the Lafayette*. Garden City, NY: Doubleday & Co., 1962.

Winegarten, Ruthe and Judith N. McArthur, eds. *Citizens at Last: The Woman Suffrage Movement in Texas*. Austin: Ellen C. Temple, 1987.

Wittke, Carl. *German Americans and the World War*. Columbus, OH: Ohio State Archaeological and Historical Society, 1936.

Wortham, Marc. *The Millionaires' Unit: The Aristocratic Flyboys Who Fought the Great War*. New York: Public Affairs, 2006.

Wythe, George. *A History of the 90th Division*. New York: 90th Division Association, 1920.

Zamora, Emilio. *The World of the Mexican Worker in Texas*. College Station: Texas A&M University Press, 1993.
Zeiger, Susan. *In Uncle Sam's Service: Women Workers with the American Expeditionary Forces, 1917–1919*. Ithaca, NY: Cornell University Press, 1999.
Zieger, Robert H. *America's Great War: World War I and the American Experience*. N. Y. Rowan & Littlefield, 2000.

Articles in Books and Journals

Abrams, Richard M. "Woodrow Wilson and the Southern Congressmen, 1913–1916." *Journal of Southern History* 22 (November 1956): 417–437.
Adler, Selig. "The Congressional Election of 1918." *South Atlantic Quarterly* 36 (October 1937): 447–465.
Anderson, Adrian. "President Wilson's Politician: Albert Sidney Burleson of Texas." *Southwestern Historical Quarterly* 77 (January 1974): 338–354.
Anders, Evan. "Thomas Watt Gregory and the Survival of His Progressive Faith." *Southwestern Historical Quarterly* 93 (July 1989): 1–24.
Barr, Alwyn. "John Nance Garner's First Campaign for Congress." *West Texas Historical Association Year Book* 48 (1972): 105–110.
Baxley, Michelle. "The Year That Changed America and Texas: The Great Influenza Epidemic of 1918." *Touchstone* 21 (2002): 35–43.
Beauboeuf, Bruce Andre. "War and Change: Houston's Economic Ascendancy During World War I." *Houston Review* 14 (No. 2, 1992): 89–112.
Boyd, Stephen and David Smith, "Thomas Hickey, the Rebel, and Civil Liberties in Wartime Times," *East Texas Historical Journal* 45 (No. 1, 2007): 41–51.
Brandimarte, Cynthia. "Using Government Documents: The Food Administration Papers for Texas." *Southwestern Historical Quarterly* 104 (October 2000): 263–281.
Buenger, Walter. " 'This Wonder Age': The Economic Transformation of Northeast Texas, 1900–1930." *Southwestern Historical Quarterly* 98 (April 1995): 519–550.
Cardoso, Lawrence A. "Labor Emigration to the Southwest, 1916 to 1920: Mexican Attitudes and Policy." *Southwestern Historical Quarterly* 79 (April 1976): 400–416.

Chatham, Russell. "World War I: The Letters of A Country School Teacher to His Girl." *West Texas Historical Association Year Book* 72 (1996): 158–170.

Christian, Carole. "Joining the American Mainstream: Texas' Mexican Americans During World War I." *Southwestern Historical Quarterly* 92 (April 1989): 559–595.

Christian, Garna L. "Newton Baker's War on El Paso Vice." *Red River Valley Historical Review* 5 (Spring 1980): 55–67.

Christian, Garna L. "The Ordeal and the Prize: The 24th Infantry and Camp MacArthur." *Military Affairs* 50 (April 1986): 65–70.

Cox, Patricia L. " 'An Enemy Closer to Us Than Any European Power': The Impact of Mexican Texan Public Opinion before World War I." *Southwestern Historical Quarterly* 105 (July 2001): 41–80.

Cumberland, Charles C. "Border Raids in the Lower Rio Grande Valley." *Southwestern Historical Quarterly* 57 (January 1954): 285–211.

Durham, Kenneth R. "The Longview Race Riot of 1919." *East Texas Historical Journal* 18 (Fall 1980): 13–24.

Eudy, John Carroll. "The Vote and Lone Star Women: Minnie Fisher Cunningham and the Texas Equal Suffrage Association." *East Texas Historical Journal* 14 (Fall 1976): 52–59.

Gaughan, Anthony. "Woodrow Wilson and the Rise of Militant Interventionism in the South." *Journal of Southern History* 65 (November 1999): 771–808.

Gerlach, Alan. "Conditions Along the Border, 1915: The Plan de San Diego." *New Mexico Historical Review* 43 (July 1968): 195–212.

Giles, Barney M. "Early Military Aviation Activities in Texas." *Southwestern Historical Quarterly* 54 (October 1950): 143–158.

Gould, Lewis L. "A Texan in London: A British Editor Lunches with Colonel Edwin M. House." *Southwestern Historical Quarterly* 84 (April 1981): 426–434.

Gould, Lewis L. "The University Becomes Politicized: The War with Jim Ferguson, 1915–1918." *Southwestern Historical Quarterly* 86 (October 1982): 255–276.

Grant, H. Roger. " 'Interurbans Are the Wave of the Future': Electric Railway Promotion in Texas." *Southwestern Historical Quarterly* 86 (October 1982): 28–49.

Grantham, Dewey Jr. "Texas Congressional Leaders and the New Freedom, 1913–1917." *Southwestern Historical Quarterly* 53 (July 1949): 35–48.

Grantham, Dewey Jr. "The Southern Senators and the League of Nations, 1918–1920." *North Carolina Historical Review* 26 (April 1949): 187–205.
Grayson, Admiral Cary T. "The Colonel's Folly and the President's Distress." *American Heritage* 15 (October 1964): 4–7, 94–101.
Green, George N. "The Texas Labor Movement, 1870–1920." *Southwestern Historical Quarterly* 108 (July 2004): 1–25.
Green, James R. "Tenant Farmer Discontent and Socialist Protest in Texas, 1901–1917." *Southwestern Historical Quarterly* 81 (October 1977): 133–154.
Hager, William B. "The Plan of San Diego: Unrest on the Texas Border in 1915." *Arizona and the West* 5 (Winter 1963): 327–336.
Harris, Charles H. III and Louis R. Sadler, "The Plan of San Diego and the Mexican-United States Crisis of 1916: A Reexamination." *Hispanic American Historical Review* 58 (August 1978): 381–408.
Haynes, Robert V. "The Houston Mutiny and Riot of 1917." *Southwestern Historical Quarterly* 76 (April 1973): 420–442.
Hays, Robert E. Jr. "Military Aviation in Texas, 1917–1919." *Texas Military History* 3 (Spring 1983): 1–13.
Hegi, Benjamin Paul. " 'Old Time Good Germans': German-Americans in Cooke County, Texas, during World War I" *Southwestern Historical Quarterly* 109 (October 2005): 235–257.
Herring, George C. Jr. "James Hay and the Preparedness Controversy, 1915–1916." *Journal of Southern History* 30 (November 1964): 380–404.
Higgs, Robert T. "The Boll Weevil, the Cotton Economy and Black Migration, 1900–1930." *Agricultural History* 50 (April 1976): 335–350.
Hilderbrand, Robert C. "Edward M. House," in Kenneth E. Hendrickson Jr. and Michael L. Collins, eds. *Profiles in Power: Twentieth Century Texans in Washington* (Arlington Heights, IL: Harlan Davidson, 1993): 1–27.
Hilton, Ora H. "Freedom of the Press in Wartime, 1917–1919." *Southwestern Social Science Quarterly* 28 (March 1948): 346–361.
Hilton, Ora H. "Public Opinion and Civil Liberties in Wartime, 1917–1919." *Southwestern Social Science Quarterly* 28 (December 1947): 201–224.
Impson, A. John. "Martin Dies, John Henry Kirby and Timber Politics, 1908–1918." *East Texas Historical Journal* 35 (Fall 1997): 20–29.
Johnson, Donald. "Wilson, Burleson, and Censorship in the First World War." *Journal of Southern History* 28 (February 1962): 46–58.

Johnson, J. Eddie. "The Economic Development of Orange County, Texas, 1906–1920." *Texas Gulf Historical and Biographical Record* 13 (November 1977): 10–27.

Karpii, Frank O. "The Last Sailing Ships Built in Texas." *Texas Gulf Historical and Biographical Record* 16 (November 1980): 55–68.

Kirby, John Temple. "The Southern Exodus, 1910–1960: A Primer for Historians." *Journal of Southern History* 49 (November 1983): 585–600.

Krenck, Henry L. "John August Hulen: Service in the Philippines Insurrection, 1899–1901." *Military History of Texas and the Southwest* 9 (No. 1, 1971): 34–48.

Lang, Herbert H. "Fort Worth's Role in the Origins of the Helium Industry." *West Texas Historical Association Year Book* 47 (1971): 125–145.

Launis, Roger D. "A New Way of War: The Development of Military Aviation in the American West, 1908–1945." *Military History of the West* 25 (Fall 1995): 167–173.

Lippman, Walter. "The Personal Diplomacy of Colonel House." *American Journal of International Law* 21 (1927): 706–715.

Maroney, James C. "The Texas-Louisiana Oil Field Strike of 1917," in Gary M. Fink and Merl E. Reed, eds. *Essays on Southern Labor History* (Westport, CN: Greenwood Press, 1976): 161–172.

McDaniel, Dennis K "The First Congressman Martin Dies of Texas." *Southwestern Historical Quarterly* 102 (October 1998): 131–162.

McDonald, Timothy G. "The Gore-McLemore Resolutions: Democratic Revolt Against Wilson's Submarine Policy." *The Historian* 26 (November 1963): 52–74.

McKay, S. S. "John Nance Garner." *West Texas Historical Association Year Book* 37 (1961): 10–20.

McMahon, Truman. "The Fight Against the Pink Bollworm in Texas." *Southwestern Historical Quarterly* 94 (July 1990): 37–64.

Matthews, Jay A. Jr. "Taps of the Bugler: Major Edwin Hutchings and the First Combat Action of the 36th Division." *Military History of Texas and the Southwest* 11 (No. 2, 1973): 71–75.

May, Irvin M. Jr. "Marvin Jones, Representative of and from the Panhandle." *West Texas Historical Association Year Book* 52 (1976): 91–104.

Miller, Thomas Lloyd. "Oscar Callaway and Preparedness." *West Texas Historical Association Year Book* 43 (October 1967): 80–93.

More, Ellen S. "'A Certain Restless Ambition': Women Physicians and World War I." *American Quarterly* 41 (December 1989): 636–660.

Neu, Charles E. "In Search of Colonel Edward M. House: The Texas Years, 1858–1912." *Southwestern Historical Quarterly* 93 (July 1989): 25–44.

Newberry, James Leslie. "The World War Diary of William S. Leslie, Pvt. 169 Aero Squadron, American Expeditionary Force." *East Texas Historical Journal* 32 (Spring 1994): 55–64.

Newby, I. A. "States' Rights and Southern Congressmen during World War I." *Phylon* 24 (Spring 1963): 34–50.

Nicholas, William E. "World War I and Academic Dissent in Texas." *Arizona and the West* 14 (Autumn 1972): 215–230.

Payne, John W. Jr. "David F. Houston's Presidency of Texas A.&M." *Southwestern Historical Quarterly* 58 (July 1954): 22–35.

Pohl, James W. "Slayden's Defeat: A Texas Congressman Loses His Bid as Wilson's Secretary of War." *Military History of Texas and the Southwest* 10 (No. 1, 1972): 43–50.

Pool, William C. "Military Aviation in Texas, 1913–1917." *Southwestern Historical Quarterly* 59 (April 1956): 429–454.

Pool, William C. "The Origin of Military Aviation in Texas, 1910–1913." *Southwestern Historical Quarterly* 58 (April 1955): 319–330.

Rainey, James W. "The Questionable Training of the AEF in World War I." *Parameters* 22 (Winter 1992–93): 89–103.

Reich, Steven A. "Soldiers of Democracy: Black Texans and the Fight for Citizenship, 1917–1921." *Journal of American History* 82 (March 1996): 1478–1504.

Rifkind, Robert S. "The Colonel's Dream of Power." *American Heritage* 10 (February 1959): 62–64, 111.

Sandos, James A. "The Plan of San Diego: War & Diplomacy on the Texas Border, 1915–1916." *Arizona and the West* 14 (Spring 1972): 5–24.

Schuler, Edgar A. "The Houston Race Riot, 1917." *Journal of Negro History* 29 (July 1944): 300–338.

Scruggs, Oley. "The First Mexican Farm Labor Program." *Arizona and the West* 2 (Winter 1960): 319–326.

Seymour, James B. Jr. "Evils More Deadly than the Carnage of the Battlefield: The Fight for Prohibition in McLennan County in 1917." *East Texas Historical Journal* 40 (Spring 2002): 58–69.

Shanks, Alexander Graham. "Sam Rayburn in the Wilson Administration, 1918–1921." *East Texas Historical Journal* 6 (March 1968): 63–76.

Skaggs, Jimmy H. "Lieutenant General John A. Hulen: Portrait of a Citizen-Soldier." *Texas Military History* 8 (No. 3, 1970): 135–143.

Smith, C. Calvin. "The Houston Riot of 1917 Revisited." *Houston Review* 13 (No. 2, 1991): 85–102.

Smith, Glen. "Drought in Runnels County, 1915–1918." *West Texas Historical Association Year Book* 40 (October 1964): 52–70.

SoRellle, James M. "The 'Waco Horror': The Lynching of Jesse Washington." *Southwestern Historical Quarterly* 86 (April 1983): 517–536.

Stamp, Major Jeff. "Lost in the Snow: The U. S. Intervention in Siberia During the Russian Civil War," in *Armed Diplomacy: Two Centuries of American Campaigning* (Fort Leavenworth, KS: Combat Institute Press, 2003), 91–103.

Steen, Ralph W. "Ferguson's War on the University of Texas." *Southwestern Social Science Quarterly* 35 (March 1955): 356–362.

Taylor, A. Elizabeth. "The Woman Suffrage Movement in Texas." *Journal of Southern History* 17 (May 1951): 194–215.

Viereck, George Sylvester. "Behind the Wilson Break," in Members of the Overseas Press Club of America, *The Inside Story* (New York: Prentice-Hall, Inc., 1940).

Vinson, Robert E. "The University Crosses the Bar." *Southwestern Historical Quarterly* 43 (January 1940): 281–294.

Wagner, Robert L. "The Congressional Career of Jeff McLemore as Seen in His Letters." *The Historian of the University of Texas* 1 (September 1962): 65–81.

Watson, Richard, "A Testing Time for Southern Congressional Leadership." *Journal of Southern History* 44 (February 1978): 3–40.

Webb, William J. "The United States Wooden Steamship Program During World War I." *American Neptune* 35 (1975): 275–288.

White, Lonnie J. "Camp Bowie." *Military History of Texas and the Southwest* 18 (No. 3, 1982): 55–87.

White, Lonnie J. "Chief of the Arrowheads: Major General William R. Smith and the 36th Division in France." *Military History of Texas and the Southwest* 16 (No. 3, 1980): 149–176.

White, Lonnie J. "From Texas to the Marne." *Military History of Texas and the Southwest* 18 (No. 3, 1982): 89–122.

White, Lonnie J. "Glory on the Aisne." *Military History of Texas and the Southwest* 18 (No. 3, 1982): 147–179.

White, Lonnie J. "Major General Edwin St. John Greble." *Military History of Texas and the Southwest* 14 (No. 1, 1978): 7–29.

White, Lonnie J. "The Call to Arms." *Military History of Texas and the Southwest* 17 (No. 2, 1982): 1–23.
White, Lonnie J. "The Formation of the 36th Division." *Military History of Texas and the Southwest* 17 (No. 2, 1982): 25–53.
White, Lonnie J. "The 71st Brigade at St. Etienne." *Military History of Texas and the Southwest* 17 (No. 4, 1982): 123–145.
Wilson, Joseph. "Texas German and Other Immigrant Languages: Problems and Prospects," in Theodore Gish and Richard Spuler, eds., *Eagle in the New World: German Immigration to Texas and America* (College Station: Texas A&M University Press, 1986): 221–240.
Winfrey, Dorman H. "The 90th Infantry Division," in *Soldiers of Texas* (Waco: Texian Press, 1973): 115–134.
Woodson, Carter, ed. "Letter of Negro Migrants of 1916–1918." *Journal of Negro History* 4 (July 1919): 190–340.

Articles in *New Handbook of Texas*

Alcott, Edward B. "Brooks Air Force Base." 1: 752.
Allen, Louise C., Ernest A. Sharpe, and John R. Whitaker. "Newspapers." 4: 1000–1002.
Anders, Evan. " Gregory, Thomas Watts." 3: 331.
Battle, William J. "Mezes, Sidney Edward." 4: 701–702.
Baulch, Joe R. "Farmers' and Laborers' Protective Association." 2: 956.
Carroll, Jeff. "*Rebel.*" 5: 473.
Coerver, Don E. "Plan of San Diego." 5: 228.
Cordozier, V. R. "Higher Education." 3: 596–600.
Cottrell, Debbie Mauldin. "Blanton, Annie Sue." 1: 587–588.
Cottrell, Debbie Mauldin. "Hopkins, May Ayres." 3: 692–693.
Cottrell, Debbie Mauldin. "Texas Association Opposed to Woman Suffrage." 6: 291–292.
De Leon, Arnoldo. "Mexican Americans." 4: 664–670.
Edwards, Margaret Royalty. "Graves, William Sidney." 3: 291.
Enstam, Elizabeth York. "Women and the Law." 6: 1046–1049.
Fleming, Richard T. "Parker, Edwin B." 5: 59.
Gould, Lewis L. "Progressive Era." 5: 347–355.
Green, Barbara L. "Scott, Emmett Jay." 5: 935.
Griggs, Joan Druesedow. "Old Glory, Texas." 4: 1134.
Hart, Brian. "Rankin, George Clark." 5: 445.
Hart, Brian. "Richardson, Wilds Preston." 5: 571.
Hunt, William. "Hickey, Thomas Aloysius." 3: 585.

Keffeler, Christine A. "Stinson, Katherine." 6: 105.
Kerr, K. Austin. "Prohibition." 5: 355.
Kleiner, Diana J. "Davis, William Leonard." 2: 535.
Kleiner, Diana J. "Houston *Informer* and the *Texas Freeman*." 3: 733.
Kleiner, Diana J. "Sulphur Industry." 6: 141–142.
Kohout, Martin Donnell. "Glenn Springs Raid." 3: 189.
Kohout, Martin Donnell. "Jordan, Louis John." 3: 1002.
Leatherwood, Art. "Barron Field." 1: 395.
Leatherwood, Art. "Benbrook Field." 1: 486.
Leatherwood, Art. "Edwards, Daniel R." 2: 797.
Leatherwood, Art. "Ellington Field." 2: 827–828.
Leatherwood, Art and Chris Cravens. "Hicks Field." 3: 588.
Legg, Josephine Hejl. "Kopecky, Josef H." 3: 1156.
Long, Christopher. "King William Historic District." 3: 1115–1116.
Long, Christopher. "Richardson, James Otto." 5: 568.
McArthur, Judith N. "Gearing, May Edna." 3: 120–121.
McArthur, Judith N. "Woman's Christian Temperance Union." 6: 1037–1038.
McArthur, Judith N. "Women and Politics." 6: 1051–1052."
Machann, Clinton. "Czechs." 2: 465–466.
Maroney, James C. "Oilfield Strike of 1917." 4: 1119.
Miller, Thomas L. "Blanton, Thomas Lindsay." 1: 588.
Minor, David. "Berry, Kearie Lee." 1: 503–504.
Minor, David. "Call Field." 1: 903–904.
Minor, David. "Hicks, Texas." 3: 588.
Myers, James M. "Barkley, David Bennes." 1: 383.
Neu, Charles E. "House, Edward Mandell." 3: 710–711.
Ochoa, Ruben E. "Macie, Texas." 4: 411.
Olien, Roger M. "Oil and Gas Industry." 4: 1119–1128.
Olson, Bruce A. "Texas National Guard." 6: 366–371.
Payne, John W. Jr. "Houston, David Franklin." 3: 715–716.
Perez, Joan Jenkins. "Truett, George Washington." 6: 578.
Perrenot, Jane Burges. "Dreben, Samuel." 2: 697.
Pilcher, Walter. "Keasbey, Lindley Miller." 3: 1043.
Price, Gary. "Ball, Thomas Henry." 1: 357.
Reed, S. G. "Lovett, Robert Scott." 4: 308–309.
Rieder, Robert A. "Electric Interurban Railways." 2: 817.
Ross, John R. "Lynching." 4: 346–347.
Smith, Wilda M. and Eleanor Bogart. "Deuell, Henrietta Eleanor Goodnough." 2: 608–609.

Snead, Ezwoh Barton. "Howze, Robert Lee." 3: 753.
Standifier, Mary M. "Cottonseed Industry." 2: 357–360.
Steen, Ralph W. "Ferguson, James Edward." 2: 979–981.
Steen Ralph W. "World War I." 6: 1077.
Storey, John W. "Religion." 5: 523–529.
Studer, Clara Trenchmann. "Trenchmann, William Andres." 6: 560–561.
Taylor, A. Elizabeth. "Woman Suffrage." 6: 1039–1041.
Thompson, John D. "McLemore, Atkins Jefferson." 4: 428–429.
Tinsley, James A. "Love, Thomas Bell." 4: 306.
Wagner, Robert L. "Culberson, Charles Allen." 2: 435–436.
Weddle, Robert. "Nimitz, Charles William." 4: 1015–1017.
Weeks, O. Douglas. "Election Laws." 2: 814–815.
Wooster, Robert. "Military History." 4: 726–730.

Newspapers

Austin American. July 1916–November 1918.
Austin Statesman. January 1917–January 1920.
Dallas Morning News. July 1914, February–October 1917, July–November, 1918.
Galveston Weekly News. February 1917–November 1918.
Ferguson Forum. April 1918.
Fort Worth Star-Telegram. April 1917, August 1920.
Houston Chronicle. February 1917–August 1917.
Houston Post. July 1916–November 1918.
Houston Press. August 1917–August 1918.
San Antonio Express. April 1918.
Waco Times-Herald. June–July 1917.

Theses and Dissertations

Adams, Richard S. "The Houston Riot of 1917." M.A. thesis, Texas A&M University, 1972.
Anderson, Adrian N. "Albert Sidney Burleson: A Southern Politician in the Progressive Era." Ph.D. dissertation, Texas Technological College, 1967.
Bailey, Richard. "Morris Sheppard of Texas: Southern Progressive and Prohibitionist." Ph.D. dissertation, Texas Christian University, 1980.

Baker, Margaret B. "The Texas Negro and the World War." M.A. thesis, University of Texas, 1938.
Bruns, Sue. "Persecution of German-Americans in Central Texas during World War I." M.A. thesis, Southwest Texas State University, 1972.
Bush, Mary Elizabeth. "El Paso, Texas, in the First World War." M.A. thesis, University of Texas, 1956.
Curtis, Donald John J. "Hard Times Come Again No More: General William S. Graves and the American Intervention in Siberia, 1918–1920." Ph.D. dissertation, Texas A&M University, 2006.
Day, Sandra D. "The Political Career of James Luther Slayden." M.A. thesis, University of Texas, 1962.
Duke, Escal F. "The Political Career of Morris Sheppard." Ph.D. dissertation, University of Texas, 1958.
Duncan, Thomas R. "A History of Kaufman County, Texas, in the World War." M.A. thesis, University of Texas, 1935.
Evans, Samuel Lee. "Texas Agriculture, 1880–1930." Ph.D. dissertation, University of Texas, 1966.
Fanton, Jonathan, F. "Robert A. Lovett, The War Years." Ph.D. dissertation, Yale University, 1960.
Glasrud, Bruce Alden. "Black Texans, 1900–1930: A History." Ph.D. dissertation, Texas Technological College, 1969.
Graham, Seldon B. "Wartime Activities of Robertson County, Texas, 1917–1919." M.A. thesis, University of Texas, 1933.
Gray, Sondra Wyatt. "The Political Career of James Luther Slayden." M.A. thesis, University of Texas, 1962.
Greer, William Lee. "The Texas Gulf Coast Oil Strike of 1917." M.A. thesis, University of Houston, 1974.
Hays, Robert E. Jr. "Military Aviation in Texas, World War I and II." M.A. thesis, University of Texas, 1963.
Hendricks, Henry G. "The Federal Food Administration for Texas, 1917–1919." M.A. thesis, University of Texas, 1925.
Hill, Forest A. "The Negro in the Texas Labor Supply." M.A. thesis, University of Texas, 1946.
Holcomb, Bob Charles. "Senator Joe Bailey: Two Decades of Controversy." Ph.D. dissertation, Texas Technological College, 1968.
Howard, Richard Winston. "The Work of Albert Sidney Burleson as Postmaster General." M.A. thesis, University of Texas, 1938.
Huckaby, George P. "Oscar Branch Colquitt: A Political Biography." Ph.D. dissertation, University of Texas, 1946.

Johnson, James E. "An Economic History of Orange County, Texas Prior to 1940." M.A. thesis, Lamar State College of Technology, 1966.
Jones, George C. "A History of Smith County, Texas, in the World War." M.A. thesis, University of Texas, 1932.
Law, Ron. "Congressman Hatton W. Sumners of Dallas, Texas: His Life and Congressional Career, 1875–1937." Ph.D. dissertation, Texas Christian University, 1990.
Maroney, James C. "Organized Labor in Texas, 1900–1929." Ph.D. dissertation, University of Houston, 1975.
McCawley, Ruth. "American Attitudes Toward England and Germany As Reflected in the Newspapers of Texas From 1914 to 1917." M.A. thesis, University of Texas, 1940.
Mathews, Mazie E. "On the Hither Edge of Free Land: Lindley Miller Keasbey and the Evolution of the Frontier." M.A. thesis, Southwest Texas State University, 1973.
Moore, Sue E. Winston. "Thomas B. Love, Texas Democrat, 1901–1949." M.A. thesis, University of Texas, 1971.
Murray, Sean Collins. "Texas Prohibition Politics, 1897–1914." M.A. thesis, University of Houston, 1968.
Park, Phocion S. Jr. "The Twenty-fourth Infantry Regiment and the Houston Riot of 1917." M.A. thesis, University of Houston, 1971.
Payne, John W. Jr. "David F. Houston: A Biography." Ph.D. dissertation, University of Texas, 1953.
Peebles, Robert. "Technology As A Factor in the Gulf Shipbuilding Industry." Ph.D. dissertation, University of North Texas, 1980.
Roades, Ora Edward. "A History of Wharton County, Texas, in the World War." M.A. thesis, University of Texas, 1938.
Rocha, Rodolfo. "The Influence of the Mexican Revolution on the Texas-Mexican Border, 1910–1916." Ph.D. dissertation, Texas Tech University, 1981.
Salas, Karen J. "Senator Morris Sheppard and the Eighteenth Amendment." M.A. thesis, University of Texas, 1970.
Scarborough, John A. L. "The University of Texas and the Great War." M.A. thesis, University of Texas, 1927.
Steen, Ralph W. "The Political Career of James E. Ferguson, 1914–1917." M.A. thesis, University of Texas, 1928.
Sonntag, Mark. "Hyphenated Germans: World War I and the German-Americans of Texas." M.A. thesis, University of Texas at Austin, 1990.

Sutherland, Julia C. "A History of DeWitt County Texas, in the World War." M.A. thesis, University of Texas, 1938.
Tinsley, James A. "The Progressive Movement in Texas." Ph.D. dissertation, University of Wisconsin, 1953.
Turner, Oran Elijah. "History of the Texas State Council of Defense." M.A. thesis, University of Texas, 1926.
Williams, David A. "The History of Higher Education for Black Texans," Ed. D. dissertation, Baylor University, 1978.
Wilson, Robert. "The Farmers' and Laborers' Protective Association, 1875–1916." M.A. thesis, Baylor University, 1978.
Wright, Robert J. "'The Texas-Oklahoma Division': A History of the 90th Division in World War I." M.A. thesis, Southwest Texas State University, 1981.

Papers at Professional Meetings

Bernstein, Patricia. "The Waco Horror: The Town, the Lynching, the Investigation and the NAACP." Texas State Historical Association, Fort Worth, March 4, 2005.
Canipe, Lee. "Preaching the Gospel in a World Made Safe for Democracy: George W. Truett, Religious Liberty, and the American Expeditionary Force." Texas State Historical Association, Austin, Texas, March 4, 2004.
Dean, Ouida. "August Tubbe: A German Immigrant in Nacogdoches in the Mid-Nineteenth Century." East Texas Historical Association, Nacogdoches, September 25, 2004.
O'Neal, Bill. "East Texans in the First World War—Oral Interviews," East Texas Historical Association, Nacogdoches, September 25, 2007.
Seymour, James B. "Fighting on the Home Front." Texas State Historical Association, Fort Worth, March 4, 2005.
Williams, David A. "Emmett Scott: Advocate for World War I African American Servicemen." Texas State Historical Association, Austin, March 6, 2004.

INDEX

Abilene, Texas, 112
Abilene Christian College, 116
Adams, Harry J., 134
American Expeditionary Force, 102, 117, 160, 168
African-Americans, in population, 12; newspapers, 16; in military service, 39–43, 105–107; supported war effort, 104–105; lynching victims, 107; in postwar years, 166–167
agriculture, 56–57, 166
Allen, Henry T., 124, 132, 160, 210
Allen, Terry de la Mesa, 140
Alpine, Texas, 112
American Federation of Labor, 109
American Protective League, 68–69
American Red Cross, 103–104
American War Mission, 64
Anderson, Adrian, quoted, 66
Andevanne ridge, 142
Arabic, 204
Archangel expedition, 149
Argonne Forest, 135, 139.141
Armaijo, Marcus B., 109
armistice, 147–148
Army, national, 35, 37, 39
Army, regular, 35, 36–37
Asquith, Herbert H., 63
Atwell, Ernest T., 104
Austin, Texas, 12, 13
Austin Daily Statesman, 11, 15, 22, 29
Austria-Hungary, 10, 11, 20, 33, 165
Axson, Stockton, 71, 210

Bailey, Joseph, 26–27, 72, 165, 167
Bailey, Thomas, quoted, 162
Baker, Newton D., presents selective service bill, 35; concerns regarding vice, 46; chairs National Council of Defense, 52; supports ten-mile alcohol-free zone, 85; appoints Emmett Scott as special assistant, 106; supports General Graves in Siberian expedition, 151–152
Ball, Thomas H., 10, 18, 51, 210
Balsley, Clyde, 117, 119–121
Baptist Standard, 115
Bantheville, France, 139–140
Barbers' Hill, Texas, 54
Barker, Eugene C., 98
Barkley, David Bennes, awarded Medal of Honor, 109, 143, 167

Barron Field, 48
Bar-sur-Aube, France, 126
Barton Dr. A. J., 89
Barton, Thomas D., 137
Baruck, Bernard M., 52
Bastrop Advertiser, 15
Battle, William J., 80, 210
Batson, Texas, 14
Baucom, Byrne, 121–122, 134
Beall, Jack Andrew, 210
Beaumont, Texas, 12, 13, 14, 53, 54, 113, 154–155
Beaumont Shipbuilding and Drydock Company, 53
Bee, Carlos, 91, 210
Behrens, Ella, 100
Belleau Wood, 128–129
Benbrook Field, 48
Berry, Kerrie Lee, 152
Berzy-le-Sec, France, 131
Bible, Dana X., 113, 210
Big Hill Dome, 55
Big Red One, 118; see also 1st Division
Big Spring, Texas, 119
Bishop, Texas, 100–101
Black Eugene, 24, 25, 73, 75, 210
Black troops, riot, 42–44; see also African-Americans
Blakely, George, 126
Blanton, Annie Webb, 90, 91, 166, 211
Blanton, Tom, 73, 75, 78, 79, 90, 211
Bliss, Tasker, 64, 211
Bloor, Alfred W., 135
Bouldin, C. W., 97
Bracht, Fred, 101
Brackenridge, Mary Eleanor, 17, 78
Brandenburg, Texas, 101
Brannen, Carl A., 128, 130, 148
Breckenridge, TX, 54
Brewster, Hugh, 134
Briggs, Clay Stone, 91
Brooks Field, 47–48
Brooks, Sidney Johnson, Jr., 48
Brownsville, Texas, 26
Bruce, Andrew D., 131, 211
Bryan Mound Dome, 55
Bryan, William Jennings, 10, 18
Buchanan, James P., 25, 73, 211
Buck, Beaumont Bonaparte, 118–119, 127, 131–132, 211

Buenger, Walter, quoted, 116, 168
Burkburnett, Texas, 54
Burgess, George F., 211
Burleson, Albert Sidney, works for Culberson, 27; recommends declaration of war, 32; appointed to Cabinet, 61, 65–66; enforcement of Espionage Act, 67; advises Wilson, 161; ending political career, 167, 211
Burns, Waller T., 97–98
Butcher, Thomas W., 142

Cabiness, George, 107
Campbell, Thomas, 88, 89
Call Field, 49
Call, Loren H., 49
Callaway, Oscar, opposed Wilson preparedness plan, 22, 23; opposes Gore-McLemore resolution, 25; defeated in re-election campaign, 27; denounces munitions makers, 30; death, 211
Camp Bowie, 40, 41, 83, 105, 126, 154, 159, 160
Camp Bullis, 46
Camp Devens, 153
Camp Dick, 50
Camp Funston, 46, 113, 153
Camp Howze, 144
Camp Hulen, 144
Camp John Wise, 50
Camp Logan, 42, 45, 106, 155
Camp Mabry, 46
Camp Marfa, 46
Camp MacArthur, 42, 45, 106, 154
Camp Mills, 125
Camp Scurry, 40
Camp Travis, 41. 92, 105, 124, 154, 160
Camp Waco, 50
Cantigny, 127
Caporetto, 64
Captain Fred Swailes and Company, 53
Carl, J. F., 51
Carlson, Paul, 59
Carranza, Venustiano, 20, 21
Chaplain, Charlie, 115
Chateau Thierry, 130
Chisos Mining Company, 55
Choctaw Indians, 138
Christian Advocate, 115
Christian, Carole, quoted, 108, 109, 167
Christian, Garna L., quoted, 46
Church of Christ, 115–116
City of Houston, 53
City of Orange, 53

City of Pensacola, 53
Civilian Advisory Commission, 50–51
Clay, Henry R., 121
Cleburne, Texas, 13–14, 114, 154–155
Clemenceau, Georges, 158
"Code talking," 138
Coffman, Edward M., quoted, 132
Cole, Charles Edward, 142
Colquitt, Oscar, elected governor, 10–11; calls special session, 18–19; sends Rangers to border, 20; runs for U.S. Senate, 27; endorses Selective Service, 36; supports Hobby, 88; heads Texas Hoover Democrats, 211
Commerce, TX, 111
Congress, debates Continental Army plan, 23–24; passes Army expansion bill, 24; declares war, 33; appropriates money, 46; creates Council of National Defense, 50; creates War Industries Board, 51
Connally, Tom, 33, 73, 75, 79, 167, 183fn, 212
Conscription, 35–39; also see Selective service
Continental Army plan, 23–24
Coolidge, Calvin, 164
Corpus Christi, Texas, 100
Corsicana, Texas, 15
Cotton, 14, 19–20, 58
Council of National Defense, 50, 52, 59, 83
Cox, James, 164
Crain, James K., 145
Crawford, William B., 107
Creel, George, 98
Croix de Guerre, 107, 120, 127, 137, 142–144
Crosby, Alfred W., 156
Crow, R. F., 57
Crowder, Enoch, 39, 212
Culberson, Charles A., chairs Judiciary Committee, 9; opposes Gore resolution, 25; re-elected senator, 26; senior senator, 72–73,; opposes prohibition, 77; opposes women's suffrage, 79; supports Treaty of Versailles, 161, 163–164; death, 212
Cunningham, Minnie Fisher, 17, 78, 86–87, 89, 212
Curtis, Will D., 137
Cyclops, 123

Dabney, Ward, 113
Dallas, Texas, 12–13, 41. 51, 154–156
Dallas, Fred W., 141
Dallas Morning News, 11, 15, 16, 22, 29
Daniels, Josephus, 19, 102
Davis, James H. "Cyclone," 22, 27, 212
Davis, William L., 104

Day, Aaron, Jr., 106
Dearing, Mary, 102
Debs, Eugene W., 68
Deep Water (Oil Company), 54
DeGrummond, Henry C., 140
Del Rio, Texas, 43
Democratic Party, 9–10
Denison, Texas, 13, 14
Desdemona, Texas, 54
Deuell, Henrietta Goodnough, 103–104, 212; see also Peggy Hull
Dickerson, Paul. 124
Dickman, Joseph T., 130
Dies, Martin, Jr., 91
Dies, Martin, Sr., committee chairman, 9; opposes Continental Army plan, 23; opposes naval expansion, 24; re-elected 27; votes for declaration of war, 33; opposes Wilson policies, 74–75; ends political career, 90; 167; death, 213
Distinguished Service Cross, 109, 127–128, 131, 134, 137– 138, 141–143
Distinguished Service Medal, 144–145
"Dixie," 116
Doughty, Walter, 90
Draft board, 37–38
Dreben, Sam, 138
Drought, 83, 185 fn
"Drys," 76
Duncan Field, 47
Duncalf, Frederick, 98
Dunlap, O. E., 51
Dunlavy, Herbert D., 128

Eagle, Joe, 25, 44, 73, 75, 91, 213
Edwards, Dan, earns Medal of Honor, 127, 131; death , 213
Edwards, Lyford C., 100
Education, 111–113
8th Infantry Regiment, 150–151
18th Infantry Regiment, 118
82nd Division, 132
89th Division, 132
Electra, Texas, 14, 54, 97
Ellington, Eric L., 49
Ellington Field, 49, 50
El Paso Herald, 15, 22
El Paso, TX, 12–13, 153, 155–156
Emergency Fleet Corporation, 52–53
Emmett, Chris, 133, 213
Entertainment, 113–115
Erwin, William P., 134

Espionage Act, 1917, 66–68, 72
Evans, R. E., 111

Fairbanks, Douglas, 115
Farmers' and Laborers' Protective Association, 96–97
Farmers' Petroleum Company, 54
Ferdinand, Francis, 10–11, 204
Ferguson, James, elected governor, 10, 18; increases number of Rangers on border, 20; supports war effort, 36; declares Texas Enlistment Week, 40; proclaims martial law, 44; appoints State Council of Defense, 43; removed as governor, 79–81, 230; runs for governor, 1918, 85, 88–90, 157; opposes prohibition, 87; aids rural schools, 111; death, 213
Ferguson, Miriam, 166
Ferris, Royal A., 51
5th Division, 124, 132, 139, 143
5th Illinois National Guard, 44
5th Marines, 118, 119, 127, 129
1st Army, 135, 159
1st Division, 118, 126, 130, 132
1st Texas Cavalry, 41–42
Fite, Gilbert, 96
Flour milling, 14
Foch, Ferdinand, 130, 132, 135
Food Administration, 56–57, 83, 94–95
Food conservation, 95
Football, 113–114
Forest Farm, 138
Fort Bliss, 40, 46, 154
Fort Brown, 40
Fort Clark, 40, 46
Fort Des Moines, 105–106
Fort Duncan, 40
Fort Ringgold, 40
Fort Sam Houston, 40, 41, 46
Fort Worth, Texas, 12, 13, 15, 41
Fort Worth Star-Telegram, 15, 21, 28–29
41st Division, 118
42nd ("Rainbow") Division, 118, 119, 126, 132, 145
Foulois, Benjamin, 46, 213
Four-Minute Men, 98
Fourteen Points, 98
France, 117–122, 124–145, 156–160
Frantz, Joe B., quoted, 188n
Freeport Sulphur Company, 55
French Flying Service, 119
Fuller, Francis O., 81

Galena-Signal Oil, 54
Galveston News, 12, 13, 14, 22, 28, 43, 113, 154–155
Gambrell, James B., 17
Gambrell, Joel H., 17
Garcia, Graviel, 109
Garner, John Nance, 33, 73, 74, 167, 213
Garrett, David E., 73, 75, 79, 91, 213
Geanapolis, George, 97
George, Lloyd, 158
Gerard, James N., 99
German, music, 92; population, 12; voters, 81
Germany, 10–11, 18, 20–22, 25, 28–29, 31–33, 35, 204
Gideon, Oscar Wesley, 124
Glen Spring, Texas, 26
Goose Creek, Texas, 14
Gore, Thomas P., 25; Gore-McLemore resolution, 24
Gosport Field, 47
Gould, Lewis, quoted, 14, 89
Grantham, Dewey, quoted, 23, 163
Graves, William Sidney, 150–152, 213
Gray, Sir Edward, 63
Grayson, Cary T., 157, 162
Great Britain, 11
Greble, Edwin St. John, 42, 125, 214
Greenville, TX, 13
Greenville Banner, 97
Gregg, Alexander W., 9, 24, 73–74, 79, 90, 214
Gregory, Thomas Watt, attorney general, 9, 61; supports Culberson, 27; legal opinion, 31; urges declaration of war, 32; enforcement of Espionage Act, 67–68; defends American Protective League, 68–69; advocates measures to control deserters, 67; ends political career, 167, 214
Gulf Oil, 54

Haley, Roscoe R., 137
Hall, Weston Bert, 120–121
Harding, Warren G., 164, 232
Hardy, Rufus, 24, 73, 75, 214
Harris, Charles T., Jr., 145
Harris, Ernest L., 152
"Hat in the Ring" squadron, 121
Hay, James, 41
Hayden, David E., awarded Medal of Honor, 134, 214
Heldenfelds, Fred and Carl, 53
Helium, 55–56
Henry, Robert L., 9, 19, 78, 214
Henry, Vida, 44
Hickey, Tom, 96, 214

Hicks Field, 48
Hilberbrand, Robert C., quoted 62, 158
Hilburn, Herbert S., 142
Hillman, Rolfe L., quoted, 131
Hobby, William P., becomes governor, 81–83; pressured by prohibitionists, 84; calls special session, 85; election campaign, 87–89; elected governor, 90, 157; postwar career, 214
Hogg, James Stephen. 62
Holman, Jesse R., 144
Hoover, Herbert, 56–57, 70, 94, 213
Hoover, John S., 136
Hopkins, May Agnes, 103, 215
House, Edward M., early career, 61–65; advises President Wilson on domestic issues, 9, 19; advises Wilson on German submarine campaign, 29; quoted, 29, 59; heads American War Mission, 64–65; recommends Burleson for Cabinet position, 65; mission to Paris, 148; influenza, 157; last meeting with Wilson, 158; final letters to Wilson, 163; ends political career, 167, 215
House, Thomas, 61
Houston, Texas: 11, 12, 13, 14, 15, 119, 154–156
Houston Chronicle, 8, 22, 28, 129
Houston Daily Post, 15, 29
Houston, David F., in Wilson Cabinet, 9, 30, 32, 61, 69–70, 99, 167, 215
Houston Texas Freeman, 8
Howze, Robert, 144, 215
Hughes, Charles Evans, 27
Hulen, John A., 136, 144, 215
Hull, Peggy, 153; see Henrietta Goodnough Deuell
Hull, Texas, 54
Humble, TX, 14
Humble Oil Company, 54
Hunter, Evelyn, 104–105
Hutchings, Edwin, 136
Hutchings, Henry, 136–137, 215
Hurley, Edward, 53

Influenza epidemic, 152–156
Illinois National Guard, 44
"Inquiry," 71

Jackson, Warren R., 117, 119, 128, 130, 147, 215
Jackson, William, 135
Jasper, TX, 154
Jester, Beauford, 140, 168, 215–216
Johnson, Donald, quoted, 67
Johnson, Douglas V., quoted, 131

Index

Jones, Jesse H., 71, 216
Jones, Marvin, 73, 75, 79, 216
Jordan, Louis J., 126–127
Jutland, 24, 205

Keasbey, Lindley M., 98–99, 216
Keith, Jeanette, 115
Kelly Field, 46–47, 83, 121
Kelly, George F., 47
Kelly No. 2, 47
Kern and Wolfe, 54
Kingsville, TX, 112
King William Street, 101
Kirby, John Henry, 53, 90, 216
Knights of Columbus, 115
Kolchak, Aleksandr, 152
Kopeckey, Dr. Josef F., 152

Lafayette Escadrille, 117, 119–120
La Follette, Robert, 30, 216
Lake, Teresa, 103
Lanham, Samuel W. T., 62
Lansing, Robert, 19, 29
Laredo, Texas, 13, 26
League of Nations, 158, 164–165
Leon Springs, Texas, 112
Leslie, William Shelton, 122
Lever Food Control Act, 56
Liberty bonds, 115
Liberty Loan, 75, 92
Link, Arthur, quoted, 29
Lipscomb, Abner E., 137
Lodge, Henry Cabot, 161–163, 216
Loescher, Frank B., 141
Logan, John A., 42
Lone Star Shipbuilding, 53
Longview, race riot, 167
Loomis, John S., 138
Looney, Ben F., 88
London, Meyer, 33
Love Field, 49
Love, Moss L., 49
Love, Thomas B., 70, 216
Lovett, Edgar O., 113
Lovett, Robert Abercrombie, 117, 123, 167, 217
Lovett, Robert Scott, 51, 70, 123, 217
Ludendorff, Erich, 126
Luebke, Frederick C., quoted, 100
Lusitania, 21, 22, 229
Lynching, 16, 107

MacArthur, Arthur, 42
Macie community, Texas, 155
Magnolia Petroleum, 54
Mansfield, Joseph J., 73, 75, 217
Mangin, Charles, 130
Manufacturing, 14
Marine brigade, 135
Marine Corps, 37, 103, 128–129
Marne, 130, 204
Marne-Asine line, 130
Marsh, Peyton C., 104
Marshall, TX, 13
Martin, Charles G., 160
Martin, Frank, 131
Mason, C. H., 138
Maverick, Maury, 133–134, 168, 217
Mayfield, Earle, 88, 217
McAdoo, William F., 69, 93, 217
McArthur, Judith, quoted, 86
McBride and Law, 53
McCammon, J. N., 53
McClanahan, Adam B., 140
McDaniel, Dennis, Jr., 90
McDonald, William, 104, 217
McLemore, Jeff, sponsors resolution, 25; vote against declaration of war 33, 71; demands black mutineers returned, 45; attacks Wilson policies, 75; defeated, 91–92; unsuccessful candidate for U.S. Senate, 217
McNealus, J. C., 21–22
McReynolds, James, 68
Medal of Honor, 127, 131, 134, 144, 167
Merchants & Planters Oil, 54
Mercury (quicksilver), 55
Metcalf, Charles B., 87
Meuse-Argonne offensive, 135–140
Mexia, Texas, 14
Mexican-Americans, numbers 12, 14; discriminated against 16; lynched, 107; workers, 108; armed service, 108–109; in postwar years, 167
Mexico, 12, 20–21, 26, 30–31
Mezes, Sidney E., 71, 217
Midland Bridge Company, 53
Miles, Nelson A., 124
Moore, Hugh B., 145
Montfaucon, France, 135
Moore, Willis, 138
Morris, Charles H., 1457
Motion pictures, 114–115
Mouzon, Bishop E. D., 89, 218
Muchet, Jules, 126

Murmansk, 149
Music, 114

Nacogdoches, Texas, city, 112; county, 154
National American Suffrage Association, 78
National Association for the Advancement of Colored People, 167, 259
National Council of Defense, 50
National Defense Act of 1916, 24, 35, 46
National Guard, 24, 39, 40–42
National Shipbuilding Company, 53
Navy, 24, 25, 102–103, 122–124
Neal, Margie, 166
Neff, Pat, 165, 232
New Orleans, 56
Newspapers, 11, 15–16, 21–22, 29; Spanish, 108
Nicholas II, 31, 206
Nimitz, Chester W., 122, 167, 218
19th Amendment, 209
90th Division, departs for overseas, 92, 117–118; arrives in France, 117, 124–125; attack St. Mihiel salient, 132; in Meuse-Argonne offensive, 139–140; crosses Meuse, 149; new shoulder patch, 160–161; occupation duty, 160; casualties, 142, 161
92nd Division, 105, 106
9th Infantry Regiment, 118, 127, 129
94th Squadron ("Hat in the Ring"), 121
Nonpartisan League, 97
Norris, George, 30

Offset, M. M., 97
Ogden, Ira C., 138
Oil, discoveries, 14; production, 54; workers' strike, 110–111; industry 165
Oklahoma, 47; National Guard, 40, 42; regiments, 133, 138–140, 141; brigade, 119
103rd Squadron, 121
117th Texas Supply Train, 119
132nd Machine Gun Battalion, 139
141st Infantry, 135–136, 139
142nd Infantry, 135, 138, 139
143rd Infantry, 139
144th Infantry, 139
148th Squadron, 121
169th Aero Squadron, 122
179th (Oklahoma) Brigade, 139, 141–142
180th (Texas) Brigade, 133, 139, 142
O'Neil, Joseph P., 160
Orange, Texas, 53–54
Orlando, Vittorio, 158
Ortiz, Conception, 109, 143
"Over There," 114

"Panther Division," 125; see also 36th Division
Paris, Texas, 13
Parker, Edwin, 52, 70, 218
Parker, James, 126, 136
Parr, Archie, 16, 90
Patenaude, Lionel V., quoted 74
Patton, Willis Earl, 124
Peden, Edward Andrew, 57, 94
Penn Field, 50
Perry, Howard E., 55
Pershing, John J., leads expedition into Mexico, 16; appointed commander of AEF, 117–118; concern over training, 125; orders attack at Cantigny, 127; plans St. Mihiel attack, 132; favors unconditional surrender, 148; allows troops more recreation, 160; after war, 218
Peterson, H. C., 96
Petrolia oil field, 55–56
Philadelphia Naval Yard, 155
Pickford, Mary, 115
Pitts, Walter E., 107
Plan of San Diego, 20, 107, 204
Pollard, Russell, 106–107
Poole, Frederick C., 149
Population, of Texas, 11–13
Port Arthur, Texas, 13, 14
Porter, Katherine Ann, 156, 218
Prohibition, 17, 76–77, 85–86
Prokosch, Edward, 99
Price, Howard C., 141

Quicksilver, see mercury

Rainbow Division, 119; see also 42nd Division
Rains County, 97
railroads, 15
Ranger, Texas, 13
Rankin, George C., 17
Rayburn, Sam, 33, 73, 75, 167. 218
Rebel, The, 96
Refineries, oil, 54
Reid, Vernon S., 110
Revenue Act, of 1913, 93; of 1916, 93
Ribot, Alexandre, 47
Rice Institute, 113
Rice, William Marsh, 113
Rich Field, 49
Rich, Perry L., 49
Richardson, Clifford, 104
Richardson, James O., 122, 167, 219
Richardson, Wilds Preston, 149–150, 219
Rich Field, 49
Rickenbacker, Eddie, 121

Roberts, Edwin, 113
Robison, Samuel S., 122
Rockport, Texas, 53–54
Roman Catholics, 18
Roosevelt, Franklin D., 56, 164
Roosevelt, Theodore, 31, 35–36
Reserve Office Training, 112
Russia, 10, 31, 149–150

Sampler, Samuel M., Medal of Honor recipient, 136, 219
San Antonio, Texas, 12, 41, 46; influenza in, 154–156
San Antonio Express, 10, 15, 22
San Antonio Inquirer, 97
San Diego, California, 46
San Diego, Plan of, 20
Sarajevo, 10
Sayers, Joseph D., 36
Scott, Emmett Jay, 106, 219
2nd Brigade, 127
2nd Division, 118, 126, 127, 130, 132, 130, 159
Selective service, 36–39
Serra, Marcelino, 109
71st Brigade, 135–136
72nd Brigade, 136
Sheppard, Morris, 25, 72–74; opposes Gore resolution, 24; leader of prohibitionists, 73, 77; supports women's suffrage, 79; supports Treaty of Versailles, 161–164; death, 219
Sherman, Texas, 13
Shipbuilding, 52–53
Shoemaker, Lonnie O., 137
Shoemacher, Max, 143
Sholars, Arthur R., 113
Siberia, 104, 150–151
Sibert, William, 118
Sinclair Company, 54
16th Infantry Regiment, 118
6th Field Artillery, 118
6th Marines, 118, 127–128, 183n
Slayden, Ellen Maury, 71, 219
Slayden, James L., 9; critical of munitions makers, 23; opposes naval expansion, 24; favors Gore resolution, 25; re-elected, 27; votes for declaration of war, 33; critical of Wilson policies, 71; defeated, 75; recommended for secretary of war post, 182n; retires, 91, 167; death, 219
Smith, Hamilton R., 131
Smith, William R. (Congressman), 9, 220
Smith, William R. (Major General), 125, 136, 138, 219

Soissons, 127, 130–131
Sour Lake, Texas, 14
Southern Baptists, 17
Southern Drydock and Shipbuilding Company, 53
Southern Methodists, 17
Spanish influenza, 153, see influenza
Speaker, William L., 119
Spindletop, 14
Sports, 113–114
Stephens, John E., 126
Stephens, John H., 9, 23, 27, 220
St. Etienne, 132, 135, 137–138
St. Mihiel salient, 132–135
Steen, Ralph W., 161
Sterling, Ross, 110, 220
Stewart, George, 149
Stinson, Katherine, 102, 220
Strickland, Riley, 141
Strikes, 110–111
Sturgeon, B. B., 83
Submarines, 21–22, 24–25, 28–29, 30–32, 124, 204–205
Sulfur production, 54–55
Summers, Hatton, 73, 75, 79, 220
Sussex, 205

Taliaferro Field, 48
Taylor, John L., 131
Tejanos, 167
Temple, TX, 43
Terlingua Quicksilver District, 55
Terrell election law, 10
Texas A&M College, 112
Texas Association Opposed to Woman Suffrage, 87
Texas City, TX, 46
Texas Company, 54
Texas Congress of Mothers, 17
Texas Enlistment Week, 40
Texas Equal Suffrage Association, 87
Texas Federation of Women's Clubs, 17
Texas Food Administration, 83
Texas Gulf Sulphur Company, 55
Texas Interscholastic Athletic Association, 114
Texas League, 113
Texas National Guard, 40, 42, 44; see also 36th Division
Texas Rangers, 20–21
Texas State Council of Defense, 51, 98
Texas Suffrage Association, 87
Texas Woman Suffrage Association, 78
3rd Division, 132

26th Division, 118
32nd Division, 42, 45, 92, 124
33rd Division, 42, 46, 92, 124
36th Division, mobilized, 40–41; overseas movement, 92, 117, 124–126; attack at St. Etienne, 137; Meuse-Argonne offensive, 135–139; casualties, 143, 161; 1st Army champions, 159; heads for home, 159
23rd Infantry Regiment, 118, 127, 129
24th Infantry Regiment, 42–43
25th Infantry Regiment, 43
26th Infantry Regiment, 118, 126
28th Infantry Regiment, 118, 127
339th Infantry Regiment, 149
357th Infantry Regiment, 133, 139
358th Infantry Regiment, 133, 139
359th Infantry Regiment, 133, 139
360th Infantry Regiment, 133, 139
Thomason, John W., Jr, 117–118, 128–130, 220
Thompson, Ernest, 168, 220
Ticonderoga, 124
Tobin, Edgar C., 121
"Tough 'Ombres," 160
Trading With Enemy Act, 67
Trenchman, William, 101
Truett, Dr. George W., 116, 220–221
Tyler, Texas; 13

U-boats, see submarines
Universal Shipbuilding Company, 53
United States Shipping Board, 52
University of Texas, 112–113
U.S.S. Pittsburgh, 123, 155
U.S.S. Nevada, 122
U.S.S. Texas, 123

Versailles, Treaty of, 158, 161–162, 163–165
Victoria Advocate, 15
Vierzy, France, 131
Villa, Francisco "Pancho," 25–26, 118, 221
Vinson, Robert E., 80–81, 221
Vladivostok, 151–152

Waco, Texas, 12–13, 42–43
Walker, Walton H., 167
War College for Women, 101
War Department, 41–42
War Industries Board, 51–52, 58
War Revenue Act, 76
War Savings certificates, 92; stamps, 92
Washington, Jesse, 107
Washington, Booker T., 106

Watson, Richard, quoted, 79
Weathered, Preston, 135
Webb, Walter Prescott, 71–72, 91, 99
Wells, James B., 16
Welsh, Sen. Thomas, 164
White, Lonnie, 41, quoted, 138, 161
Whitworth, Pegram, 136
Wichita Falls, Texas, 13–14
Wilhelm II, 63
Williams, Edith, 166
Willis, Paul, 138
Wilson, Edith Bolling Galt, 204
Wilson, Ellen Axson, 204
Wilson, James C., 27, 73, 75, 221
Wilson, William B., 108
Wilson, Woodrow, 9, 11; endorses Thomas Ball, 10, 18; criticism of 19; protest over *Lusitania*, 20; preparedness plan, 22, 24; orders Mexican expedition, 25; re-elected, 27; peace without victory, 28; saddened by U-boat campaign, 29; Zimmermann note, 31; recommendation for war, 32–33; selective service, 35–36; mobilization, 50; urges increased production, 56; message from French president, 47; meets with Colonel House, 62; supports women's suffrage, 78; criticizes Slayden, 91; promises to send troops to Europe, 117; sends House to Europe, 146; supports General Graves, 152; 1918 election, 157; illness in Paris, 157–158; last meeting with Colonel House, 158; submits Treaty of Versailles to Senate, 161, 163; suffers stroke, 162; hopes for 1920 elections, 164; death, 158, 221
Woellert, Lola Bracht, 100–101
Wolters, Jacob, 89
Woman's Christian Temperance Union, 17
Women's suffrage, 77–79, 86–87
Women, Texas, 17; impact of war upon, 101–103
Wooden ships, 52–54
Wool, 58–59

Young, Charles G., 106
Young, James, 73, 75
Young Women's Christian Association, 17

Zeppelins, 55
Zimmermann, Alfred , 30–31

www.ingramcontent.com/pod-product-compliance
Lightning Source LLC
Chambersburg PA
CBHW030313080526
44584CB00012B/551